Pam Cullen

*Liberty and Licence
in the Indian Cinema*

Liberty and Licence in the Indian Cinema

Aruna Vasudev

VIKAS PUBLISHING HOUSE PVT LTD
New Delhi Bombay Bangalore Calcutta Kanpur

VIKAS PUBLISHING HOUSE PVT LTD
5 Ansari Road, New Delhi 110002
Savoy Chambers, 5 Wallace Street, Bombay 400001
10 First Main Road, Gandhi Nagar, Bangalore 560009
8/1-B Chowringhee Lane, Calcutta 700069
80 Canning Road, Kanpur 208004

ISBN 0 7069 0625 X

1V02V1601

Printed at Roopak Printers, K-17 Navin Shahdara, Delhi 110032

To the memory of
Paul Ronder
with whom I grew up in film

Acknowledgements

Acknowledgements for help received takes many forms. There are not simply those who very graciously provided practical help with time and material, but those who over many years did so much towards shaping a way of thinking and being.

An initial, and superficial, interest in film grew into a passion inspired by the friendship of two great people of the cinema—Lotte Eisner and Willard Van Dyke. B. D. Garga, through both his example and his generosity with the wealth of his knowledge and carefully collected material, directed that passion into practical channels—first a thesis and now a much expanded book.

The Ministry of Information & Broadcasting throughout was of constant help, which was extended to and by the Censor Boards at Bombay, Calcutta and Madras. I regret very much that it is not possible, because not permissible, to name individuals, but I hope they will understand how much I appreciated their most generous assistance. The Indian Institute of Mass Communications and its director M.V. Desai offered active support at a crucial stage, making all the difference between a mass of shapeless material and its emergence as a finished piece of work. P. K. Nair, Curator of the National Film Archives at Poona, not only listened and answered endless questions with exceptional patience, but offered all possible help by way of archive material, both films and books.

At the Institute Francais de Presse in Paris where the thesis was prepared, Professor Fernand Terrou took on the task of directing my studies and by his interest in, and curiosity about, all things, provided vital stimulation. Madame Hertzmann was her gracious, kind and always helpful self. I am most grateful to Professor Pierre Albert who, at a moment's notice, took over when Monsieur Terrou most sadly and suddenly succumbed to a heart attack.

I can never adequately express my thanks to all the friends who whether they liked it or not, found themselves involved in my early efforts to cope with Paris, French and Indian film censorship—to Catherine Larène, Michel de Cooman, Gonzalo and Simone Estrada, Abdoulaye Yerodia, Francois-Xavier Gillier, Deshraj Singh, Anil de Silva, Aida Diop-Gerard. To Eddi Ploman, for offering constant intellectual excitement. To Sunil Roy, who read, re-read and re-reread the manuscript with inexhaustible patience, making invaluable suggestions and corrections.

Above all to my parents who have never failed to encourage the pursuit of any interest, any profession, and have always been ready to provide a much-needed haven.

To my sister Uma. She did not read the manuscript. But then, without her endless bullying, there would have been no manuscript to read.

I am grateful to Hari Ram Jindal for typing the manuscript.

New Delhi   ARUNA VASUDEV

Introduction

Five hundred and seven feature films were produced in India in 1976, making it the largest film producing country in the world. One million people are employed in the film industry whose yearly box office receipts total Rs 300 crores of which 60 per cent goes to the public exchequer in the form of taxes. An estimated 8 million spectators a day fill its 9000 plus cinemas to capacity.

From the day the first film was shown in India in 1896, its popularity was established. From 1913 when the first feature-length Indian film was made, its extraordinarily rapid expansion began. The early fascination with the cinema, its remarkable hold on audiences and its unrivalled potential for informing, influencing and shaping public opinion has engaged the careful attention of successive governments from colonial times onward. Thus an understanding of the rise and development of control over the Indian cinema can only emerge from an understanding of the motivations of the powers that imposed it, and the political, economic and socio-cultural climate in which its policies were formed.

The period of the Emergency from June 1975 to March 1977, interrupted an otherwise continuous pursuit of democratic freedoms since Independence in 1947. As such, it need not enter into the wider context of a general survey of control over the cinema. However, it illustrated graphically the total vulnerability of the cinema to pressures from the central government and the distortions that can take place when decisions are based on individual, personal or narrow political considerations. The one positive aspect was that in terms of the media it has led to a more emphatic, more urgent rethinking on questions of public accountability, freedom and responsibility, liberty and licence.

Even though in recent years, technological advancement and changing economic, social and cultural standards had brought about an awareness of the important role played by communication and information channels in any society, it was the abuse of these under the Emergency that has accelerated a transformation in the area of government control over mass media. Today there is a positive move towards freeing the radio, television and even Films Division from total subservience to the government and setting up independent corporations for all three. Freedom of the press has been restored and efforts are being made to reframe and update the Dramatic Performances Act of 1876 by which the theatre is still governed.

The film industry, in principle free and independent, was for the first time, brought face to face with the disastrous consequences of its repudiation of responsibility for its actions, and its complacent acceptance of government control. However, despite the immediate post-Emergency determination of the industry to establish some form of self-regulation, it is doubtful if this will ever come about as from a historical survey of cinema and censorship, emerges the astonishing fact that while the film industry has frequently chafed against a too great government interference and control over the cinema, at no stage has there been any concerted action for the abolition of censorship per se. From time to time, a handful of individuals have demanded its removal; but the majority, while deploring the manner of its application, have admitted that in view of the complexity of social conditions in the country, some form of government control is inescapable and even desirable.

The roots of this complaisance lie in attitudes that were formed with the inception of the cinema and which help explain this attitude and the acceptance of a condition that has aroused heated controversy in other free societies. From the very beginning cinema was treated with a scornful disdain by the educated, cultured, political and conservative segments of society. In fact, in India as elsewhere, "for about 20 years, writers, men of letters, political and prominent men, were ashamed to be seen in a Cinematograph Hall, considering it a shame and a depravation, compared to the theatre," wrote Aloysio de Vincente in 1929, in the *International Review of Educational Cinematography*. The reaction ranged from the contemptuous to the patronizing to the frankly suspicious. It was silent, therefore non-literate and unworthy of serious consideration; since it was a popular form which reached wider and more heterogenous audiences and was not confined to the urban theatre patronized by the intellectual and cultural elite, it was dismissed as a vulgar form of mass entertainment. And, because it was an entirely new medium, a product of contemporary technological achievement not sanctified by centuries of tradition, it was regarded with hostility by conservative opinion.

Since film as a medium developed in an India under colonial domination, censorship was introduced by the rulers along the lines of what existed in their own country and was grudgingly accepted in India as part of the larger web of Imperialist control. Nor was there any protest against it by those who led the independence movement, as they did not consider cinema a worthwhile cause. As the years of British rule drew to a close, the film industry rejoiced at the coming of independence in the hope that political freedom for the country would signify an end to the humiliating controls exercised by an alien authority. But an infrastructure of film censorship had been built up and, along the whole administrative apparatus, was taken over by the new national government.

The attitude of this government in 1947 was marked by a desire to revive the Hindu/Indian ideals of asceticism and simplicity. Many of the men now in power had spent a large part of their lives as political prisoners, and their approach was governed entirely by values of hard work and duty. To them the idea of entertainment was anathema. They "looked upon the pleasure derived from seeing films as bordering on the sinful" and regarded the cinema as "an instrument of moral degeneration."[1]

By 1947 the cinema had in fact degenerated into a form of mindless entertainment—a view sedulously fostered by the industry itself. But its popularity was unquestionable. Since, therefore, it could not be wished away, the Government determined to exercise strict control over its content in terms of moral value judgements, and to derive financial benefit from it through the imposition of exorbitant taxes.

The film industry itself did perhaps more harm to the cinema than the reformist zeal of the new government. In insisting only upon the entertainment aspect of film, the producers themselves completely rejected the concept of public responsibility that is attached to any medium capable of moulding and influencing minds. Concerned primarily with box office success, they regarded as the province of government all responsibility for the impact of their films. It is significant to note that in 1948, producers and directors of an earlier era, shocked at the level to which cinema had fallen, exhorted the government not to hesitate to censor films on moral grounds.

In the thirty years that have followed, neither the Government nor the commercial cinema has basically altered its position. The notion of film as mere entertainment has persisted, with eminent producers like B. R. Chopra determinedly espousing the theory that "people just do no want anything but escapist entertainment, an entertainment that lifts them to the realm of pure miracle and make-believe, in which they see themselves singing and dancing with their favourite stars. A producer has no other gods but the people, and if people like escapist entertainment, well, we just can't do anything about it." To the argument that such films can prove harmful in the long run, he replied—"I do not subscribe to this view because I believe people do not take such films seriously."[2]

It was precisely this attitude that the Government Film Enquiry Committee in 1951 had condemned, saying in its report: "Those who look upon the film as a means of providing relief from the burdens of the day, ignore the fact that even anodynes can have unpleasant and even dangerous effects."[3]

Since producers felt they were providing escapist entertainment of the kind that had proved popular with mass audiences, they preferred to stick to the tried formula. Not interested in experimenting with content in view of the steadily rising costs of production, they continued to propagate stereotypes in set patterns— the hero and the villain, the good girl and the bad girl, the fool, the upright upholder of the law and the comic policeman—all of them two-dimensional characters, with a veneer of glamour glossing over all shadings. As long as it remained on this level, the Censor Board had little to say. However, in the last few years, entertainment has turned increasingly towards crime, vendetta, brutality, sadism;

the boy-meets-girl in song-and-dance sequences giving way to rape, assault, and various forms of sexual vulgarity.

Deeply disturbed by this destructive development, the government's efforts to curb it have grown in proportion to the increasing dominance this exercises over the cinema. The film industry maintains its claim that it only reflects the actual situation, while catering to the fantasies of its audiences. It discounts the objection of the authorities that these films are aimed at the lowest common denominator and as such must be discouraged whatever the cost. To the producer this is not an acceptable standpoint when the financial risks are so high that only 25 per cent to 30 per cent of the pictures released every year recover their costs. A Tamil producer gave the example of one of his films which enjoyed great success. It contained a liberal dose of "sex, violence, vulgarity, sexual innuendo, dialogue with double meaning" which he was surprised to find that even the women in the audience caught on to, and thoroughly enjoyed. Another film he made which was also an "entertainment" film but with songs and dances and no fights or sex, did not do half so well.

The clashes continue between producers who insist that they are providing much-needed entertainment in the form people enjoy, and a government that is concerned about the anti-social nature of this kind of "entertainment." But even here, while rejecting the government's point of view, the film producers accept the continuance of censorship. An explanation of this shelving of responsibility on the part of the filmmaker lies perhaps in conditions peculiar to the Indian scene. In a country composed of as many disparate elements as India, with deeply divisive ethnic, religious and linguistic differences, and a largely illiterate, volatile and easily swayed population, some one person or group of persons will always find something objectionable in every film. Complaints received by the government range from the objection of *dhobis* to their image in a particular film, to violent state-wide agitation against what was thought to be slighting references to segments of their society. As recently as 1973, a colourful song-and-dance melodrama *Yeh Goolistan Hamara* (This, My Garden), passed by the Censor Board for universal exhibition, was withdrawn from circulation in seven states by the Central Government because the people of these states protested that it "injured the feelings of the Naga community." Also in 1973, the Hindi film *Prabhat* (Morning) was recalled and released again only after the names of the hero and heroine were changed from Ram and Sita to Ramesh and Sarita.

The film maker is vulnerable—to law suits, to court cases, most of all to brick-throwing expressions of anger and disapproval—and he knows it. In all of this, a government seal of approval in the form of a censor certificate offers a measure of protection.

In spite of controls, in spite of censorship, side by side with the conflict-ridden, entertainment-oriented commercial cinema, the last few years have also seen a steady rise in the number of high quality films, particularly in the regional languages. Efforts by state governments to provide encouragement and incentives through subsidies and cash awards for outstanding films in regional languages, are beginning to show positive results. On the national level, the graduates of the Film and Television Institute have made a considerable mark with their low-budget, off-beat films giving rise to talk of a New Wave Indian cinema.

The Film Finance Corporation since it was set up in 1960 has financed 100 films, opening up possibilities for a fresh approach by new film makers, who would otherwise have been lost in the commercial rat race. Small independent producers and state governments have been inspired to emulate this example and the result is a small nucleus of films that can justifiably lay claim to being judged as art not commerce. The Directorate of Film Festivals, established in 1973 with a view to promoting Indian films abroad and organizing international and interregional festivals at home, has made it possible for a growing class of discerning film-goers to see the best of world cinema. The National Film Archive has been collecting international and national film classics since 1964 for the benefit of researchers and students. Many of them trained at the Film and Television Institute set up in Poona in 1961. The Film Society movement started by Satyajit Ray in Calcutta in 1947, now comprises 125 cine clubs, all with more than 65,000 members over the country. The exposure of constantly increasing numbers of film goers and film makers alike to a language and quality of film rarely found in the Hindi cinema is leading not only to a spread of film culture, but a demand and a search for improvement in the tone and texture of the Indian film as well.

With no competition from any other medium of entertainment or information, with nothing to threaten its position, the film industry has continued to grow every year. But it is only now, 30 years after independence, that the Indian cinema is showing signs of emerging from the stranglehold of commercial constraint into the free atmosphere of creative expression.

In this context, the role of censorship accused of being the most intransigent in the world, assumes great significance: what are the reasons and need for its continuation, in what manner it has interfered with the liberty of the film maker and to what extent it has hampered the flowering of this huge cinematic output into a form of art.

Notes

[1]*Film Enquiry Committee Report*, para 127, p. 41.
[2]B.R. Chopra, "Film and the Censor," *Filmfare*, 1 December 1972.
[3]*Film Enquiry Committee Report*, para 130, p. 42.

Contents

1

Birth and Bondage

An Art is Born

If a precise date could be given for the beginning of cinema, it would probably be 14 April 1894, when Thomas A. Edison's Kinetoscope was installed for public and commercial showings in New York. Edison had made a decisive step forward by inventing the modern film format of 35 mm and the Kinetoscope ran 35 mm perforated films 50 ft in length. But it was a small machine through which only one person at a time could look.[1]

Immediately following the installation of the Kinetoscope dozens of inventors all over Western Europe and North America attempted to project films on to a large screen. For their experiments they used copies of Edison's films which were available for sale or films of the Edison format which they printed on chronophotographs—imitations of the Frenchman Jules Marey's invention.

Almost two years of frenzied experimentation were to pass before the Lumière Brothers unveiled their cinematograph in the basement of the Grand Café in Paris on 28 December 1895. For the first time, moving pictures were projected on to a screen where they could be seen by several people at once. Within weeks of the Paris triumph the Lumière Brothers sent their operators all over the world to popularize their invention.

The cinematograph succeeded in captivating audiences wherever it was shown, and it was shown everywhere. In Russia, where there was a command performance for the Tsar and Tsarina, in Morocco, Bombay and Hong Kong, people came in growing numbers, fascinated with the cinematograph by which name this new spectacle was to become established as the Seventh Art. On 7 July 1896, just six months after the Paris demonstration, and three months after the first public showing in New York of Edison's newest invention, the Vitascope, on 23 April 1896, Indian audiences too were introduced to the moving picture.

The first few showings were held four times a day, at Watson's Hotel. They were so popular that on 14 July they were moved to the Novelty Theatre. Here they continued for a month with several changes in their daily programmes. The curiosity and interest generated was such that a special Indian arrangement was soon introduced and boxes in the theatre were reserved for "*purdah* ladies and their families only."

Indian Interest in the Cinematograph

Although these first showings attracted largely British audiences along with such educated Indians who identified their interests and tastes with those of the British, on a few Indians the impact of these early films was electrifying. One of these, Harishchandra Sakharam Bhatvadekar had opened a photographic studio in Bombay in the 1880s. On seeing the Lumiere show, he immediately ordered a motion picture camera from London. When it arrived, he photographed a wrestling match in Bombay. The film had, naturally, to be sent to London for processing. While waiting for it to be returned, he acquired a projector and also became an exhibitor of imported films. In 1901 he filmed what was later termed the first "newsreel event" in Indian film chronology; an Indian student R.P. Paranjpye had won special distinction at Cambridge University in England. His triumphant return to India was the occasion for great jubilation and the expression of a sort of nationalist pride in his achievement. This was the first of the historic and significant events that Bhatvadekar filmed before giving up production for exhibition.

In the meanwhile, several other exhibitors and inventors had come from America and Europe, bringing their motion picture making and projecting machines. Events moved quickly and enterprising Indians too began to import films, projectors and cameras, turning out such items as *Poona Races 98, Train Arriving at Bombay Station, Great Bengal Partition Movement, Tilak's Visit to Calcutta and Procession,* and *Terrible Hyderabad Floods.*

These films were shown in theatres, usually after plays, concerts and magic shows. In Calcutta, Hiralal Sen in 1898 filmed scenes from plays presented at the classic theatres. This has led some to claim for him the honour of being the first Indian film maker since what he filmed were not simple documentary events, but stories with actors. This point is, however, disputable. Later, in 1909, some members of a dramatic club in Bombay attempted a filmed version of one of their most popular plays *Pundalik.* They managed to raise the finances through friends, and technical equipment as well as an English cameraman from the British company, Bourne and Shepherd. Although *Pundalik* (Pundalik) was merely a play filmed entirely as it was staged, the finished film was 8000 ft long and earned for its director R.G. Torney, the distinction of being the first feature film maker in Indian cinema. But after this initial achievement, Torney faded into obscurity and produced nothing memorable. Today it is not he but his immediate successor the great D.G. Phalke who is celebrated as the first real film maker of India.

A significant step in the growth and popularity of the cinema was the travelling cinema show, held in tents or out in the open. The greater majority of Indians lived outside the cities and were used to open-air performances of folk theatre and music. It was consequently a logical move for the film exhibitor to take his show from village to village for the immensely popular one-night stand. The practice of travelling cinema shows continues to be an important feature of village life.

Jamshedji Framji Madan was the first of these showmen. In 1902, having bought the requisite equipment from an agent of Pathé Frères, he held a "Bioscope" show in the central park of Calcutta. This was for him the beginning of a film production-distribution-exhibition empire that for three decades dominated the scene in the whole of British India, which at that time also included Ceylon and Burma.

Another flamboyant film personality—Abdulally Esoofally—began as a tent showman. From 1901 to 1907 he held shows in Singapore, Sumatra, Java, Burma and Ceylon, and from 1908 to

1914, exhibited throughout India. In 1914, Esoofally settled down in Bombay, taking over the Alexandra Theatre with Ardeshir M. Irani as his partner. In 1918 they built the Majestic Theatre where in 1931, the first Indian talking film *Alam Ara* (Beauty of the World) produced and directed by Ardeshir Irani, was premiéred.

The films presented by these early film exhibitors were acquired from several different sources—France was the leading supplier, and, since in the silent era language was not a barrier, films from America, Italy, England, Denmark and Germany were all seen and enjoyed even by largely uneducated Indian audiences.

In 1910, the technique of making films was a jealously guarded secret, and for the Indian anxious to learn this new craft, it was not easy. Even if he had the money and resources to go to Europe or America, it was by no means certain that he could get into any of the big film manufacturing companies as they were called then (e.g., Hepworth Manufacturing Co., or Edison Manufacturing Co.). Those that were prepared to accept apprentices, demanded huge sums of money from them. There was naturally no way of learning the craft in India, nor were there any laboratories for processing film.

D.G. Phalke, First Indian Film Maker

Some time around 1910, D.G. Phalke, Sanskrit scholar, painter, photographer, printer and magician, dissatisfied with all these as a profession, realized that his future lay in film. He spent two years studying magazines and catalogues on the subject, and took a trip to Europe to look at and buy equipment. He went to see the editor of *The Bioscope* in London who was so impressed by the knowledge that Phalke had acquired on his own, that he arranged for him to spend some time at the immense Hepworth Manufacturing Company, visiting its 18 workshops and watching rehearsals and actual shooting on the sets.[2]

On his return to India, all Phalke could raise money for was to shoot a little film on the growth of a pea into a plant, but it did help to get him the finances he needed for a major film, and on 8 May 1913, *Raja Harishchandra*(King Harishchandra)had a triumphant premiére at the Coronation Theatre in Bombay. Phalke chose the life of Raja Harishchandra as the subject of his first film for several reasons, the principal one being that as a story from the

Mahabharata, it was well-known throughout India and had in fact, often been performed as a folk play. This was an important consideration as it meant that the film could be seen and understood everywhere even though the subtitles, in both English and Hindi, were meaningless to the vast majority of Indians who were illiterate. As it is, immediately after the first show in Bombay and Poona, screenings of the film were held in Calcutta and even in Colombo and Rangoon where the masses were familiar with stories from the Hindu epics.

One of the more harmful effects of foreign rule is the imposition of the ideals of the rulers on the ruled. There had been a growing emphasis on English education between 1880 and 1901. Since only those who were educated in these new schools were eligible for government jobs, the indigenous school system suffered a rapid decline and in 1911 there was 94 per cent illiteracy in India.[3] The avowed aim of those who had wanted education in English for India was to "substitute Western culture for the Indian" and, at the same time, to create a class of Indians who would be "Indian in blood and colour but English in tastes, in opinion, in morals and in intellect."[4] In this they succeeded so well that for a while the English-educated Indian turned his back on all things Indian—on arts and crafts, on literature and history, on his own language itself. In Mahatma Gandhi's opinion, "This English education in the manner it has been given has emasculated the English-educated Indians; it has put a severe strain upon the Indian student's energy, and has made of us imitators."[5] Apart from this newly-created, anglicized Indian bourgeoisie which learnt to glorify and idealize British rule while deprecating India's own history and achievements, were the highly politicized freedom fighters on the one hand and the vast illiterate mass on the other. Both felt the need to cling to *their* culture, *their* religion—a need that *Raja Harishchandra* fulfilled in large measure. It also set a trend of mythological films popular even today where mythology and tales from the epics hold for the average Indian both a vivid reality and a religious significance.

Raja Harishchandra was released in May 1913. Its stunning popularity encouraged other Indians already engaged in film activity of one kind or another, to take the plunge into the uncertain hazards of feature film making. Dhiren Ganguly, known familiarly as "D.G.," member of a well-to-do family of Calcutta, at an early age became principal of the Nizam of Hyderabad's Art College on a then princely salary of Rs 1,500 a month. Interested in photography as well as art, he published a book of photographs in 1915, and sent it to J.F. Madan in Calcutta. By 1918 he had given up his very lucrative job, and disowned by his horrified family, was living in a Rs 7 a month room in Calcutta, deeply involved in trying his hand at films.[6] In 1920 his first film *England Returned* was released. A delicious satirical comedy, it started D.G. on a long career of comedy and satire, which has still not ended.

The enthusiastic expansion of the cinema was checked by the outbreak of war in Europe. The manufacture of raw film became restricted and equipment harder to come by. For the exhibitor too, there were fewer and fewer European films to import. Less affected by the great War of 1914-18, America moved with alacrity into this vacuum, flooding the market in India with American films.

Measures of Control: Introduction of Censorship

By this time the popularity and spread of the cinema had achieved such disquieting proportions that the British authorities determined to bring it under some kind of governmental control. In England, France and America, a form of censorship and control had been in practice for some years. In France, although no Parliamentary legislation has ever been passed for controlling the cinema, in January 1909 a Ministerial Circular addressed to all *Préfets*, classed cinema as a *spectacle de curiosité* and reminded the *Préfets* of the power of the *Maires* to forbid them. Another Ministerial Circular on 19 April 1913 reminded the *Préfets* that the *spectacle de curiosité* into which category[7] the cinematograph unquestionably falls, remained governed by the already existing legislation, (i.e., Article 4, titre XI of the Law of August 16-24, 1790 in the following terms: *spectacles publics* may not be permitted and authorized except by municipal officials").

Although theatrical censorship had been abolished in France in 1906, and although film is more comparable with drama, as the film industry pointed out again and again, for many years after its beginning, cinema was not so much a serious dramatic art form as a series of one-reel farces, *actualités* and melodramas, shown mainly at fair grounds and in music halls. The actions of *Maires* and *Préfets* based on these *arretés* were continually contested and control and censorship of films went through many changes and modifications.

In America, local censorship of films was first introduced in 1907. Chicago passed an Ordinance on 4 November 1907 requiring police inspection and licensing of all films to be shown in the city. A permit could be withheld by the Chief of Police, if a film was considered "immoral" or "obscene."[8]

In 1909, a group of citizens in New York formed the National Board of Censorship (later called the National Board of Review), to preview and judge films before their release. This Board was set up with the object of heading off government censorship. With the moral and financial support of the film industry, which agreed to abide by its decisions, government control was put off until 1921 when New York State passed a licensing law.

In 1911, Pennsylvania enacted the first censorship law, followed in 1913 by Ohio and Kansas, and in 1916 by Maryland. Although at that time the US Supreme Court upheld the constitutionality of these laws, Federal authorities have taken little active part in film censorship. In a country where legislative power is divided between the Federal Government and the States, censorship was centralized only by means of the film industry's own system of self-regulation.[9]

In England, by 1907, the making and exhibition of films had become a highly organized business. This organization and expansion of cinema meant that the majority of buildings in which films were shown no longer came under the licensing powers of the local authorities, who began an attempt to obtain wider powers from Parliament. The campaign to obtain the powers played upon the fear of fire during cinematograph exhibitions. The film trade showed great naiveté in not opposing this move, for should a Parliamentary Act give powers to a local authority to license places of exhibition for films, the danger was that these authorities[10] might attempt to improve upon Home Office regulations.

On 1 January 1910, the Cinematograph Act (1909) came into force. But already in December, the Theatres and Music Halls Committee of the London Country Council had recommended that licenses issued under this act should forbid the opening of Cinema Halls on Sundays. Thus, even before it was promulgated the Act passed "to make better provision for securing safety at Cinematograph and other exhibitions" began to be used for a purpose other than the one stated.

Little by little, the local authorities extended their powers by making the granting of licenses conditional upon various grounds until, inevitably, the subject matter of film also began to be taken into consideration. The public attitude to the cinema was also becoming hostile. On 29 December 1910, *The Bioscope* wrote: "One can hardly peruse a daily or weekly paper without reading something in the nature of an attack on moving pictures."[11]

The idea of a trade censor of films began to be mooted by exhibitors. Tired of the contempt with which their efforts were being greeted, they sought respectability and acceptance. In July 1912 the Cinematograph Exhibitors Association passed the motion that "censorship is necessary and advisable," and on 7 November 1912, the British Board of Film Censors came into being, as a form of self-regulation by the film industry.[12] The Board was recognized but not given official support by the Home Office. Power still lay with the local licensing authorities and could not be taken away from them without an Act of Parliament. Although the Board worked according to general principles with no code and only two specific rules—"no nudity, and no portrayal of Christ"—a set of rules was drawn up by the Home Office and the local licensing authorities which recognized the existence of the Board of Censors. But efforts to bring the licensing authorities and the British Board of Film Censors together under one set of guiding principles proved abortive. A somewhat ambiguous situation prevailed for some time, with local authorities keeping their privilege of banning films approved by the Board. In 1917 the Cinema Enquiry Commission published a report favourable to the British Board of Film Censors. Under its then President T.P. O'Connor, the Board's decisions began to be recognized by both the film industry and the local licensing authorities. But the 1909 Act remained in force with some amendments until the widespread use of safety film rendered obsolete the fire prevention hazard on which it was based. A new Cinematograph Act was passed only in 1952.

The Great Awakening

The turn of the century, when Bombay audiences thrilled to the Lumière cinematograph saw a great national awakening in India, a rising political awareness, the resurgence of a pride in being Indian, an increasing impatience with British rule.

Two international events had a profound effect on Indian politics as well. Two occidental powers suffered military defeat; in 1896 Italy lost to Abyssinia and in 1905 Russia was driven back by Japan. In this atmosphere, nationalism became almost a religion for the Indian youth.

In India, a severe famine in 1896 was only one of a series brought about as much by ruinous land taxation and rent collection as by natural disaster. Appalling conditions in the countryside, plague, drought and hunger, were met by British indifference. For over a 100 years the peasants had suffered with nowhere to go and no one to turn to for help. But by the end of the nineteenth century the climate in India was changing. More educated men with a concern for social justice emerged on the national scene, and the systematic impoverishment of the country and its people augmented the growing anger with British rule.

A free and lively press was largely responsible for stirring up nationalist sentiment. The first session of the Indian National Congress in 1885 was closely related to the development of the press as the founders and editors of some of the leading newspapers were also prominent among the founders of the national political organization. Dadasaheb Naoroji was editor of *Rost Goftar*, Narendranath Sen, editor, *Indian Mirror*, G. Subramania Iyer, editor, *The Hindu*, Ranade, founder-editor of *Indu Prakash*. At the turn of the century the Indian National Congress was in the hands of a Moderate group that hoped to bring about social and economic reforms without violent confrontation with the British. The platform of the Congress was thus denied to the Extremists who turned to the press to express their urgent demands for self-government.

The press had suffered many vicissitudes since the first newspapers were founded around 1820. Press Laws had been passed, amended, annulled and passed again, according to the political leanings of successive Viceroys. The major English language papers, still in existence today—*The Times of India, The Tribune, The Hindu, The Madras Mail, The Amrita Bazaar Patrika*—started publication in the second half of the nineteenth century in different parts of Indian—Bombay, Lahore, Calcutta, Madras. Although a few papers had been started earlier, it was the great reformer Raja Rammohan Roy, who really founded the nationalist press. His *Sambad Kanmudi* in Bengali around 1821, and the *Mirat-Ul-*

Akhbar in Persian in 1822, were the first publications with a distinctly nationalist and democratic progressive orientation.[13]

From 1823 till 1853, fairly stringent press restrictions were in force. A period of freedom was then enjoyed until the Indian Mutiny of 1857, when a very repressive Press Act, known popularly as the Gagging Act, was passed. But in the face of violent opposition and protest, it remained in operation for one year only. The Press and Registration of Books Act 1867 which restricted freedom of printing and publication of books, and the Vernacular Press Act 1878, imposed firm restrictions on the vernacular press which was growing rapidly and becoming the organ of nationalist views, critical of the British government. In December 1881, the liberal Viceroy, Lord Ripon, repealed this Act and until 1908 the Indian press enjoyed considerable freedom.[14]

It was in this climate of leniency that in 1889 B.G. Tilak, militant nationalist, denied admission to the moderate Indian National Congress, founded *The Kesari* in Marathi and *The Maratha* in English. In his hands, these two papers became potent weapons for the spread of disaffection. The young, the militant, the Extremists, rallied to his stirring call: "Swaraj (self-government) is my birthright, and I shall have it." In 1897, Tilak was sentenced to 18 months rigorous imprisonment for his "seditious" articles in *The Kesari*.[15] The publication of the paper was, however, not banned. The Press continued to grow and in 1908 when the most restrictive Press Act yet was passed, there were 708 papers in English and the vernacular languages.[16]

The means of disseminating information at the end of the nineteenth century were very limited. Apart from the newspapers which reached only a small, literate, urban group, there was only the theatre. A folk theatre, presenting mainly folk tales and stories from the epics in the form of dance dramas, had existed for many centuries. The classical theatre in Sanskrit was again limited to educated urban audiences. A modern theatre, dealing with contemporary concerns and performed in the spoken languages was born only towards the middle of the nineteenth century. This was the time also that a social awareness in themes, and simpler realistic acting came into being.

A Bengali play—*Neeladarpana*—performed in the 1870s in Lucknow by National Theatre of Bengal, so incensed the Europeans in the audience that they attacked the players.[17] The Dramatic

Performances Act, 1876, was the direct outcome of this incident. This Act authorized any magistrate to stop a performance and arrest the actors if it was found that the performance was "scandalous, or defamatory, or likely to excite feelings of dissatisfaction towards the Government, or likely to cause pain to any private party." In actual practice, the Act was interpreted by police inspectors who in their zeal, censored even words such as "motherland" or "mother India."

After *Neeladarpana*, the Indian theatre assumed a sociopolitical colouration, expressed through comedy and historical-mythological plays. A favourite character was the anglicized Indian who aped British customs and manners.[18] Theatre became a platform for the expression of national pride as well as entertainment. The veiled symbolism in the mythologicals was at once recognized by the people. Their influence was far-reaching because they attracted large numbers of women who did not otherwise visit the theatre. In *Keechakvadha* (1906), a Marathi play based on an incident in the *Mahabharata*, the audience immediately recognized the fiery Tilak in the person of the hero Bhima, while the unpopular Viceroy Lord Curzon was unmistakable as the villain Keechak. This was one of the 150 plays banned on the Marathi stage alone under British rule.[19]

Establishment of Censorship in India

Until 1918, the film maker and the film exhibitor in India enjoyed total freedom. Occasionally even films that had not been approved by the controlling authority in their own countries were imported into, and exhibited in, India. A form of local control did exist before 1918, but "the existing law on the subject was for the most part framed long before the cinematograph was dreamt of and is altogether inadequate a deal with films which may be objectionable."[20] The laws by which control was exercised came under the Indian Penal Code and the Criminal Procedure Code, and were concerned mainly with obscenity, wounding religious susceptibilities or inciting disaffection against the Government.[21] No uniformity in judging a film was possible because "the authority which decides whether an exhibition is objectionable is a single local official whose judgement may differ very widely from that of a similar authority in another town."[22]

Measures to control cinematograph exhibitions had long been in force in Burma. Notifications had been issued under the Burma Towns Act 1907 and the Burma Village Act 1907 declaring that these exhibitions could only be given under a license issued by the authority appointed to do so. In Rangoon, censorship was entrusted to the Commissioner of Police, assisted by a committee appointed by the local government. The committee consisted of six official members and 12 non-official members. The actual work of censorship was carried out by sub-committees, each consisting of one official and two non-official members.[23]

Introducing the Cinematograph Bill in the Legislative Council on 5 September 1917, Sir William Vincent said :

Most other civilized countries have found it necessary to revise and supplement the existing law for the control of spectacular entertainments with special reference to this form of exhibition. Two points are to be considered : (*a*) Safety of the audience: and (*b*) Prevention of objectionable films being exhibited. It is obviously necessary to guard against the exhibition of indecent and improper films, or those which wound religious or racial feeling.... If it had not been for the preoccupation with the War, the Bill would have been brought before the Council earlier.

The Bill was not passed without spirited objection from some Indian members of the Legislative Council : "There is no word in the Bill itself to indicate what is improper or objectionable.... There is the likelihood of this Bill working unnecessarily harshly, and any film that may not suit the taste of the censoring officer will be prohibited.[24] I look upon this Bill as a humiliation sought to be imposed upon the liberties of the people."[25]

An attempt was made by Kharpade, an Indian member of the Legislative Council, to make it possible to appeal against a decision, not to the Provincial Government, but to a Court of Law on the grounds that: "In matters where the liberty of the subject is to be curtailed, it has always been the rule that the final decision should rest with a Court of Law."[26] In his reply Sir William Vincent insisted that the liberty of the subject was not really curtailed. He went on to add : "So far I am aware, there is no precedent for such an appeal, nor is there in England any appeal whatever. Again, although in many of our Acts the authorities are authorized to impose restrictions on such things as public processions in towns, I do not know of any case in which a right of appeal to the High Court is given. If we ask the Court to decide questions of this kind, without evidence, we shall be placing them in an impossible position, and if a decision on these appeals is to be delayed until the evidence is forthcoming and affidavits filed, the maximum amount of delay, expense and inconvenience will be caused."[27]

The possibility of extending the Dramatic Performances Act 1876 to cover the cinema was considered, but not adopted. According to this Act, power was vested entirely in the hands of the District Magistrate or the Commissioner of Police to prohibit performances that might be considered as being (*a*) of a scandalous or defamatory nature; (*b*) likely to excite feelings of disaffection with the government; (*c*) likely to deprave and corrupt persons present at the performances.

Referring to this Act, Sir William Vincent had said:

It is partly because we are averse to purely official control that we have refrained from amending the Dramatic Performances Act of 1876 so as to cover the cinematograph. The Act does give some powers of censorship but it contains no provisions for the safety of audiences, and if we had attempted to amend it to meet modern requirements, it would really have been necessary to recast it altogether.[28]

Other existing laws enabling local authorities to enforce protection against overcrowding, fire and other dangers in places of assembly were scattered over a number of provincial enactments. But their powers did not extend to travelling film shows, nor did they cover the whole of India. Fires were a definite danger. In November 1917 a fire in a Calcutta Theatre destroyed 100,000 ft of film.[29] Since the auditorium at that time was empty, nobody was injured. However, with memories of the great fires in European theatres[30] it was considered essential to enact regulations affording some form of protection against the hazard of fire.

The Cinematograph Act 1918

For all practical purposes, therefore, film censorship began in India with the passing of the Cinematograph Act in 1918. The Act declared that :

No person shall give an exhibition by means of a cinematograph elsewhere than in a place licensed under the Act. (Section 3)

Licences were to be granted by the District Magistrate or by the Commissioner of Police. (Section 4)

No film should be exhibited unless it had first been certified by the prescribed authority as suitable for public exhibition. (Section 5 [2])

The Governor-General in Council would by notification in the Gazette of India, constitute as many authorities as he might think fit for examining and certifying films with the certificate of such an authority to be valid in areas specified in the notification, (Section 7 [1])

However, the exhibition of a film could be suspended and its certificate annulled in any Province, on the authority of the District Magistrate or Commissioner of Police, pending the order of the Provincial Government, which could uncertify the film for the whole or part of the province. (Section 7 [5] & [6])

If an authority refused to certify a film, the person applying for the certificate could appeal within 30 days of the decision, for consideration of the matter by the Local Government. (Section 7 [3])

From May 1920, in accordance with the terms of this Act, and with the concurrence of smaller provincial towns,[31] Censor Boards were set up in the four seaport towns of Bombay, Calcutta, Madras and Rangoon,[32] where foreign films could be submitted for approval immediately upon their arrival in India. These were also the four major cities in British India, and as such were the centres for the exhibition, and later, production, of films. The northern city of Lahore was not a port, but it was an important town where, as a concession to the growing local film production, a Censor Board was established in 1927.

During the following decade, censorship was applied with varying degrees of severity, reflecting the attitudes and reactions of the areas where the Boards were located. The composition of each Board also differed considerably, although the procedure adopted for examining films was more or less similar.

The Bombay Board consisted of (1) the Commissioner of Police, who was the President ex-officio, (2) the Collector of Customs, (3) a member of the Indian Educational Service, (4) a prominent Hindu citizen of Bombay, (5) a prominent Muslim citizen, and (6) a prominent Parsi citizen. All members were appointed by the Government of Bombay. No European as such was appointed as it was considered that European interests were adequately safeguarded by the official members, some of whom would in any case be European. The Board met twice a month, and each member received a small fee for each meeting and each film examined. A part-time Secretary, who was Indian, was paid a regular monthly salary of Rs 350. The films were examined by an Indian Inspector who was paid a maximum salary of Rs 500 per month plus a travel allowance. The Inspector was required to have a good University degree, and to have travelled in the West. The procedure adopted for certifying a film was that on receipt of an application, the Secretary or the Inspector examined the film within the period prescribed by the Board from time to time, and submitted his report to the Board. On the basis of the report, the Board would award or withhold a certificate. The Board could ask for the film to be re-examined by a Committee of its members before giving a final decision if it was thought necessary.[33]

The Calcutta Board consisted of (1) the Commissioner of Police, President ex-officio, (2) the Station Staff Officer, (3) a European lady representative, (4) and (5) one representative each of the Bengal Chamber of Commerce, and the Calcutta Trades Association, (6) a Jewish merchant, (7) a Muslim representative of the Education Department, and (8) a Hindu lawyer, representing the Calcutta Corporation. A Deputy Commissioner of Police, with a monthly allowance of Rs 100 was the ex-officio secretary. The Calcutta Board had a part-time European Inspector with an allowance of Rs 300 a month and an Indian Inspector with a maximum salary of Rs 150 per month plus a travel allowance. The members of the Board and the Secretary received a small fee for attending Board meetings and for examining films. The procedure for certifying films was the same as in Bombay, except that the period between receiving an application and examining a film was fixed at seven days.[34]

At Madras too, the ex-officio president was the Commissioner of Police. The Board consisted of one military representative and four Indian gentlemen of whom one had to be Muslim. The full Board was seldom required to meet. There was no Inspector of films and each film was examined by a member of the Board. The fees levied for certification were equally divided among the members of the Board who were given no other allowances. The Madras Board adopted the certification procedure followed by Bombay and Calcutta with the difference that the President himself or a member deputed by him, examined the film within seven days of the date of its delivery to the Board.[35]

The Censor Board at Rangoon was composed of (1) the Commissioner of Police, as President ex-officio, (2) the Assistant Commissioner of Police, ex-officio, who also acted as the Secretary, (3) a military representative, (4) a European medical man who represented the Vigilance Society, and (5) three Burmese gentlemen and one Burmese lady. The Board normally met once a week and each member was paid a fee for attending meetings and certifying films. There was no Inspector of films, and each film was examined by a sub-committee consisting of not less than two members who were appointed by the President.[36]

The Lahore Board (instituted in 1927) was to have five members with the Director of the Information Bureau as Secretary of the Board. Films would be seen by the Inspector and the Superintendent of Police, both of whom were to be on the Board. No remuneration would be given to any of the members and the Board was to be alloted only Rs 500 for its monthly expenditure. The Lahore Board would adopt the standard followed by the other Boards, and be guided by the Instructions to Inspectors which had been formulated by the Bengal and Bombay Censor Boards.[37]

To assist the Inspector in his work, the Bombay Board of Censors drew up a list of points to be kept in mind while examining and judging a film for certification. The "Suggestions to Inspetors of Films" begins with the statement of some general principles:

No generally and rigidly applicable rules of censorship can be laid down.

It is essential to be consistent but impossible to aim at strictly logical decisions.

Each film must be judged on its own merits.

Nothing should be approved which in the Inspector's honest opinion is calculated to demoralize an audience or any section of it.

Inspectors should consider the impression likely to be made on an average audience in India which includes a not inconsiderable proportion of illiterate people, or those of immature judgment.

The "Suggestions" also included, with one exception,[38] the list prepared by the British Board of Film Censors in 1916, of subjects that might be considered objectionable. These had become famous as T.P. O'Connor's (the President of the British Board of Film Censors) 43 Rules, and they were taken over practically word for word by the Indian Boards. But the ambiguity in the phrasing of certain Rules led the Censors in their zeal to err on the side of severity rather than leniency. Rules such as "No vulgar accessories in the staging," or "offensive vulgarity and impropriety in conduct and dress," or "references to controversial politics," were bound to be interpreted by the censors according to their own lights.

The Calcutta Board in its turn issued circulars to all principal managements of theatres, and to importers and exporters, giving the chief points which might render a film "undesirable for exhibition in British India."

(1) Rape
(2) Leading young girls astray
(3) Prostitution
(4) Feminine nudity
(5) Scenes showing women in a drunken state
(6) Exaggerated scenes of debauchery at cabarets and saloons
(7) Scenes based on the desecration of religious places of worship
(8) Torture or cruelty scenes by whites versus blacks or vice versa

Four principles were to be kept steadfastly in view, viz. Moral, Racial, Religious and Political. These rules were framed while keeping in mind the kind of films being imported, principally from America. In a letter to the Secretary, Government of India, H.L.

Stephenson, Chief Secretary to the Government of Bengal, explained that: "The Board has exercised strictness in the certification of the propaganda type of films produced chiefly in America, in which scenes of an exaggerated nature are introduced, i.e., white men and women shown in a state of extreme drunkenness in order to portray the degradation caused by drink. Such scenes do not convey the moral intended, to a half-educated audience, but simply give an erroneous idea of Western manners and ideals."[39]

Notes

[1]R.S. Randall, *Censorship of the Movies: The Social & Political Control of a Mass Medium*, University of Wisconsin Press, 1968, p. 10.

[2]Satish Bahadur, "Some Aspects of Phalke," Film Institute of India, Poona, 1970; "Swadeshi Moving Pictures"—an article on Phalke published in *The Kesari*, 19 August 1973, translated by Narmada Shahane, *Studies in Film History*, Film Institute of India, Poona, 1970.

[3]A.R. Desai, *Social Background of Indian Nationalism*, Popular Book Depot, Bombay, 1946.

[4]Lord Macaulay, "Minute on Education," *Cambridge History of India*, Vol. VI, p. iii, Reprinted in New Delhi, S. Chand & Co., 1968.

[5]*Collected Works of Mahatma Gandhi*, Vol. XX (April-August 1921), Publications Division, Ministry of Information and Broadcasting, New Delhi, 1966, p. 42.

[6]D.G. Ganguly in an interview with the author, Calcutta, April 1975.

[7]In 1901 the *Prefet* of Paris had banned final sections of Zecca's "Histoire d'un Crime." See *Jeanne et Ford: Historie Encyclopedique du Cinema*, Vol. I, p. 78. Also, N.M. Hunnings, *Film Censors and the Law*, Allen & Unwin, 1967, p. 333.

[8]Hunnings, *ibid.*, p. 151, and Randall *op. cit.*, p. 11.

[9]Randall, *ibid.*, p. 12.

[10]Their position here was similar to the *Maires* in France. Hunnings, *op. cit.*, p. 46.

[11]Hunnings, *ibid.*, p. 65.

[12]*Ibid.*, p. 52.

[13]S. Natarajan, *History of Indian Journalism*, Publications Division, Ministry of Information and Broadcasting, Delhi, 1955, p. 98.

[14]*Ibid.*, p. 93.

[15]*Cambridge History of India*, Vol. VI, p. 551.

[16]*Ibid.*, p. 681.

[17]B. Gargi, *Theatre in India*, Theatre Art Books, New York, 1962, p. 109.

[18]*Ibid.*, p. 110.

[19]*Ibid.*, p.126.

[20]*Indian Cinematograph Committee (hereafter ICC) Report*, 1927, para 13.

[21]Legislative Council Debate, 5 September 1917.

[22]*Ibid.*

[23]Letter from F.W. Rice, Chief Secretary to Government of Burma to Secretary to Government of India, Home Department, 2 September 1918.

[24]Legislative Council Debate, 5 March 1918, Hon'ble Mr Ayyangar.

[25]*Ibid.*, Hon'ble Mr Kharpade.

[26]*Ibid.*

[27]Legislative Council Debate, 5 March 1918.

[28]*Ibid.*, 5 September 1917.

[29]*Ibid.*, 6 February 1918.

[30]Eg. the cinema-theater of the Bazaar de la Charite in Paris, May 1897, and earlier in Covent Garden, London 1856, St Petersburg 1836 and Ring Theatre in Vienna, 1881.

[31]Eg. letter from Mr H. Mc Pherson, Chief Secretary to Govt. of Bihar and Orissa, to Secy. Govt. of India, Home Department, 20 June 1918. "With the exception of occasional exhibitions by Calcutta firms in one or two of the larger towns, cine exhibitions are unknown in Bihar & Orissa. The Lt. Governor therefore feels that he is not in a position to assist the Govt. of India with an opinion based on these exhibitions. He would have no objection to accepting the certificates of the examining boards which will be constituted at the Chief seaport towns." Proceedings of the Home Department, February 1920.

[32]Press communique, Delhi, 31 January 1920.

[33]*ICC Report*, 1927, paras 228-238, Central Publications Branch, Calcutta 1928.

[34]*Ibid.*

[35]*Ibid.*, paras 228-238, pp. 106.

[36]*Ibid.*

[37]*Evidences*, Vol. II p. 11-12; Evidence of Mr Muzaffar Khan, Director of Information Bureau, Punjab.

[38]"The effects of vitriol throwing."

[39]Home Department, file 71 of 1922, Subject of Tightening up of Film Censorship.

2

Imperial Preference

Reactions to Foreign Films Exhibited in India

All through the twenties, there were strong protests both in England and among the English residents in India, against the kind of films that were being shown in India. Questions were asked in the English Parliament, and articles and letters in the press as well as individuals and citizens groups, demanded tighter control and stricter censorship for a variety of reasons. In 1921 W. Evans, a "cinema expert", was asked by the Government of India to make a survey of the cinema industry in India. In his report he stated that the existing Boards of Censors were "weak and inexperienced," and he suggested that the Government of India should urge the Provincial Governments to "stiffen up and raise to reasonable efficiency the present censorship which is largely nominal." From 1921 onward the general trend of criticism was as stated by a Bishop at a conference in England in 1926 : "The majority of films which are chiefly from America[1] are of sensational and daring murders, crimes and divorces, and, on the whole, degrade the white woman in the eyes of the Indians." An article in the *Times* of London on 23 August 1923, said :

There has recently arisen a good deal of dissatisfaction among British residents in our possessions in the East on account of the unsuitable nature of many of the films that are being shown in cinemas frequented by the native population. A great many films that are sent to India and other countries are quite unsuitable for exhibition to natives. Either they are actively injurious, as when scenes of violence or passion are exhibited, or they are passively harmful, as when they exhibit the white man in a foolish or contemptible light. The native never seems to grow up mentally, and the average audience at these picture theatres is, therefore, composed of those who are mature in body and very immature indeed in mind. To them are exhibited "sex films" made in American studios, and films in which violence is the main theme. With these may be sandwiched a comic film showing a white man carrying out a series of ridiculous antics. The result is inevitable, and a little while ago there was definite proof that the abduction by natives of an officer's wife was suggested by a serial film in which scenes of violence occurred.

The Westminister Gazette wrote a piece on "The Cinema in India" on 17 November 1921:

One the great reasons of the hardly veiled contempt of the native Indians for us may be found in the introduction and development of 'moving pictures' in India. A visitor to an average cinema show in England will be treated to a more or less sensational drama in which somebody's morals have gone decidedly wrong, a thrilling but impossible cowboy film and, of course, will be afforded an opportunity to appreciate (or not) our marvellous sense of humour as displayed by Charlie Chaplin squirting inoffending people with soda syphons, or breaking innumerable windows.

Now imagine the effect of such films on the Oriental mind. Like us, the Indian goes to see the 'movies,' but is not only impressed by story of the film, but by the difference in dress, in customs, and in morals. He sees our women on the films in scanty garb. He marvels at our heavy, infantile humour—his own is on a higher and more intellectual level. He forms his own opinions of our morals during the nightly unrolled dramas of unfaithful wives and immoral husbands, our lightly broken promises, our dishonoured laws. It is difficult for the Britisher in India to keep up his dignity, and to extol or to enforce moral laws which the native sees lightly disregarded by the Britons themselves in the "picture palaces."

The cinema provoked another response as well. *The Manchester Guardian* on 4 September 1923, was amused at the violent reactions to the cinema, saying:

Hot water seems to be the natural element of the kinema industry; it has always done, or is about to do, something that gravely shocks the conscience of the community which it is preparing to enslave. If a film renter were to establish a branch office at the North Pole there would probably be an indignation meeting of polar bears within 15 minutes of the conclusion of his first (trade) show. And what is more, according to their native lights, the bears would probably be right. But perhaps the real explanation of why the kinema finds itself so often in trouble is the same for the East and the West. It is altogether too successful. When it does give offence, it delivers the offence like an avalanche. Pictures reach so many and tell their tale so fast that those who object to the tale cannot but take notice of its tendency. They might deplore in silence the errors of the printed word, but there is no ignoring the films with their instantaneous message to all sorts and conditions of men.

Implementation of Censorship

The Censor Boards were certainly not ignoring the power of the cinema nor did the government show any inclination to encourage the growth of an Indian film industry. Its attention was entirely focussed on coping with the influx of imported films above.

In 1921-22, of the 1320 films exhibited in India only 64 were Indian.[2] In 1920, the Calcutta Board made cuts in 49 films, and refused certificates to 13.[3] The Boards were particularly sensitive to nudity, passionate or suggestive love-making, women in a state of drunkeness, anything that might show the white man in a bad light, scenes of western women in any contact with "Oriental men" and, of course, any reference to political activity or ideology. Portions that were required to be entirely deleted included scnes such as: "woman on bed beckoning to man on couch," "the dinner scene showing the man and woman drunk and fondling each other," "the husband kissing the wife's toes while she is in bed," and "scenes where hero is shown holding heroine by the bust." In sub-titles the word "ravisher" was to be ommitted whenever it occurred (this is an American film of 1925, called *The Rape of Helen*). Cuts were ordered in a number of Biblical films released in the '20s, e.g., "Omit Adam quite nude walking quietly across picture," "scene showing temptation of Joseph by the wife of the Pharoah," "scene of Eve leaning over the body of Abel, where her breasts can be seen." Another reason for scenes being cut is illustrated in rulings such as: "Cut scene showing Mohammedan brigand holding and fondling white woman," "a European embracing a Tibetan girl in a dancing den," "scenes showing Chinaman throttling white woman," or even "omit dance between white girl and coloured man." Nothing was permitted that might throw any doubt on the inherent superiority of the white man e.g., "Omit scene showing a squad of British soldiers with fixed bayonets driving back a crowd in Constaintinople," "scene showing English priest mad with thirst," "omit subtitles 'Lawless Ireland,' and 'Police Reprisals in Ireland' and scenes relating thereto."

On another level, reflecting another kind of apprehension, subtitles to be omitted included the following:[4]

And my poor brother's only sin was to love his native land. (*Bright Shawl*, USA 1926)

We are fighting for freedom from tyranny as your country once did. (*Hutch of the USA*, USA 1926)

Gandhi, notorious Indian agitator, imprisoned. (*Pathé Gazette*, France 1922)

If we do not succeed by peaceful means, we shall not hesitate to use force. (*Revenge of the Pharaoh*, Germany 1926)

Damn the law. We are the people. We are the law. (*The Light in the Clearing*, USA 1928)

Comrades, how long shall we suffer intrusion by these foreigners? (*The Flight Commander*, England 1928)

Occasionally the Censor Board asked for sub-titles to be changed, e.g., For: "Dreamed of a day when the Government would be a government of the people, for the people," substitute "Dreamed

of a day when peace and contentment would prevail in the land."
For: "But that is murder, they are our own people," substitute
"Must I obey your orders, Sir?" (Both examples from *Hutch of the
USA*, USA 1926)

There was rarely any appeal to the Provincial Government
against a decision of the Board. From 1924 to 1928, only two
appeals were made in Bengal of which one film was passed after
excisions and one was dismissed. In Madras, one appeal was
made against a decision of the Board, but the film was approved
after examination by the full Board. One appeal in Burma in 1924-
25 was dismissed by the Provincial Government. However, between
1924 and 1928, a number of films that had been passed by the
Boards, were declared uncertified by the Provincial Governments
under Sub-section (6) of Section 7 of the Cinematograph Act:[5]

Bombay		United Provinces	
1924-25...	3	1924-25...	15
1925-26...	3	1925-26...	3
1926-27...	I	1926-27...	4
1927-28...	1	1927-28...	7
Bengal (*Calcutta*)		Central Provinces and Berar	
1924-25...	2	1924-25...	12
1925-26...	1	1925-26...	2
1926-27...	nil	1926-27...	nil
1927-28...	nil	1927-28...	5
Burma (*Rangoon*)		Bihar and Orissa	
1924-25...	2	1924-25...	19
1925-26...	1	1925-26...	4
1926-27...	4	1926-27...	6
1927-28...	2	1927-28...	8
Madras		Assam	
1924-28...	nil	1924 ...	4
		1925 ...	1
Punjab (*Lahore*)		1926 ...	1
1924-25...	11	1927 ...	1
1925-26...	8	Delhi	
1926-27...	4	1924-25...	16
1927-28...	13	1925-26...	4
		1926-27...	6
		1927-28...	9

Certain films both foreign and Indian, were approved in one region and rejected in another. There were some legitimate reasons for this. Lack of contact between the regions, divergencies in customs and manners and in the degree of education, sophistication, urbanization, all created major differences between the provinces. These had to be taken into careful consideration by the Censor Boards when approving or rejecting a film, for reasons which had less to do with the film itself than with the nature of the audiences. W. M. Hailey, Chief Commissioner of Delhi, reported in 1926 that "The whole question of exhibition of undesirable films is of interpretation and sentiment. A film which would attract no attention in Bombay might cause a riot up-country. I myself have had to stop at Delhi the exhibition of a film containing a bullfight which no censor at Calcutta or Bombay would have dreamed to be objectionable, and which had been shown without incident throughout the rest of India."[6]

A number of films suffered from this anomaly as, for example, *The Virgin of Stamboul* (1920), passed by the Burma Board, was banned by the Bombay Board which felt that "certain ideas are likely to offend the Mahommedan community." *The Prince of Bharat* (1921), approved by the Bombay Board was banned in the entire country by the Secretary of State for India who felt that it was "likely to offend Europeans." *The Lion's Claw*, or *Moonchild* (1921), passed by both the Bengal and Burma Boards was rejected by Bombay because "it depicts an African ruler attempting to stir up rebellion in Africa with the help of a proclamation of the Sultan." It was subsequently uncertified in the whole of India by the Home Department "on political grounds."[7]

Bhakta Vidur (Saint Vidur, India 1921) passed by the Bombay Board was uncertified by the District Magistrate, Karachi, and by the Local Officer for Bombay State on the grounds that "it is likely to excite disaffection against the Government and incite people to non-cooperation," since the film was thought to be "a thinly veiled resumé of political events in India, Vidur appearing as Mr Gandhi clad in Gandhi cap and *khaddar* shirt. The intention of the film is to create hatred and contempt and to stir up feelings of enmity against the government." *Razia Begum* (Queen Razia) India, passed in March 1924 by the Bombay Board, was rejected in Punjab, Delhi, UP, Bihar and Orissa on religious grounds, as "immoral, indecent and offensive to Mahommedans." *Exploits of*

Submarine U-35 (1925) passed by Burma, was rejected by Bengal as "likely to injure British prestige." *Poona Raided* (1925) passed in Bombay, was banned in Burma and in Bihar and Orissa as it "could create disputes and ill-feeling between the local Hindus and Mussulmans." *Triumph of the Rat* (1927), passed by Bombay, was banned in practically all the provinces on the recommendation of the Government of Bengal that "the film is unsuitable for public exhibition in India on account of its low moral tone, and its protrayal of the degradation of European men and women."

D.W. Griffiths' *Orphans of the Storm* (1923), was approved by Bombay and Madras City only, but rejected in Burma, Bengal, Punjab—all other provinces in facts—on "political grounds," as it "deals with revolutionary propaganda,"[8] and his *Broken Blossoms* (1924), passed by Bengal, was banned by Bombay, Burma, Punjab, Delhi, Madras, as "it depicts cruelty, and sensuality, and draws an invidious comparison between East and West."[9]

Some films were banned altogether in the whole of India. In the beginning no reasons were given but by 1926 we find that a film is rejected because:

It deals with an undesirable theme, depicting in a very unpleasant light both from the point of view of their moral and general character, two Englishmen and two Englishwomen, as compared with a Chinaman who is generally shown in a favourable light. It also introduces the vexed question of marriages between Western women and Orientals." (*The Chinese Bungalow*, England 1926)

It is throughout of exceedingly low moral tone, and contains revolting sex scenes. (*Variety*, Germany 1928)

It preaches class warfare and eulogizes assassins and murderers. (*Rose of Blood*, USA 1928)

It deals with the overthrow of an established form of government. (*Siberia*, USA 1926)

This film tends to lower the prestige of the Government in the eyes of the uneducated cinema-goers. (*Guilty Conscience*, USA 1926)

Sadie Thompson (USA 1929), was refused a certificate because it "is unwholesome, and of low moral tone," and *The Hunchback of Notre Dame* (England 1927), because "this picture is bound to

offend the religious susceptibilities of a large section of the public."
Battleship Potemkin (USSR 1925) was banned because "it depicts
scenes of brutality and mutiny and the tyranny of successive governments, driving a people to rebel." Other films now considered
classics, were first banned then released with a large number of excisions: *Metropolis* (Germany 1928) 18 cuts; *Birth of a Nation* (USA
1925) 19 cuts.

With regard to Indian films, the cuts were mostly on political or
religious grounds: *The Great Sikh Procession* was banned by the
Calcutta Board on the grounds that it was "likely to cause communal
friction." In *Chandrarao Moray*, (Chandrarao Moray) in the sub-
title "My sons! Die in freedom rather than live in Shivaji's service,"
the Bombay Board deleted the words "in freedom" because they
were thought to be politically inflammable. The words "Swaraj"
(self-government), "crescent" and "flag" were also deleted where-
ever they occurred.

However, even in Indian films certain cuts were ordered which
are very interesting in the light of the attitude of the censors today.
In an Indian film, *Laila Majnu* (Laila Majnu) 1922, the producers
were told to "reduce the length of the kissing and the dance," and
later, in *Krishna Kanta's Will* (1926) to "omit the scene where the
heroine's busts are exposed."

The Question of a Central Board of Censors

On 9 November 1921, in the English Parliament Sir Charles Yate,
MP, asked the Secretary of State for India what had been the result
of the introduction of film censorship in India, who were the censors,
and what had they done. In his reply, the Secretary of State said:
"I understand that the Government of India has recently had its
attention drawn to the matter, and suggestions have been made to
it for making the censorship in each place more efficient."

On 11 October 1923, in a despatch to the Government of India,
the Secretary of State wrote that having considered in Council
(the Council of State) the reports submitted to him, he found indi-
cations of considerable variations in the procedure of the several
Boards; it appeared that the actual examination of films was not in
all cases made by the Board itself, and that a film was frequetly
passed for exhibition merely upon the report of an Inspector. He
felt that it was perhaps this situation that explained the continued

statements made in the English press that unsuitable films, mainly of American origin, were so often exhibited in India. He requested that "it may be considered whether any action can usefully and effectively be taken in regard to films such as those mentioned, like *Life of the Buddha*, and those which embody stories that have the effect of bringing Europeans into contempt. Those of the former type seem to be dangerous on religious grounds; those of the latter, politically undesirable. I observe that the Burma Board of Censors has susepnded the exhibition of *Life of the Buddha*, but the important matter, in my opinion is that a film of which the exhibition has to be suspended ought probably not to have been licensed at all."[10]

Life of the Buddha was an Indian film, produced by Madan and Company, and in the line of productions such as *Life of Christ*. No objection to it was raised in Bombay or Bengal. In Burma, the local press judged it inoffensive, but the Buddhists of Burma objected to it on the ground of the Buddha being represented on the screen by a human being, and therefore the film was refused a certificate.[11] As a result of the reaction in Burma the film was banned in Madras, Punjab, CP and Berar, Bihar and Orissa, and Delhi.[12]

However, even before the question of variations in Censorship proceedings was raised by the Secretary of State, the Government of India had already examined the advisability of setting up a Central Board of Film Censorship, with its headquarters in Bombay. The other Boards were, firmly against this idea. The (Indian) Secretary to the Government of Madras, wrote to the Home Department on 24 March 1922, that "a Central Board of Censors would be undesirable not only for reasons of delay in transmission of films for censorship, but it would be impracticable for provincial public opinion to be properly represented on such a Board."

The Chief Secretary to the Government of Burma wrote on 13 April 1922 that a Central Board at Bombay was "out of the question for a province like Burma with its own port of entry, and with manners and customs which requires a different angle of vision in its cinema censors." A letter from Major R. W. Macdonald, Commissioner of Police, to the Chief Secretary to the Government of Burma, had this to add: "The Rangoon Board has to be convinced that the existing Board at Bombay has shown efficiency in tackling the serious question of film censorship. Several films passed by Bombay have been turned down—whole, or in part, at Rangoon;

some due to differences in local conditions, others because the Rangoon Board considered them unfit to be shown in any civilized country."[13]

The Chief Secretary to the Government of Bengal, Calcutta, said merely that "His Excellency (The Governor) considers it impracticable to establish a Central Board for all India on account of delays, and of the divergencies in conditions existing in different provinces."[14]

There was another aspect to the question of establishing a Central Board. The Amendment in 1919 to the Cinematograph Act of 1918, had made film censorship a function of the Provincial Governments, and the appointment of a Central Board would be in direct infringement of the Act. The attempt was, in view of all these difficulties, temporarily abandoned. Some action was, however, taken to tighten up the censorship of films. In consultation with local governments and administrations, the following measures were adopted:

(1) Local governments were impressed with the necessity for a stricter system of certification, and more systematic methods for prompt handling of undesirable films.

(2) Importers and exhibitors of films were apprised of the nature of films which were likely to be found objectionable, and which they should not import or exhibit.

(3) District Magistrates and local authorities were instructed to exercise greater vigilance and to submit prompt reports to local governments for the suspension of objectionable films.

(4) Local governments were requested to notify other local governments as soon as a film was declared to be uncertified in any province.[15]

The Secretary of State for India had also asked in his Despatch of 11 October 1923, "whether any arrangements exist for the control of the production of films in India, for exhibition either locally or in other countries or, in the alternative, for the examination and control before export of films so produced."

The Government of India found that it had no means of discovering what films were made in India. "No authority at present exists under which Government can, as a matter of right, be kept informed of the production of films in this country, and in order

to vest them with necessary authority, legislation seems necessary."[16] This question of legislating with a view to secure some
control over production was fully considered by the Government,
but was dropped in 1926 as "the experience we had gained since
August 1923 is not such as to demonstrate the necessity for undertaking legislation now.[17]

As the cinema continued to grow,[18] so also did the conflict,
controversy and criticism surrounding it. In the Council of State,
on 22 January 1926, Sir Ebrahim Haroon Jaffer moved a resolution that "in place of the various existing Provincial Boards a
single salaried Board be appointed for the whole of India to
regulate the import into India of cinema films and to exercise a
stricter control over cinemas generally." In support of his resolution, he spoke of the "altogether erroneous impression made on
the Indian mind of the social life of England, America and other
Western lands by many of the cinema films permitted to be
shown."

The Home Secretary, J. Crerar, while referring to "the gross
misrepresentation of Western morals, of Western culture, and
Western civilization which have not infrequently found their way
into cinema exhibitions," reminded the members of the Council
of State that in the Cinematograph Act control of cinemato-
graphs had been made a Provincial subject, and he quoted instances
where it had been found necessary to ban in one province a film
found unobjectionable in another. He also emphasized the great
inconvenience to the trade of a Central Board.

The resolution was negatived.

On 21 March 1927, V. Ramdas Pantulu, in the course of a
speech in the Council of State, deplored the "scenes which are
calculated to corrupt public morals" in the films that come mostly
from America, and recommended an improvement in the "system
of censorship and control over cinemas and other public resorts of
amusements." In the discussion that followed, U. Rama Rao
asserted that "the growing increase in crimes and the moral depra-
vities of man and women in India are partly the outcome of the
so-called educative value of these cinema shows." He referred
also to the "abominable love scenes which lead the unfortunate
youngesters astray."[19]

The Home Secretary, H.G. Haig, agreed that it was desirable
to improve the system of censorship, but he defended the censors,

saying that "the films which are shown in India represent an alien civilization interpreted by these crude and vivid methods, to an audience which in many cases comprehends very imperfectly the social conditions presented. That makes the effect of the cinema particularly difficult to determine," and "the censor has to decide not only what is tolerable from a Western standpoint in the representation of Western manners, but what is tolerable from an Estern standpoint, or even what is tolerable from the standpoint of probable error or misrepresentation."[20]

The resolution was adopted and was to result in the appointment of the Indian Cinematograph Committee later that year. But in neither of these debates was any voice raised to deny that the cinema was having a harmful effect in the country.[21] In the winter of 1926-27, a British Social Hygiene Delegation visited India and wrote in their report: "In every province that we visited, the evil influence of the cinema was cited by educationists and representative citizens as one of the major factors in lowering the standards of sex conduct, and thereby tending to increase the dissemination of disease."[22]

British Prestige

By far the greater number of films exhibited in India were American. In fact, in 1926, 80 per cent of the films shown in India were American, and only 10 per cent were British. Since the production and exhibition of films had become an important industry, the Federation of British Industries began to be concerned regarding the "monopoly enjoyed by foreign concerns in cinema programmes in the Empire."[23]

The Federation considered the American monopoly to be "very deterimental to British prestige and prejudical to the interests of the Empire...as they contain large coloured populations."

The Indian Daily Mail commenting on this statement on 22 April 1926 said:

India will not share the feelings expressed by the Federation of British Industries in its statement to the Board of Trade. The anxiety of the Federation is quite understandable when it is considered that the production and exhibition of cinema films has become an important industry in the past few years, paying large profits and giving employment to thousands of men and women. The cinema, however, unlike ordinary industries, has great value as an instrument of propaganda. The Federation lays particular emphasis on this aspect of the matter. Its argument seems to be that films produced in America take no account of the importance of maintaining the white man's prestige, and show him in the most unfavourable light, exaggerating his weak points and bad qualities. It considers that this will destroy the respect and fear of the white skin among brown and black men on which, in its view, rests the foundation of Empire. This is the weakest argument that the Federation could have brought forward to support its claim for the encouragement of British films. It is absolutely out of place in cinema halls where people go to be amused and not to drink in the glory and might of Britain or any other country. The censorship of cinema films on the ground of the colour of the people who go to see them has as little justification as the censorship of books which analyze the weaknesses of western society. The attempt to make all cinema films shown to coloured audiences represent the white man as something above all faults and who considers it his sole duty to guide brown and black man along the paths of peace and virtue will be a deplorable failure.

The Times of India, on 21 April 1926 said that it depreciated the practical monopoly that American films enjoyed mainly because "it was bad business on the part of Britain to leave such a valuable market in American hands. American films should certainly be fought by business competition, but to try to suppress them by a hypocritical plea for Imperial welfare is merely ridiculous."

Both newspapers found the American films technically far superior to British films, but the *Daily Mail* considered that Indian audiences would patronize neither if there were more Indian films produced and exhibited. The Federation of British Industries had suggested that the American film monopoly might be considered by the forthcoming Imperial Conference. The *Daily Mail* suggested that "If it comes up before the Conference the Indian representatives should make the position of this country clear. American and British films exhibited here should be judged on their merits and if any encouragement is to be given it should be to the Indian, and not to the British Industry."

The question was indeed taken up at the Imperial Conference in 1926, and certain "remedial measures" were proposed, among which were that effective customs duties should be levied on "foreign films," while free entry should be allowed for films produced within the Empire. A minimum quota was also required to be imposed on the renting or exhibition of Empire films. No mention was made of measures to encourage the Indian film industry. However, on 15 September 1927, a resolution was presented in the Legislative Assembly that: "A committee be appointed to examine and report on the censorship of cinematograph films in India, and to consider whether it is desirable that any steps should be taken to encourage the exhibition of films produced within the British Empire generally, and the production and exhibition of Indian films in particular."[24]

In his speech introducing the Resolution, the Home Member J. Crerar, recognized that the cinema had become "one of the great forces for good or evil now operating upon society. We have to deal with what is not only a great force, but what may be a great art."[25]

Regarding the Resolution of the Imperial Conference, he thought it would be premature to say whether it would be at all possible to proceed along these lines and that the question would have to be carefully examined. He, in fact, recognized the importance of encouraging the Indian film industry.

He countered the criticism levelled against the machinery of censorship, saying that however efficient it may be "it is by no means a final answer to the various problems which the cinema sets up." The need for a Committee to examine all its many aspects was clearly indicated as, he continued, "We have now reached a stage where the ordinary method of examining questions of public importance by correspondence between the Government of India and Local Governments, and between the Local Governments and the various subordinate authorities have been nearly exhausted."

In the course of the ensuing debate a number of points were raised and widely differing views expressed. Col. J.D. Crawford said that he had received very many complaints from his own community regarding the misrepresentation of the conditions of western life in films shown in this country. Lala Lajpat Rai objected in his turn to the misrepresentation of Asiatics in general and Indians in particular, in films he had witnessed abroad. In Mohammed Yamin Khan's opinion, Indians attached little importance to scenes of western life in the imported films, but some films were objectionable from the point of view of school-children, youths and women because, "though some things may not be considered objectionable in western countries...on account of the different social customs prevailing here (in India), they are really objectionable." He added further: "Indian ladies have now started to see the cinematograph and I like it very much. But it would not be desirable that Indian ladies, after coming out from *purdah* should see such kinds of films that are exhibited nowadays."

Although the debate was not concluded, there was unanimity on the need for the appointment of a Committee that would examine the question of censorship as well as consider steps for the further encouragement of the Indian film industry. Controversy persisted over the vexed question of British Empire films.

On the following day, a resolution in indentical terms was moved within the Council of State by the Home Secretary, H.G. Haig. In the course of his introductory remarks, he said: "I think we are probably all agreed that the Cinematograph is an influence with great potentialities for good or evil, an influence that requires to be watched very carefully. I think we are probably all agreed that in some respects at the present time that influence is not good, and we want to see whether we can eradicate the evil aspects of the cinematograph and improve the good."

He then reviewed the main problems that the Committee would be asked to consider: Whether film censorship should remain as at present on a Provincial basis, or whether it should be certralized : "that will be the first and perhaps the main problem that the Committee will have to consider;" The constitution of whatever censoring authority they decide is required and, in particular, how non-official opinion should be brought to bear on this work of censoring; How far it is possible to develop the production and exhibition of Indian films because "(*a*) the problem of censorship would be largely simplified if we could increase the number of Indian films showing Indian stories in an Indian setting and, (*b*) it seems desirable that the audiences...should have presented to them pictures which give them their own social conditions, their own culture. In that way the cinema may become an instrument of great educational and moral value."

The committee was asked also to consider the question of the encouragement of Empire films.

Indian Cinematograph Committee of 1927

The Indian Cinematograph Committee was appointed on 6 October 1927. It consisted of an Indian Chairman, T. Rangachariar, Lawyer, High Court Madras, and five members (two Indian, three English) all of whom were Government officials or Members of the Legislative Assembly. Among them were A. M. Green, Collecter of Customs and a member of the Bombay Board of Film Censors, and J. Coatman who was the Director of Public Information. The film industry was not represented.

The Committee completed its report in May 1928, having studied in detail all aspects of film production, distribution and exhibition, public reaction, views of the industry and aspects of government supervision. On the matter of censorship it was found that almost all the witnesses they examined, and who represented various fields of interest, overwhelmingly favoured strong censorship. Even those who said they generally disapproved of censorship maintained that it was necessary for India. The producers too, did not take a strong stand against censorship. Ardeshir M. Irani, (who was to go on to make the first Indian sound film in 1931) said, when questioned by the Committee, that "For the present, we have no difficulty with censorship. It is quite satisfactory."[26] He however, asked for two things: "We should like Indian pictures to be seen by a Board of Indian Censors, and when pictures are banned a reason should be given." The Chairman posed most of the questions as for example :

Question: I see a statement here from a report on censorship that the reason given is 'Rough handling of white girl by Moor is undesirable in India.' Is that sort of information enough?
Answer: Yes, fine. But usually a picture is banned and two months later when it is published in the Government Gazette, we know the reason why. The reason should be given immediately. The Inspector should say so-and-so is objectionable. We might remove it there and then and give it to him. He should say, 'This is what we don't like. Are you going to cut it out?'
Question: And you welcome that? Because we were rather

puzzled the other day at some of the excisions in that list of films. But if you and the Inspector are both agreed, you prefer to cut out than be delayed for anything up to a week while sanction is being obtained?

Answer: Quite.

Question: Have you ever approached the Board for hearing?

Answer: We have, and we have been satisfied.[27]

Occasionally it was the quality of the questioning, usually by the Chairman himself, that practically forced the producer to concede, albeit reluctantly, that he was not happy with censorship, as in the following exchange:

Question: You are asked to omit the sub-title: 'Oh God, I have always been a man of peace. But the ways of peace seem to have gone wrong. Please guide me.' Do you think it will encourage the director of a film to develop freedom in his own line if he is asked to do that?

Answer: Well, I think he would resent it.

Question: Do you think that a scenario writer who is asked to omit these words—do you think it will encourage him?

Answer: I cannot exactly say why the censors object to it.

Question: I want your view as a director.

Answer: I think it does interfere with the freedom to a certain extent.

Question: In another case, you are asked to omit the words 'in freedom' in 'My sons, die in freedom rather than living in Shivaji's service.'

Answer: I think it is very wrong of the censor. I do not know why the words 'in freedom' should be omitted.

Question: Do you think that such interference by the censor is conducive to the development of the art?

Answer: It is not conducive to the art of the cinema.[28]

In a written answer to the questionnaire sent out by the Committee, the Bombay Cinema and Theatres Trade Association, in collaboration with the Indian Motion Picture Producers Association, stated that "From the point of view of this Association, we feel that the present system of censorship though rigid, is satisfactory."

There were a few protests of a general nature: "The business of the censor is more to prohibit than appreciate a work of art. The very name savours of sickening restriction, and it is the hand of death if it touches a work of art." But more typical was the attitude: "Unduly interfere with the artistic and inspirational development? This is bosh! There is neither art nor inspiration in such pictures. They are gross and vulgar."

In its report, submitted in May 1928, the Committee stated that it had found that "Censorship is certainly necessary in India, and is the only effective method of preventing the import, production and public exhibition of films which might demoralize morals, hurt religious susceptibilities or excite communal or racial animosities"; that the existing censorship had yielded on the whole satisfactory results, but that "its machinery is capable of improvement."[29] It had discovered that most of the criticism of the functioning of censorship had been of a general nature and much of it was ill-informed, and sprang from persons who were either not conversant with Indian conditions or who had fixed convictions not based on facts.[30] It maintained that the overwhelming majority of films exhibited in no way tended to demoralize the Indian public,[31] or to bring western civilization into contempt. In fact, the Committee quoted in its report the evidence of N. P. A. Smith, an officer of the Imperial Police Service, as admirably summing up the whole matter: "If any slight misunderstanding exists, and lowers the public conception of Western civilization, it is surely wiser to let time and education provide a truer perspective and a saner demand rather than to attempt to sanctify a civilization which, like all others, is humanly imperfect."[32]

It found that though certain film scenes showing passionate love-making had a tendency to demoralize the youth of the country[33] it agreed with the complaint that communal, racial, political and even colour considerations were treated with too much sensitivity.[34] Finally, the members of the Committee believed that conflicts of opinion between the Boards were most exceptional, but there were dissensions between different Boards and provinces and that "a Central Board would obviate all genuine difficulties."[35] They proposed that this Central Board be located in Bombay, and consist of seven or nine members with a majority of Indian non-officials, and with a non-official Indian Chairman. There should be a Deputy Censor in Calcutta for the censorship of imported films, with Provincial Boards where necesssary, for the censoring of locally produced films. The Committee, in fact, laid out in great detail the functioning of censorship, should such a system be adopted.[36]

On the question of "Imperial Preference," it stated firmly that "it is not recommended that any steps be taken for giving any special preference or encouragement to films produced within the Empire." It had arrived at the conclusion that "If too much exhibition of American films in the country is a danger to the national interest, too much exhibition of other Western films is as much a danger.[37] The British social drama is as much an enigma to the average Indian audience as the American. In fact, very few Indians can distinguish American manners and customs from British manners and customs. If the cinema, therefore, has any influence on the habits, lives and outlook of the people, all western films are likely to have more or less the same kind of effect upon the people of this country." It consequently felt that "it is no good to India to substitute artifically one class of non-Indian films for another. Our aim will be and should be, to remove the non-Indian grip on the screen."[38] With these words, the Indian Cinematograph Committee dismissed the idea of Imperial Preference. Instead, it urged extreme measures for the encouragement of the Indian film— measures that would only be taken up very many years later in independent India. Among its recommendations the Committee suggested the establishment of a Cinema Department under the Ministry of Commerce,[39] Government loans and financial aid to producers, the building of more cinemas, encouraging travelling cinemas to take more Indian films,[40] Government scholarships for film study and training abroad,[41] Government award for the best production of the year, and finally, the abolition of all import duty on raw film stock.[42]

The Report included one more proposal, one that led to a Minute of Dissent by the three British members of the Committee who did not agree with the recommendation that all Indian theatres should be required to show a proportion of Indian films. The Report stated that "It is an unsatisfactory feature, not to be accepted as permanent, that Indian films should be excluded from any theatre."[43] The three British members did not feel that this should be made mandatory, nor did they agree wholly with the proposal to extend financial support to Indian producers.

But all these points remained academic, for His Majesty's

Government of India put aside the Report. Not one of its recommendations was enacted into law. The Committee had, while advocating sweeping changes in the censorship system, expressed itself reasonably satisfied with the arrangements as they existed. It had rejected Imperial preference, which the Government was interested in, and recommended instead concrete support for the film industry in India, which the Government was not particularly concerned with implementing. A Resolution was introduced in the Legislative Assembly in February 1929 proposing that "with a view to fostering the growth of the Indian film industry and the protection of the Indian cinema trade from exploitation by non-Indians, immediate effect be given to the recommendations of the Indian Cinematograph Committee, by the imposition of the quota system...."[44] But this Resolution was negatived due, no doubt, to the Minute of Dissent by the British members of the Committee.

However, the lack of governmental interest in the recommendations of this Committee could have been due equally to another factor of infinitely greater significance. Even before the Committee began its investigation, fundamental changes had convulsed the international film world. On the same day as the Committee was appointed, on 6 October 1927, *The Jazz Singer* the world's first talking film, had its première in New York. By the time the report of the Committee was published, the film industry in India as elsewhere, was engulfed by a new set of problems, a new set of preoccupations. It was to take almost four more years for India to acquire the expertise and the material to handle this new development in the cinema. But at last, in 1931, with equipment obtained in the United States, equipment that was virtually "junk,"[45] Ardeshir M. Irani of the Imperial film Company in Bombay, completed the first Indian sound film *Alam Ara,* and ushered in perhaps the most interesting period of Indian cinema—the decade of the 1930s.

Notes

[1] 80 per cent of films shown in India in the '20s were from America, *ICC Report 1927*, para 219, p. 103.

[2] *Ibid.,* Table 9, pp. 184-186.

[3] Calcutta Censor Board Records.

[4]A despatch from the Government of India to the Secretary of State dated 1 June 1922 pointed out that "The object of censorship is not merely to prevent the exhibition of obscene films but also of films that are politically objectionable." Government of India, Home Department, File No. 71—Jails, 1922.

[5]*ICC Report, 1927*, Tables 19 to 21, pp. 196-197.

[6]L M Hailey, Home Department (Political) 1926, File No. 168-III-26.

[7]*Evidences* Vol. IV, pp. 368-403.

[8]The Punjab Board saw other censorable matter in *Orphans of the Storm* as is shown in the oral evidence of Parkinson, member of the Punjab Board, before the ICC in November 1927.

Mr P.—Generally speaking, I cut out all passionate love scenes and scenes of debauchery. There was a film named *Orphans of the Storm* which had very objectionable scenes.

Q.—It is being publicly exhibited?

Mr P.—It was stopped.

Q.—The film was censored at Bombay?

Mr P.—Yes

Q,—It has been entirely banned?

Mr P.—Yes. In the Punjab.

[9]*Evidences*, Vol. V, pp. 368-403.

[10]Home Department (Political) File 308 of 1923. *The Manchester Guardian*, 4 September 1923, took this opportunity of having another dig at the 'kinema'; "We have no information about the precise details in the film *The Life of the Buddha* which has given offence to Rangoon, but it is very easy to imagine that they exist. The metaphysical subtleties of Buddhism, do not sound exctly the safest of subjects for the kinema . . . there is a certain incongruity about an attempt to project the light of Asia through a kinematograph machine."

[11]*Evidences*, Vol. IV, p. 400.

[12]*Ibid.*, pp. 373-403. See also *ICC Report 1927*, para 251, p. 120.

[13]Government of India, Home Department (political), File No. 308 of 1923.

[14]*Ibid.*

[15]*Ibid.*

[16]R.L. Bajpai, Director, Public Information, in *ibid*.

[17]C.W. Gwynne, File No. 168-III-26 Home Depertment (Political) 1926.

[18]In 1927 there were 360 permanent cinemas and 37 "seasonal cinemas as compared with 148 altogether in 1921. *ICC Report*, paras 32-33, pp. 18-19.

[19]*Ibid.*, Para 13, p. 7.

[20]*Ibid.*

[21]*Ibid.*, para 13, p. 8

[22]The *ICC Report 1927* conclusively proved that this statement was a total fabrication. See *Report*, para 248, p. 117.

[23]Statement of Federation of British Industries to the Board of Trade, *The Indian Daily Mail*, 22 April 1926.

[24]*ICC Report*, p. xi.

[25]Legislative Assembly Debates, 14 September 1927.

[26]*Evidences*, Vol. I, p. 185, A.M. Irani and D. Bhavnani of the Imperial Film Company.

[27]*Ibid.*, p. 187.

[28]*Evidences*, Vol. I p. 191; Oral Evidence of M. Bhavnani.

[29]*ICC Report*, para 223, p. 105.

[30]*Ibid.*, para 245, p. 114.

[31]*Ibid.*, para 243, p. 111

[32]*Ibid.*, para 243, p. 113.

[33]*Ibid.*, para 246, pp. 114-115.

[34]*Ibid.*, para 251, pp. 119-120.

[35]*Ibid.*, paras 252-254, pp. 120-123.

[36]*Ibid.*, para 255, pp. 123-125.

[37]*Ibid.*, para 211, p. 99.

[38]*Ibid.*, para 218, p. 102.

[39]*Ibid.*. para 98, p. 49.

[40]*Ibid.*, paras 130-132, pp. 62-64.

[41]*Ibid.*, paras 135-142, pp. 65-69.

[42]*Ibid.*, paras, 51-52, pp. 26-27.

[43]*Ibid.*, para, 145, pp. 70.

[44]Legislative Assembly Debate V-I, 28 Jan to 23 February 1929.

[45]E. Barnouw and S. Krishnaswamy, *Indian Film*. Columbia University Press, New York 1963, p. 56.

3

Brief Interlude

The Sound of Hindi

The mood in which the Indian film world entered the '30s was one of dismay and uncertainty. In 1929 Madan Theatres of Bombay had introduced India to sound cinema with a screening of the American film *Melody of Love*. And it was Madan Theatres again that became the first Indian producers of sound films. They made a number of shorts and put them together in one programme. It was, in a sense, like the beginning of cinema all over again. But this time the period of experimentation was very brief and in March 1931 *Alam Ara* the first "all-talking, all-singing, all-dancing" film (in Hindi) was released in Bombay. Twenty-six other films in Tamil, Hindi and Bengali were released later that same year.

The problem facing the Indian film makers at this stage, was no longer only one of acquiring new equipment, building sound studios and learning new techniques for both performers and technicians. Language too, became an important factor. Up to now, the market of the Indian producer had been the whole of India, Burma and Ceylon. Some films had been exported to Malaysia, East Africa and South Africa.[1] But now, in a country of 14 major languages, it seemed as if, instead of his film-market expanding, it would have to limit itself to the region of its language. Among the three major centres of film production, Bombay was the capital of 21 million Marathi speaking people. Calcutta could cater for 53 million Bengalis, and Madras, where film production was just making a hesitant start, had a potential market of 20 million Tamil speaking people in Southern India, with a few million in Ceylon and Malaya. Tamil could generally be understood in the Malayalam, Telugu and Kannada language regions in South India, but for the 26 million Telugu speaking people, there was no film centre. There was, and still is, no language common to the whole of India. Curiously there was no major film centre in the North and Central regions of India which, with a 140 million Hindi speaking inhabitants, in 1931 comprised the largest single linguistic zone. Lahore, in the North, located in the Punjabi-Urdu speaking area (both of which languages bear some relation to Hindi) although it boasted of a Censor Board, never became important as a centre of film production. Many years later, in 1947 after Independence and Partition, when Lahore became a part of Pakistan, the enterprising Punjabis moved en masse to Bombay which had become the major centre for Hindi films. But in 1931, the language problem was acute. Apart from these three language areas where film studios were already established, there were the smaller language pockets—Gujarati 10 million, Punjabi 16 million, Kannada 11 million, Malayalam 7 million, Assamese 2 million, Oriya 10 million, and several other smaller areas.[2]

The language issue eventually resolved itself as it became clear that the greater number of films would have to be in Hindi—the language spoken and understood by the largest majority of the people. Bombay's geographically central position, its heterogenous population, and the fact that it had the most facilities to offer, made it the natural centre for Hindi film production. But as the demand for films continued to grow, a need was felt for more films in the other Indian languages as well. An increasing number of films began to be produced in the regional languages. They were made on a such smaller scale, and too often they took their cue from the Hindi cinema to the extent sometimes of bringing out a local language version of a commercially successful Hindi film.

But the problem facing the cinema in 1931 seemed so insurmountable that a number of smaller film production units folded up. This was to result a few years later in the establishment of the

big studios which were to dominate the film scene from the early
'30s, until Independence brought yet another set of fundamental changes, another set of problems. However, in 1931, for
the courageous film producers who were willing, and able, to
gamble on the switch to sound, the rewards were overwhelming.
The delirium with which *Alam Ara* had been greeted by surging
crowds did not abate. Huge crowds thronged the theatre, thrilled
at the idea of hearing pictures. Ruby Meyers who as Sulochana was
one of the great stars of the era, wrote later that "the lay masses
were so overpowered when they saw their favourite gods talking
on the screen that even the bullock carts advertising pictures about
these divinities were profusely garlanded."[3] By 1933, *Indian
Filmland* was able to write: "What with scanty resources, step-
motherly Government aid, with keen competition from privileged
foreign films, with few technically qualified men...with actors and
actresses scarcely able to spell their names (for it was thought a
disgrace by society people to be associated with the screen), with no
market excepting India, with censuring censors, with discourage-
ment to the right, cheap sneers to the left, despair in front and
criticism from behind, the Indian film industry, thank God, has
marched on and on to the field of victory, battling against a
thousand other misfortunes."[4] With those problems, and that excitement, it is not surprising that neither the film industry nor the
Government had a thought to spare for report of the Indian
Cinematograph Committee! But the surge in the popularity of the
cinema brought out the worst in the nervous "censuring censors."
Films continued to be cut and banned, with an increasing severity
that was reflected in all Government reactions, partly due to the
dramatic events taking place on the political scene.

Escaping the Worries, Escaping the Facts

In December 1929, the moderate Congress Party changed its
stand. With Nehru as President, it demanded "complete freedom
from British imperialism."[5] In April 1930, Mahatma Gandhi for-
mally launched the Civil Disobedience Movement on a massive
scale with the 240-mile march to Dandi, in protest against the Salt
Law. On 5 May, Gandhi was arrested. The number of political
prisoners rose to 90,000 as nationalists resigned Government
offices, withheld taxes and began the economic war with the

boycott of British goods. In March 1931, three young nationalists were arrested and sentenced to transportation for life for throwing a bomb and propaganda leaflets in the Central Legislative Assembly while it was in session. While in jail Bhagat Singh, Rajguru and Sukhdev were accused of the murder of the SP of Lahore and sentenced to death.

Outspoken press comments, criticism, and exposures of the atrocities committed, led the Government to enact the Indian Press (Emergency Powers) Act to prevent publication of the inflammatory matter and incitement to violence. The execution of Bhagat Singh, Sukhdev and Rajguru, all in their early 20s, captured and stirred the imagination of the whole country. "The corpse of Bhagat Singh will stand between as and England," said Nehru after the death sentence was carried.[6] But these events and emotions were to find an echo in the cinema only in the 1940s. In the early '30s, film makers were still only beginning to come to grips with the demands made upon them by the latest developments in their medium. Also, the nervousness of the authorities in the face of this new politicization among the people was such that even newsreel items regarding all national figures, particularly Gandhi, were banned e.g., (1) Mahatma Gandhi's Historic March; (2) Mahatma Gandhi's Return from London; (3) Topical of Mahatma Gandhi and others; (4) Bombay Welcomes Mahatma Gandhi; (5) Mahatma Gandhi's Return from the Pilgrimage of Peace; (6) Forty-fifth Indian National Congress at Karachi[7]; (7) Message by Babu Rajendra Prasad (deals with controversial politics); and (8) Pandit Jawaharlal Nehru's Message (deals with controversial politics and likely to forment social unrest and discontent).[8]

A few attempts were made in feature films to bring in the political mood of the country, but those scenes were immediately cut out by the censors. In *Sone Ki Chidia* (Golden Bird), 30 August 1934, the following dialogue had to be omitted: "Yes, it is a rare opportunity that we get to serve our nation or country, and then we must sacrifice our business and prosperity," and "May sacrifice for our country become our aim in life. Instead of living without feeling it is better to die like this." The film *Mahatma* (The Great Soul) was banned on the grounds that "it deals with controversial politics." The authorities were also unhappy at the title *Mahatma* with its unmistakable reference to Gandhi. The film was ultimately allowed to be exhibited with several cuts and a new title—

Dharmatma (The Pious One).[9] In *Iman Farosh* (He who sells his Conscience), February 1937, the producers were told to "omit all cries of *Inquilab Zindabad* (Long Live the Revolution) uttered by crowds."[10]

Even in foreign films, anything with a political flavour had to be removed. In *Captain of the Guard* (USA, June 1936) it was "Death to all who refuse to take the oath of independence" and "Our guns will spit, the blood of the aristos will flood the streets, France will be free," that had to be removed. In *Knight Without Armour* (England, August 1937), it was: "In scene of bomb outrage, omit all dialogue showing Russian students taking part in revolutionary activities...also the preliminary discussion about method of preparing bombs...actual bomb explosion can remain." In *"Kid Millions"* (USA, February 1935) "cut all scenes where a person dressed exactly like Mahatma Gandhi is shown."[11]

Apart from politics, anything that might incite any section of the community to question its condition, and to rebel against it, was taboo. A film that became a minor *cause célèbre* in 1935, dealt with mill-workers in a factory. It was first presented to the Censor Board on 5 February 1935, with its original title *The Mill or Mazdoor* (Labourer). Based on a novel by the well-known Hindi novelist Premchand, it was banned for being "a travesty of mill life and management, the effects of which are likely to be harmful to the relations between employers and workers in India." In its revised version and new name *Seth ki Ladki* (The Merchant's Daughter) on 19 March 1935, it was prohibited again because "there is running throughout the film the idea of the conflict of capital and labour; that much of the film depicts the squandering by members of the capitalist class of money earned by labour, in contrast with the squalid conditions under which labour lives; and that it is a direct incitement to discontent in labour circles."[12]

None of the film producers had the financial resources to rest on their principles. A mere *'succès d'éstime'* could spell financial ruin and so, in March 1936, *The Mill or Mazdoor* was released as *Daya ki Devi* (Goddes of Mercy) with the following excisions:

(1) All scenes of rowdyism on the part of millhands, such as the beating of the mill officers entirely omitted.

(2) All scenes of mob incitement considerably toned down.

(3) Scenes showing mill-hands and their leaders being shot by mill-owner together with later references to shooting.

(4) Scenes of seduction of women workers in the mill by mill management.

(5) Scenes showing workers going on strike, the employment of black legs to break the strike and picketing by strikers, reduced to a minimum.

And, thrown in for good measure, all scenes of drinking in dance halls and toddy booths had to be reduced, and scenes showing Mohammedans drinking were to be omitted entirely.[13]

When socially aware producers tried to get away with strong statements by setting the film in an earlier period, such as *Benarsi Thug* (Benares Gangster) June 1936, set in the late fifteenth early sixteenth century) scenes of oppression of peasants by State Officers demanding land revenue from famine stricken peasants, peasants holding meetings and making inflammatory speeches, all had to be eliminated.[14]

In *Sant Tulsidas* (Saint Tulsidas) February 1934, the producers were ordered to "omit entire scenes referring to questions of admittance of low-caste persons to a Hindu temple."[15]

An American film *Black Fury* was banned in June 1935 because it "seeks to justify during industrial strikes, direct action by workers, even to the extent of using explosives to destroy their employers' property."[16]

In *The Road Back* (USA, September 1937) : "Drastically curtail mob scene showing the crowd (hunger stricken) taking the law into their own hands, looting shops, defying authority, and the police and military shooting down people."[17]

No reference was permitted to poverty, or the exploitation of the poor by the rich. Dialogue to be cut included words such as:

Is humanity in the grip of evil? When men, children of the same maker, live on the blood of their follow-men. The rich feed themselves on the poor. While the poor eat dust and live at the expense of the dogs." (*Bala Joban* [Youth on Fire] Indian, May 1934) or : "Why should the poor die like rats in their holes. Why should the nobles eat off the fat of the land? Why should we endure this injustice? Food for the poor, food for the poor. . . . " (*The Affairs of Voltaire*, USA, March 1934).[18]

All these examples, however, concern a very small number of

films, quite insignificant in the mainstream of commercial film-making. But they do give an indication of why the general run of pictures dealt with uncontroversial topics, where producers attempted to attract audiences with offers of sensational scenes of seduction, sadism and crime. They went to the censor boards prepared to cut out immediately all scenes that were thought to have gone beyond tolerable limits. For them, there was no problem of compromise with principle, or with artistry. The sooner a film could be released the sooner the money would start coming in.

Pictures in the American Style

Thus, in the main, cinema continued to demonstrate its normal preoccupations. Mythological films became more and more popular. With words added to images other less universally known stories could be put on film. But apart from the epics which provided an unending fund of source material, the problem for the producer was to find stories for his films. As audiences grew more accustomed to the cinema, they also became more knowledgeable and less naive about it.

Rabindranath Tagore, whose towering figure dominated the literary scene until his death in 1941, had written 25 volumes of poetry, five novels, 15 plays, five volumes of essays. He was awarded the Nobel Prize for literature in 1913. Kinghted by the British (he renounced this honour in 1919 in protest against the massacre of Indians by British troops at Jallianwalla Bagh), he was a painter, a public speaker, a social reformer. He founded Santiniketan, a place of study dedicated to the ideals of freedom and the arts, and stood as a symbol of humanity, tolerance and freedom in Indian and international political issues.

In December 1929, a film made from one of his stories *Bicharak* (The Judge) was banned for its "low moral tone," in dealing with the fate of a widow who, cast off by her family in accordance with the treatment meted out to widows in orthodox Hindu society, is forced into prostitution to provide for herself and her child. The Indian member of the Calcutta Censor Board J.N. Bannerjea, found it necessary to justify his recommendation to ban the film in a three-page letter to the head of the Board. He emphasized his admiration for Tagore but said that the film "hurts our delicate sentiments in presenting realistically a morbid and abnormal situation, which, though of immense value to social reformers is at least on the screen, unwholesome and hence unpresentable." The English member, J.H. Henderson, agreed with this view, but added a note: "*Bicharak* is open to further objection because it shows one of His Majesty's judges in an unfavourable and damaging light."

The film may will have been a travesty of Tagore's story. Since it no longer exists, there is no way of verifying this. But the censors seemed to find fault with the subject itself, and the "air of stark realism in its presentation." The situation was not "abnormal" as Bannerjea found it: in fact, the fate and status of widows was one that social reformers were deeply concerned about. The film was eventually permitted to be exhibited some months later, in a very mutilated form.[19]

With nowhere else to look, the film maker turned to imitating the films that were being imported, the greater majority of which were American. Stories were plagiarized, customs and manners openly imitated. A 1930s poster of *Gentleman Daku* (Gentleman Bandit) shows the very popular star Leela Chitnis, in white tie and tails, top hat, cigarette in a long holder, looking very like Marlene Dietrich in *Morocco*. Indian films frequently had titles in English which were derived directly from the popular American comedy and crime films—*Benarsi Thug, Whose Darling, Dynamite, Mr X, Double X, Fashionable Wife, Indira M.A., Educated Wife. 300 Days and After* was advertised as "India's first picture in the Americn style."[20]

"Films in the American style," is what led to a sarcastic comment in *Filmindia* in April 1938 under the heading "Some Absurdities in our Pix":

> The West may be taking large strides towards stripping the fair sex of all clothes by slow but sure degrees, but it must be remembered that the West is West and the East is East. The Sari and Dhoti have survived the ages. The East is not accustomed to dress its daughters in the dress with which they are born at home or on the stage. Why should the producers then attempt an impropriety in this direction by presenting them before our eyes either semi-naked or with an apologetic dress?

The cinema was reaching out to influence manners and customs to a degree that some found alarming. Young people particularly, slavishly copied the styles of hair and dress affected by their favourite stars. *Filmindia*, a year later deplored the possible impact of crime films. An editorial in the April 1939 issue, chided the film maker in the moralizing tone that Indians have a tendency to adopt all to readily:

The ever increasing tendency among Indian producers to produce crime pictures is to be deplored. Instead of doing real social and national work by producing pictures that would elevate the moral standards of our people, and educate the nation on the right lines through this all-important instrument of visual education, they are falling over one another to establish a crime school in India after the style and fashion pursued by the Americans. It does not need much intelligence to imagine the sad effect of such pictures on the minds of our growing younger generation. . . .

In fact, whatever the film maker did was wrong. The main problem with the cinema seemed to be its success. When the film did take up more serious topics, it came up against the censor. In September 1939, the *Journal of the Film Industry* took exception to the unjust and severe censorship on behalf of *The Only Way*, produced by Sagar Movietone, which had shown "a few Indian soldiers in a camp hospital (during World War I it is on record that Indian soldiers were given bad food, hopeless medical treatment etc.) raving about the cruel madness of the war, and wondering why they should have come all that way to face German bullets. This scene was deleted from the film in the Punjab, Sir Sikandar Hayat Khan [then Governor of the Punjab] being one of Britain's strongest allies, and recruiter of study Punjabis. This ban is objectionable because it discourages producers from dealing, even remotely and in an indirect and apologetic manner, with vital political realities."

The Morality of Publicity

Protest by and on behalf of the film industry was exceptional. Much more common were protests against films. These had never stopped. In the Legislative Assembly in September 1933, Sheikh

Sadiq Hasan had drawn the attention of the Government to the "great resentment among the Muslim public when scenes of harem life are depicted in films, and especially when historic Muslim queens and princesses are shown making love."[21] Jagan Nath Aggarwal asked if "the attention of Government has been drawn to the various cinema films, passed by the Censors, to which objection has been taken by religious bodies, both Hindu and Muslim, on the ground that they offended their religious susceptibilities, or that they portrayed religious personages in an objectionable manner."[22] Both these members, one Muslim, the other Hindu, demanded stricter vigilance from the Censors.

At a meeting in Karachi in December 1934, the All India Women's Conference called upon local governments to appoint at least one woman member on every censor board. At the same time it reiterated "the urgent necessity of a far more rigorous censorship of films and posters."[23]

The question of submitting posters and other material advertising films, had been taken up intermittently by the authorities, and by various citizens' groups. In June 1934, the Executive Committee of the Bengal Welfare Association, Calcutta, had also "requested the Police Commissioner of Calcutta to stop the ill-practice of pasting of placards by commercial concerns, especially the demoralizing cinema posters, on walls of houses to the unavoidable gaze of even the unwilling public...as it has an equally harmful effect on the community and the individual."[24]

The Government discussed at length the possibility of amending the Cinematograph Act of 1918 to "provide for the censorship of advertisements and posters relating to cinema films." The question had been taken up by the ICC 1927. The Committee had found that the posters were often more lurid than the films they advertised, even referring at times to scenes that had been excised; and "occasionally these posters are distinctly suggestive and as they are posted in public places may, and at times do, offend the cultured, and possibly do moral harm to the ignorant and the adolescent." The Committee thought that some of the criticism of films was a result of the posters alone as "sometimes the critic had never seen the film at all."[25] However, the Committee had concluded that in spite of the considerable body of opinion, with which it agreed, that wanted greater control over posters and publicity material, pre-censorship would be administratively very difficult as well as very inconvenient for the trade. It satisfied itself with recommending that "the Magistracy or Police should be given power to direct any poster which appears to be objectionable to be forthwith removed, and that disobedience to such an order should be punishable with a fine." When the issue of legislation to censor posters came up in 1934 there was an outcry from the film trade. The industry objected to it on grounds of delay of publicity, that mid-week changes in programmes would not be possible, and that obscenity and indecency any way came under the purview of the Indian Penal Code. In spite of these protests, the Bill was passed by the Council of State, but was finally dropped because it was felt that "though there might be a case for legislation to introduce censorship of posters, the matter was not at the time of such urgency as to justify legislatiion.[26]

Perhaps even the authorities concerned had come to realize that there were enough safeguards and means of control in existence. Perhaps they were also influenced by the articles in the press. One of these preserved in Government files, wrote of the "idiosyncrasies of the Censor Boards" whose "anxious concern about the 'morals' of the people has proved a great hindrance in the development of the film industry..."[27] After this, no substantial changes were made in the censorship until 1949.

In 1935, a new Constitution was drawn up, which placed theatres, dramatic performances and cinemas on the Provincial List, and the sanctioning of cinematograph films for exhibition on the concurrent list. This did not affect the existing situation, but provided for the possibility of a central censorship Board later on. Under the terms of this constitution, Burma was separated from India.

Burning Topics of the Day

In spite of these and other related harassments and frustrations, the much maligned and sorely-tried film industry continued to prosper and flourish. In 1939 it was the eighth key industry in the country. To the immense popularity of the mythological and the crime film, another genre had been added—the "stunt" film, or the "action-thriller." These were also imitative of an American form—the serials of Pearl White and Eddi Polo, and the exploits of Douglas Fairbanks. A box office triumph in 1935 was *Hunterwali* (The Huntress) produced by the Wadia brothers' company

Wadia Movietone. *Hunterwali*, based on *The Mark of Zorro*, is the story of a princess who sets out to rescue her father who is being held captive by a scheming minister. She disguises herself as a man and roams the countryside, robbing the rich to feed the poor. In her adventures she falls in love with a peasant boy. They fight side by side against overwhelming odds and eventually rescue the king. The tremendous success of this film led to a series of stunt films. But according to J. B. H. Wadia who took an MA in English Literature and a law degree before founding Wadia Movietone, "The stunts and the comedy were only a veneer. Into these stories I wove the problems of the day, like untouchability, Hindu-Muslim unity which was a favourite topic of mine, emancipation of women, anti-fascism, literacy campaign. Into every film which I wrote I brought in the burning topics of the day."[28]

These issues had become the "burning topics of the day" as a direct result of Mahatma Gandhi's emphasis on social reform. Rabindranath Tagore had been an early instigator of reform, and M. N. Roy's humanism had attracted many followers, including J. B. H. Wadia. But in the early '30s it was Gandhi who inflamed the passions of the entire country. A significant outcome of both his political action and his drive for reform in society, was the evolution in the role and status of women. Indian society, when cinema began in 1913, was confined within the bounds of a strict orthodoxy. The women, particularly, led severely secluded lives, and did not often appear in public. Social mixing between the sexes was rare and limited to a small section of the westernized upper classes, and to the revolutionary reformists of the Brahmo-Samaj movement in Bengal. Though spearheaded by M. N. Roy and Tagore, Mahatma Gandhi, with his widespread call to all Indians to join the non-violent struggle for freedom, was responsible for breaking down these barriers, as women from all over the country responded to his call. "Thousands of them, many being of good family and high educational attainments, suddenly emerged from the seclusion of their homes, and in some instances actually from *purdah*, in order to join Congress demonstrations and assist in picketing. . . ."[29]

The new-found freedom enjoyed by the women, led them into several fields. It also gave them the courage to brave the social stigma attached to film acting. In its Report the Indian Cinematograph Committee of 1927 had said; "It is a deplorable fact that many of the actresses now in the field, came from a class of people who unfortunately have not the best reputations,"[30] and regretted "the sad want of cooperation from the educated classes.[31] But in the '30s, the situation began to change and by 1938 the film industry was pointing with pride to the background of some of the actresses:

Leela—Belongs to a respectable Maharashtrian family of Kolhapur.
Uma Shashi—Comes of a respectable family...
Leela Desai—First Society lady with a BA.[32]

The shift in social behaviour led to a shift in emphasis in the theme of films as well.

The Studio as Super Star

Alongside the rapidly expanding popular cinema another style of film making had been steadily growing. Gradually, in small numbers, young people from good families, finally succumbing to the potential and fascination of this still new medium had started to enter the film world. Educated, cultivated, concerned with political and social behaviour, theirs was an angry response to the complacent assumptions of an unbending morality. Centuries old ideas, rituals and customs—these were the questions that provided the subjects of many of their films.

In the thirties, with the switch to sound demanding much larger investments than they could handle, many of the smaller producing companies collapsed and the studio system came into being. Actors and actresses, writers and musicians, producers, directors and technicians, all worked regularly for a monthly salary. Sabita Devi, one of the highest paid actresses of the period earned Rs 3,000 a month, princely salary compared to the Rs 60 some of the other performers received. Dominating the studio scene were the Big Three—Prabhat in Poona, New Theatres in Calcutta and Bombay Talkies in, where else, but Bombay.

In 1930, B. N. Sircar, son of the then Advocate-General of Bengal, returned home with an engineering degree from Glasgow. His intention was to make a career in engineering and construction. One of his first jobs was to construct a cinema, and this contact with the film world proved conclusive. He built and managed a cinema for himself for some time, without the knowledge of his family, until an enterprising journalist learnt of it and published the story. But once his father discovered it, he accepted it and in fact, helped his son to start his own production company, International Film Craft. It produced two silent films *Chorekanta* (Sly Thorn) and *Chasar Meye* (Farmers' Daughter). But the talkies arrived just then and with them, B.N. Sircar launched New Theatres.[33] He quickly built and equipped a first-class studio and laboratory and gathered round him a host of talented people—some who were already in films, some were new-comers—all were to make the name of New Theatres memorable for innovative craftsmanship, style, theme, acting and directing. A number of these New Theatres' films were to become classics of Indian cinema.

D.G. Gangulee, the satiric comedian and director had formed his own company in the 20s, British Dominion Films. This collapsed with the coming of sound. He joined New Theatres for whom he made a number of satiric comedies, one of the most sussessful of which was *Excuse me, Sir*. Debaki Bose had worked with 'DG' in British Dominion. In 1920, stirred by Mahatma Gandhi's call, he had left college to join the non-cooperation movement. His father, who himself had no difficulty in cooperating with the British, was outraged and disowned him. In the mid-'20s, when he was assistant editor of a Congress weekly *Sakti*, he met DG, wrote a script for him, and *Flames of Flesh* became the first production of British Dominion. But it was New Theatres and working with sound that brought out the real talents of Debaki Bose. He became known for his lyrical dramas and creative use of sound. In *Chandidas* (Chandidas), background music was used for the first time. Another of his films, *Seeta*, with Durga Khote was in 1934, the first Indian film to be shown at the Venice Film Festival, while *Puran Bhakt* (The Devotee) the previous year, had created a sensation and spread the fame of New Theatres throughout India. The themes of his films too were revolutionary. *Chandidas* is the story of a poet-priest of the sixteenth century who is excommunicated by his fellow Brahmins for his love of a washerwoman. Many years later at a film seminar in Delhi in 1955, Debaki Bose said that "films, to make millions escape from the worries of everyday life have also made people escape from the facts of everyday life." In none of his films can he be accused of having done that.

In 1934 another New Theatres film, *Bhāgyachakra* (Wheel of Fate) introduced playback singing to Indian cinema. Nitin Bose had been the cameraman on *Chorekanta*. Now, as technical chief of New Theatres, he kept abreast of the latest developments in film technique in the West. Impressed with the rich possibilities of playback singing, he asked the New Theatres' Music Director R.G. Boral and sound engineer Mukul Bose to try it out. They experimented with great success in a song-and-dance number for *Bhāgyachakra* which Nitin Bose himself directed. Playback singing had come to stay. But the man who played perhaps the most spectacular role in the history of New Theatres was Prince Barua. Son of the Raja of Gauripur, he had innumerable interests and more than enough money to indulge in them. But it was film that caught his imagination. He too, had worked with DG and Debaki Bose. For a while he had his own company, Barua Pictures, in Calcutta. But in the end he also threw in his lot with New Theatres, attracted by B.N. Sircar's creative producing which smoothed the path for directors and allowed them to work in an atmosphere free of irritating constraints. He made a number of films for New Theatres but the one that caused a lasting sensation was *Devdas* (Devdas). Sarat Chandra Chatterji's classic novel of the same name appealed strongly to Barua, matching as it did his own tragic view of a life in which there are few happy endings.

Devdas, to an extent, was a film of social protest. When the girl he loves is given away in an arranged marriage while he is away at university, Devdas find refuge in drink and eventually dies of a broken heart, a victim of his surroundings, of a bigoted society in which no protest was admissible. It was a film that touched a chord in many people, virtually a generation is said to have wept over it. The romantic, tragic hero had an intense attraction for the young for whom Devdas became almost a cult figure and Devdasiyat a condition to be envied, imitated, cultivated and revelled in.

First shot in Bengali in 1935, with Barua playing the lead, it was followed the same year with a Hindi version in which New Theatres' sensational discovery K.L. Saigal, was Devdas. These two names became inseparably linked and together with Barua's achieved permanent fame. Both the Bengali and the Hindi versions were directed by Barua. In both, the cameraman was Bimal Roy who made his own version of it in 1956 with Dilip Kumar, and

Vijayantimala in the role made famous by Jamuna. In 1936 New Theatres produced a very successful Tamil version of *Devdas* and today it is being made yet again by Gulzar, with Dharmendra and Hema Malini.

Practically all of Barua's pictures had this melancholy, doomed quality. Another of his films, *Mukti* (Liberation) in taking up the theme of adultery, was provocative indeed. Barua himself plays the role of the romantic young husband who simulates a perfect suicide in order to leave his wife free to marry the man she loves. He disappears into the forest where they all meet accidentally years later when the wife with her new husband comes there on a hunting trip. He is finally killed while rescuing his ex-wife from kidnappears, thus giving her *mukti* a second time. About this film a contemporary critic, probably accustomed to a diet of gangster, stunt and mythological films also prevalent at the time, wrote: "The theme of this story is provocative and is good for those who indulge in thinking as a pastime!"[34]

In Poona, in those days, was another group making films that "indulged in thinking as a pastime." The Prabhat Film Company had been launched in 1929 by the 28-years-old V. Shantaram, together with four partners. Shantaram had been drawn to the cinema through his fascination from childhood with the films of Phalke. His first sound film *Ayudhya Ka Raja* (The King of Ayudhya), was in fact that the story of Phalke's *Raja Harischandra*. Shantaram however, 18 years after Phalke, was able to get a "high caste girl" Durga Khote who was hailed as the most spectacular new-comer of the year to take the role of the princess which in Phalke's had been played by a young man.

Prabhat had started at Kolhapur with no trained personnel, very few facilities and much enthusiasm. S. Fathelal, one of the partners, described the conditions under which they functioned: "We set up a studio made of canvas and only years after had a tin-built studio at Kolhapur....We depended on ourselves and some-how learnt direction, art direction and cinematography, editing and processing...." They employed permanent stars and invited local people in to participate as extras for the fun of it. Later when they shifted to Poona in more affluent circumstances, more stars were engaged but, "there was not any gradation—their salary being the same. We taught them how to speak dialogue, or walk in a scene, and when they were not required for shooting, they were taught swimming, horse riding, motor driving and even sword fighting, and work or no work they were required to present themselves at the studio at 9 A.M. and stay till 7-8 P.M."[35] The same conditions applied to technicians, musicians, writers. They even ended up with a little zoo where tigers, horses, dogs, deer and birds were trained! As a gesture of goodwill the Agfa and Kodak companies installed the machinery for a processing laboratory and trained the Prabhat technicians who in their turn trained others. Today the Film and Television Institute stands on the sprawling magnificent grounds of the old Prabhat Company in Poona.

For the ambitious young founders of Prabhat, well-known mythological and devotional strories seemed the safest starting point. In 1936, Shantaram's *Amar Jyoti* (Eternal Light) was shown at Venice, but in 1937 it was *Sant Tukaram* made by V. Damle and S. Fathelal that became the first Indian film to be ranked among the three best pictures at the Fifth International Exhibition of Cinematographic Art, Venice. Shantaram soon began to experiment with social protest and is in fact, best remembered for his stories on contemporary problems. *Duniya Na Mane* (The Un-Expected), 1937, bears a slight resemblance in theme to Barua's *Mukti*, but it goes beyond the personal tragedy of *Mukti* to deal with the rights of women. In it the old husband, brought to an awareness of the injustice of a society that has forced a young girl into marriage with him, commits suicide in order to free her. But it is the young wife's own strength and fearlessness that liberates her in the end.

His *Admi* (Life is for Living) was, however, made as a direct answer to *Devdas*. As he himself said: "*Admi* was my own reaction to the theme of frustration and tragedy of *Devdas* in which the lover, failing to get his beloved, starts drinking and visiting a prostitute and ultimately dies. As a result, hundreds of college Romeos whenever jilted in love resorted to drink . . . . The reaction of the audience was so strong that I felt the necessity of making a film stressing the fact that a woman's love is not everything in life. And I had the satisfaction that I had fulfilled my responsibility when I got a letter from a young man saying that after seeing *Admi* he decided not to end his life as a result of disappointment in love. This letter, which credited me with having saved one life gave me far more satisfaction than anything else."[36]

The third in the group of the Big Three of the '30s was Bombay Talkies. Its founders, Himansu Rai and Devaki Rani, both from well-established, "good" families, had met and married in London. Himansu Rai had a law degree from Calcutta University and had also studied at Santiniketan. In London, he was supposed to train as a lawyer, but could not see tear himself away from the theatre and film. He managed to persuade the Emelka film Company in Munich to co-produce, with Indian finance, a film on the Buddha. *The Light of Asia* was a triumph in Europe in 1925, but had only limited success in India.[37] At the time they met, Devika Rani having graduated from the Royal Academy of Dramatic Art, had taken up architecture, when Himansu Rai won her over into film. They made two more Indo-German co-productions in the silent era, before shooting *Karma* (Fate) in English, and with Devika Rani and Himansu Rai acting together. The London prèmiere was a great success for Devika Rani who had the press rhapsodizing over her "large velvety eyes that can express every emotion." The film brought them many more offers but Himansu Rai decided it was time to go home, saying, "Let us learn from these people, but let us put the knowledge to work in our country."[38]

Carrying a print of *Karma*, Devika Rani and Himansu Rai arrived in Bombay in 1933. This was the beginning of Bombay Talkies and a series of film that stand out in Indian film history.

Unlike New Theatres and Prabhat who started with mythologicals, Bombay Talkies' first produced light comedies. But their best known and best remembered film, the one that made a star of Ashok Kumar in 1936, was *Acchut Kanya* (Untouchable Girl). Caste was the taboo touched upon in this film—the impossible love of a high caste Hindu boy for an untouchable girl. But having no solution to offer, this, as so many others "socials," ended with that most convenient way out of all problems—death.

But important issues were being raised, and the social films of the '30s were not afraid to attack the established canons of Hindu society. In Madras, K. Subrahmanyan formed Madras United Artists Cooperation in 1936, and started making films in Tamil and Telugu, later including Malayalam and Kannada as well. Subrahmanyan, one of the few Brahmin producers in those days, outraged his community by making *Balyogini* (Child Saint) which dared to criticize the treatment of widows in orthodox Hinduism. B.N. Reddy's *Sumangali* (Fortunate Girl) in Telugu, also focussed attention on the problem of widowhood, without offering re-marriage as the solution. A number of early Tamil films had an anti-caste, anti-Brahmin attitude which won them a wide popular following and which was to have quite surprising repercussions in the '60s.

A few other studios were engaged in social criticism. Chandulal Shah, had started the trend of "socials" in the early '20s, and one of his first talkies *Radharani* (Radharani) exposed the gross injustice of society towards women. In the '30s he founded Ranjit Movietone in partnership with his star "Glorious Gohar." The company concentrated on socials, comedies in both Hindi and Gujarati, and enjoyed a decade of uninterrupted successes with films such as *Gun Sundari* (Why Husbands Go Astray) and *Typist Girl*.

Looking back on that period today, 40 odd years later, one perhaps invests these films with greater significance than was felt at the time. However, an article in *The Hindu* on 19 May 1939, commemorating the 25th anniversary of the Indian films did say that "It has unsettled the placid contentment of the Indian masses, it has filled the minds of youth with new longings and it is today a potent force in national life."[39] There is no doubt that the people involved in the making of these "socials," given their background, could not have remained untouched by the mood and temper of the country as the movement for Independence gathered strength. K. A. Abbas, esteemed film maker, critic, journalist and author, believes that these films were the response of a literate, concerned people whose creative conscience was limited by the kind of censorship prevalent at the time. Unable to attackle the bonds that held the country in political captivity, they turned inwards to challenge the precepts of their own society whose inflexible rules represented another kind of slavery. In an article in *New Age*, 24 July 1958, on "The National Theme in Indian Cinema" he wrote :

Just as British imperialism had affected India on three levels—political enslavement, economic exploitation and social stagnation—the freedom movement too, was carried on three levels. The agitation for democratic rights, the struggle for a living wage, and the movement for social reform were carried on simultaneously. In the cinema all three forms were reflected but, because of censorship, the political and economic struggles could be depicted not directly but only by means of suggestion and symbolism. The main emphasis was on social reforms. As a growing number of intellectuals infiltrated into film studios, they began to give the films not only a finer aesthetic and cultural tone, but also a definite social purpose. A great many films were produced which attacked the rampant social evils, sometimes not hesitating to expose economic inequalities and injusice. However, the treatment of social themes in these films was not fully scientific but subjective, emotional and sometimes only vaguely progressive. A more direct attack on existing society was not possible under the existing censorship.

In another article he wrote: "In the general atmosphere of growing anti-imperialism, the theme of Democracy and the people's rights to revolt against tyranny was subtly introduced even in mythologicals—as for instance in *Gopal Krishna* (Lord Krishna) (1938), the cowherd Krishna's struggle against the tyrant Kansa could not but strike a patriotic chord of defiance in the hearts of the cinegoers."[40]

In general, as long as the political status of Britain was not touched (occasionally, even demonstrations against a film for reasons of religious susceptibilities could create a "law and order" problem) they permitted anything.[41] Thus not one of the 150 odd pictures produced by New Theatres was ever subjected to cuts by the Censors.[42]

The Indian film world at the end of the thirties had come into its own, and begun to be organized as an industry. The Motion Picture Society of India had been formed in 1932, followed immediately by regional associations—in Calcutta the Bengal Motion Picture Association, (1936), in Bombay, the Indian Motion Picture Producers Association (1937), in Madras, the South Indian Film Chamber of Commerce (1938). Each of these began to publish journals and bulletins. Fan magazines and film periodicals also made their appearance. In 1938, there were 68 periodicals devoted to the cinema of which half were in English, half in various other Indian languages.[43] Film makers could also take pride in some of their achievements; New Theatres' *Seeta* (Seeta) had been shown at the Venice Film Festival in 1934, and Prabhat's *Sant Tukaram* won an award in 1937. In 1938, the Imperial Film Company that had made the first sound film *Alam Ara*, produced another first *Kisan Kanya* (Farmer's Daughter) in colour.

In view of the immense influence of the cinema, it is a source of constant amazement that the political leadership of the country never took advantage of its vast potential as a means of propaganda. B.N. Sircar had close family ties with Subhas Chandra Bose, who became Congress President in 1938. Later, impatient with the slow, non-violent struggle for independence, he became the idol of the young as he took to more militant ways. Arrested by the British, he escaped to Germany from where he made his way to Japan, eventually training the Indian National Army in South East Asia to fight the British. He died under mysterious circumstances in a plane crash in 1945. When asked if Bose had never discussed with him the possibility of using film for political purposes, Sircar replied that "the Congress never realized the potency of the film medium."[44] In fact, it consistently looked down upon it. In 1938 when a Bombay trade paper asked Gandhi for a message to the film industry on its 25th anniversary, it received this answer from Gandhi's Secretary: "As a rule Gandhi gives messages only on rare occasions, and these only for causes whose virtue is ever undoubtful. As for the Cinema Industry he has the least interest in it and one may not expect a word of appreciation from him."[45] Occasionally a word of appreciation did come as when Mrs Sarojini Naidu, the poet-politician who became the first woman Governor of a State in independent India in 1947, said about Baburao Painter's *Savkari Pash* (Savkari Pash) (1925): "A remarkable film that portrays with perfect art the moving and tragic story of Indian peasant life. It is a more eloquent plea on behalf of the villager than a hundred speeches made from public platforms." The film industry itself, recognizing the power of film to mould opinion, was very incensed at the portrayal of India in some American and British films made in the thirties. A campaign was launched in *Filmindia* in 1939 against films like *The Drum*, *The Siege of Lucknow*, *The Black Hole of Calcutta*, *The Tiger of Krischnapur*, *Gunga Din* (Gunga Din). They demanded a protest by the Secretary of State for India against the misrepresentation of India and Indians in these films. Although the subject was discussed in England's House of Commons, nothing came of it. But it does show that at least a section of the film industry was concerned with more than just making money.

Just as the film industry was beginning to experience a sense of confidence in itself, its was once against overtaken by external events.

Indian Cinema during the Second World War

On 3 September, 1939 when Great Britain declared war on Germany, Lord Linlithgow, Viceroy of India, declared India too, to be at war with Germany. The Indian National Congress took strong exception to this, saying that such decisions could only be taken by the Indian people. The Congress, while expressing its abhorrence of Fascism and Nazism, declared that "India cannot associate herself in a war said to be for democratic freedom when that very freedom is denied her . . . a free democratic India will gladly associate herself with other free nations for mutual defence."[46]

Since Congress leaders made clear their "determination to boy-cott the war, British censorship tried to maintain a blackout of the Congress."[47] Casually, in the background, Congress symbols began to be introduced into films: the spinning wheel (Gandhi's motif), a photograph of Nehru or Subhas Chandra Bose, a calendar with Gandhi's portrait, the Congress Flag, on the sound track a Congress song. Often these had no relevance to the story of the film, but audiences recognized and cheered them. The Censor Boards recognized, and cut them. In 1942, with Gandhi's cry to the British to "Quit India," the freedom movement gathered momentum, and no allusion to Gandhi was permitted in films. "But," pointed out the *Journal of the Film Industry* "excision of photographs of Congress leaders is not going to remove them from the hearts of their followers."[48] Even knowing those scenes would be cut out, films continued to introduce references to freedom, war, the Congress, leading to Censor Boards' decisions such as:

(1) In scene where the two servants of the hero are shown talking together, omit the part of their conversation referring to anti-war views (*Amar Asha* [Eternal Hope], India, June 1942).

(2) In part of the dialogue where a comparison is made between Hitler and Mahatma Gandhi omit all references to Gandhi. (*Pritam* [The Loved One], India, August 1942).

(3) *a.* Omit references to Mahatma Gandhi.

b. Omit Congress salute given by Raja before Mahatma Gandhi's statue.

c. Omit part of Raja's speech where he is shown using strong language in emphasizing his preference for Hindi as against

English language. (*Raja* [King], India, April 1943)

(4) Omit the words *Vande Mataram* (Hail to the Motherland) and the Congress National Song. (*Maze Bal* [My Child], India, May 1943).

(5) *a.* Delete scenes showing photos of national leaders.

b. Cut two lines of song which convey the meaning 'Take by force the thing you need, for this is not the Age to ask for something before taking it. (*Naya Tarana* [New Melody], India, October 1943).

(6) Omit all parts showing picture of Subhas Chandra Bose in the wallet of the hero. Also cries of *Mahatmaji ki Jai*. (*Sangam* [The Meeting Point], India, December 1943).

(7) Omit from the three concluding Hindi songs all parts of the scene showing India in chains, as also all words referring to India in chains. Omit following words: (*a*) *Bhuke Mare Bangal* (Bengal can Die of Hunger); (*b*) *Vande Mataram* (Hail to the Motherland); (*c*) *Inquilab Zindabad* (Long Live the Revolution); (*d*) *Akhand Hindustan*(India United). (*Gajabhau*[Brother], India, August 1944).

(8) "Omit the scene where an American soldier's car was stopped by school children and street urchins and he was heard shouting *Jai Hind* with them." (*Avijatri* [The Voyager] India, December 1946).[49]

The same judgements held for foreign films too. Thus *Hangmen Also Die* (directed by Fritz Lang, written by Bertold Brecht, USA, 1943) was banned because "its entire theme is the lauding of political assassination." Even in newsreels e.g., *March of Time No. 11 "India at War,"* USA, October 1942, all shots referring to either the Indian National Congress or its leaders had to be omitted. Another *March of Time* in June 1945, referring to the Irish question was banned because it "deals with controversial political questions on which feelings between certain subjects of H.M. are strained."[50]

During the war, film shows were arranged for the entertainment of the troops. The Wadia Movietone stunt films that continued to be immensely popular, were an obvious choice. But the unexpected response of the soldiers made the authorities suspicious. They became aware of the themes underlying the action, and the films were withdrawn from circulation because of their "revolutionary content."[51]

Another genre of films appeared at this time—the historical. Conceived on a grand scale with a huge cast, *Sikandar* (Alexander) was the first film to be made on a historical theme. Sohrab Modi had been a Shakespearean actor touring India with his theatrical company. With the coming of sound, he turned to the cinema. His first film was *Hamlet* which he had played so successfully on the stage. This was followed by *Henry VI*—both in Hindi. From Shakespeare's history to India's history was not such a big step, and "I thought Indians should know about our glorious past," he said. In his spectacular *Sikander* he showed Alexander's campaign up to the borders of India from where he had to turn back. The film was passed by the Censor Board, but was later uncertified for theatres in Army cantonments. Its appeal to nationalism was considered too direct. Although as history *Sikander* remained fairly superficial, for the grandeur of its spectacle, it was compared favourably in a London paper with Griffiths' *Birth of a Nation*,[52] and Sohrab Modi went on to specialize in historical dramas.

Various devices were resorted to in an attempt to fool the censors and communicate a sense of national pride directly to the audience. Thus when the British Government asked producers to make anti-Japanese films during the war, the imaginative song writer, Pradeep, composed a rousing chorus song for the film *Kismet* (Destiny), a song that was ostensibly addressed to the Germans and Japanese... "Door Hato..." (Go back, go back, you foreigners, whether you be Germans or Japanese, India belongs to us). But by the way the audiences cheered it, it was clear that the song applied equally to the British.[53]

Another war effort film, K. Subrahmanyan's *Manasamrakshanam* (In Defence of Honour), was approved and released and only the spirited audience reaction made the authorities realize that here again, in saying "Go away" to the Japanese, the film could be echoing the Congress slogan "Quit India" addressed to the British. The film was removed from circulation by some local authorities.[54]

This political censorship was in addition to normal censorship on the usual grounds of "low moral tone," "drink," "distasteful, cruel, sexy," even "bathing scenes," "mixed dancing" "bedroom scenes" and "ridiculing the police."[55]

But the years of the British Raj were drawing to a close, and war-time censorship had less effect on the film industry than other simultaneous developments. The British Government in India understood the value of film as a medium for informing and shaping public opinion. In 1940 a Film Advisory Board was set up, to make and encourage war effort films. In America the Government had invited Hollywood directors to come to Washington to make war propaganda films. In 1942-44 a successful series of films called *Why We Fight* was made by Frank Capra who at the time was one of the biggest names in Hollywood. But this was not India's war, and Alexander Shaw, documentary film specialist, was brought from England to set up this documentary film unit in Bombay. Though most leading Indian producers supported the Congress position, some others, moved by reports of Nazi brutality and apprehensive about the Japanese advance, thought otherwise. Thus when the Film Advisory Board was set up, J.B.H. Wadia accepted its chairmanship. At the same time, the Government also took up the production of newsreels. By 1943 the showing of documentaries and newsreels in the theatres had been made compulsory.[56] This Government control over the production and distribution of propaganda films which the theatres were not only obliged to show but also had to pay for, was to play an important and controversial role in independent India.

The war also delivered into the hands of the Government another weapon to be used against the film industry. Raw film became a scarce commodity and to ease the situation, the Government put a limit of 11,000 ft on the length of feature films.[57] As the shortage and difficulty of obtaining raw stock increased, the Government also took the allocation of film into its hands. In India today, this is still an important form of control over the film industry. At that time, the Government decided that to receive regular allocations of film, a producer, or the studio must make every third picture on a "war-effort" theme. Apart from the painful position into which this put the producers of having to support the (British) Government, it led to some disastrous films—Bombay Talkies' *Char Aankhen* (Four Eyes), about nurses, was a total failure, and New Theatre's *Dushman* (Enemy) on tuberculosis, was only a little better. But a film that proved both successful and interesting was Shantaram's *The Journey of Dr Kotnis*. Written by K.A. Abbas who was now launched on a film career after several years as a journalist, it was the story of an Indian doctor who went with an Indian Medical Mission to China. Seven doctors had been sent by the Congress as a gesture of support and sympathy to serve with Mao Tse Tung's 8th Army. The project had been sponsord by Nehru, but since the story was anti-Japanese, the British supported it as a war effort theme.[58]

The most momentous development on the film scene of the middle forties was also indirectly caused by the war. The war brought sudden wealth to speculators and black marketeers. This was not legal money that could openly be reinvested, and the black-marketeers began to look for ways of putting their money to use.

Film was an industry that could not and did not show concrete proofs of investment. But there was money in it. So they began to speculate with film. They enticed away stars from the studio to act in independent productions. Stars were offered huge amounts, half of it in "black," undeclared, non-taxable income. Star fees shot up from Rs 20,000 to Rs 200,000 per film. From a pre-war average of Rs 90,000 the cost of production escalated to a post-war average of Rs 500,000, wrote the *Journal of the Film Industry* in April 1950. Offers of exorbitant fees were soon extended to another key figure in film—the music director. Fly-by-night producers sprang out of nowhere, made their money on one film, and disappeared. "With black money and corruption abounding in the country, businessmen began to think in terms of easy money and quick returns. The inflationary war boom has been the greatest encouragement for all and sundry to enter the various branches of the film industry."[59] More and more films began to be made on this basis. But there was no corresponding increase in the number of theatres, as wartime shortages extended to building materials as well. Power passed from the studios into the hands of the distributors and exhibitors who could now choose the kind of film they wished to handle. Their aim was easy money and quick returns, and they laid down the criterion for what they thought would be a surefire hit at the box office: a star, six songs, three dances. The formula film was born.

This approach to film signified inevitably a loss in quality. The great advantage of the studio system had been that, functioning as an office with everybody including stars, directors, musicians and technicians on monthly salaries, risks could be taken with "serious" films that might not bring in as much as a "popular" film, that may sometimes even be a total failure at the box office. But experimenation in a limited way had been possible. This was now ended. There was to be no more "social realism." The emphasis from now on was to be on glamour, gloss, escapism and the star. One by one the studios began to close down. Kanan Devi, who starred in a number of New Theatres' films in the '30s, described the end: "The star system met with great success in the abnormally strained atmosphere of the war. It grew in size and in the huge deluge that it produced, the producer, the technician, the writer and others were washed away."[60] Chimanlal Desai, founder of Sagar Movietone in the '30s declared sadly: "No other course was left to us but to close down and so we did."[61]

In 1945 an independent group of young people from the theatre got together to produce a film which has become something of a legend. All the prints and negatives were destroyed in a fire that gutted the laboratory where it was lying. Years later a print of it was discovered in a Calcutta bazaar along with other discarded bits of film that were being sold by the weight. It was bought up for Rs 10 by the members of a film unit who recognized it and that print, scratched and badly damaged, is now with the National Film Archives at Poona.

In 1946 however, *Neecha Nagar* (Lower Depths) was the first Indian film to win the Critics Award at the first Cannes Film Festival after the war where the second prize went to David Lean's *Brief Encounter. Neecha Nagar* is the allegorical tale of a rich industrialist whose downfall is wrought as much by the peoples' non-violent, non-cooperation movement as by his daugher who has an emotional attachment to the fiery young leader of the people. For those who cared to look for it, the references to the British Government, Gandhi, Nehru, the Indian elite—symbolized by the daughter—were unmistakable. The censors did not see it that way and passed the film.

Made on a shoe-string budget, it was Chetan Anand's first attempt at film direction. It was based on a novel by Hayatullah Ansari who was at that time editor of Jawaharlal Nehru's Urdu paper *Qaumi Awaz* (Voice of the Nation) in Lucknow. The dancer Rafiq Anwar played the main role and it was financed and produced by his brother who had made his money as a wrestler in England.

As a Hindu-Muslim venture, it could not find a distributor in those troubled days. The bitter communal strife which was to culminate in the bloody riots at independence a few short months later, had already begun. No Hindu distributor would touch it because the producer was a Muslim, no Muslim distributor would take it because the director was a Hindu. Eventually the film was shown in a little suburban theatre of Bombay, where the audience broke up the chairs, threw things at the screen. They had not come to see a stark, grim tale of suffering. They were not interested in what it had to say. They wanted their money back. The film was withdrawn and never released again. It had one prestigious showing before it disappeared—at the First Asian Conference in Delhi in 1949, Jawaharlal Nehru had it specially screened for the delegates.

In 1946, shortly before Independence, another film was made that was to be the last of the socials of the era, and provide a fitting epitaph to it—*Dharti Ke Lal* (Children of the Earth). Produced as a cooperative venture by the Indian People's Theatre Association and directed by K.A. Abbas, it was the harrowing story of a peasant family in the great Bengal famine of 1943. Commercially it was a complete failure, though it brought him great prestige. The people had shown that they definitely preferred the escapist formulas of the musical romances.

The escapist formula was to be the norm of the Indian film in the years to come, once again invoking the scorn and disdain of the educated elite. Apart from a handful of distinguished exceptions, it would not be until the '70s that Indian cinema would attempt to break out of the commercial stranglehold and once again create films of significance and relevance.

Notes

[1] *Evidences,* Vol I, p. 167.

[2] E. Barnouw and S. Krishnaswamy, *Indian Film,* Columbia University Press, New York, 1963, p. 56. *Census of India 1931* Vol. I, Part I, Report, Delhi, Manager of Publications, 1933.

[3] Ruby Meyers, "Ordeals of Stardom," *Indian Talkies 1931-56,* p. 126.

[4] S. Rangaswami (Ed), "Who is Who in Indian Filmland," Happy India Office, Madras, 1933.

[5] Presidential Address of Jawaharlal Nehru, Lahore Congress 1929.

[6] B.D. Garga, "One Man's Crusade for Social Justice" (Article in brochure on K.A. Abbas as film maker, printed for Abbas Film Retrospective, 1974.).

[7] 1 to 6: *Journal of the Motion Picture Society of India,* August 1937.

[8] 7 to 8: Bombay Censor Board Records.

[9]*Ibid.*

[10]*Ibid.*

[11]*Ibid.*

[12]Calcutta Censor Board Records.

[13]*Ibid.*

[14]Bombay Censor Board Records.

[15]*Ibid.*

[16]*Ibid.*

[17]*Ibid.*

[18]*Ibid.*

[19]Calcutta Censor Board Records.

[20]*Filmindia*, April 1938.

[21]Legislative Assembly Debates, 4 September 1933.

[22]*Ibid.*

[23]"Stricter Censoring Needed," *Amrita Bazar Patrika*, 26 June 1934, quoted in Home Department (Political) File 1934.

[24]*Ibid.*

[25]*ICC Report*, p. 118.

[26]Home Department (Political) File 1934.

[27]F. Malik, "Muzzling the Cinema Industry," *Daily Herald*, 9 July 1937.

[28] .B.H. Wadia to the author, Bombay, May 1975.

[29]Ram Gopal, *British Rule in India*, Asia Publishing House, Bombay, 1946, p. 336.

[30]*ICC Report*, paras 174 & 177, pp. 82-83.

[31]*Ibid.*

[32]B.D. Bharucha (Ed), *Indian Cinematography Yearbook*, 1938, Bombay Motion Picture Society of India, Bombay, 1938.

[33]B.N. Sircar to the author, Calcutta, April 1975.

[34]*Filmindia*, June 1938.

[35]S. Fathelal, "Prabhat was a Training School," *Indian Talkie* 1931-56, p. 139.

[36]V. Shantaram, "New Wave, Nude Wave and All That," *Illustrated Weekly of India*, 1 October 1972, and *Film Seminar Report*, 1955.

[37]Oral evidence of Himansu Rai: "Lbelieve that in the years 1925-26 there was not another picture, whether American, German or English which had more reputation than this."

[38]Barnouw and Krishnaswamy, op. cit., p. 93.

[39]*Ibid*, pp. 96-97.

[40]K.A. Abbas, "Film & Society" *Yojana*, 15 October 1974.

[41]J.B.H. Wadia to the author, Bombay, May 1975.

[42]B.N. Sircar to the author, Calcutta, April 1975.

[43]*Yearbook of Indian Cinema*, 1938, p. 14.

[44]B.N. Sircar to the author, Calcutta, 1 April 1975.

[45]Reported in *Dipali* 16 June 1939, quoted by Barnouw & Krishnaswamy, p. 111.

[46]A.K. Azad, *India Wins Freedom*, Orient Longmans, Calcutta, 1959, pp. 26-30.

[47]Barnouw and Krishnaswamy, *op. cit.*, p. 118.

[48]*Journal of the Film Industry*, February 1944.

[49]Bombay Censor Board Records.

[50]*Ibid.*

[51]J.B.H. Wadia to the author, Bombay, May 1975.

[52]Sohrab Modi to the author, Bombay, May 1975.

[53]K.A. Abbas, "The National Theme in Indian Cinema," *New Age,* 24 July 1958.

[54]Barnouw and Krishnaswamy, *op. cit.,* p. 125.

[55]Madras Censor Board Records.

[56]"On 15 Sept 1943 the Government of India issued an order under Rule 44A of the Defence of India Rules making it compulsory for exhibitors to show a minimum of 2000 ft of films approved by Government," Panna shah, *The Indian Film,* Motion Picture Society of India, Bombay, 1950, p. 208.

[57]*Journal of the Film Industry*, May 1942, p. 5.

[58]K.A. Abbas, interviews with the author between 1970 and 1975 in Bombay and Delhi.

[59]*Journal of the Film Industry*, September 1947, p. 11.

[60]Kanan Devi, "Rise of the Star System," *Indian Talkie*, p. 135.

[61]Chimanlal Desai, "Sagar was Ten Years Ahead," *Ibid.*, p. 127.

4

The Imperatives of Freedom

Independence

Independence Day 15 August 1947, was welcomed with as much joy by the film industry as by the rest of the country. But the euphoria was tempered by stories of unbelievable massacres perpetrated in the communal frenzy that accompanied it. The first months after independence were months of darkness for the Indian subcontinent; partition, refugees, half a million dead in the state of the Punjab alone; the assassination of Mahatma Gandhi in January 1948, war with Pakistan.

But freedom was at last a reality, and in spite of these momentous and tragic events, in the first flush of independence there was pride, a sense of achievement, of national identity. With Nehru as Prime Minister, the political ideology of the country veered naturally towards the democratic and the liberal. In this context, all press restrictions were lifted, and the Indian press became one of the most independent and outspoken in the world.

But the cinema had always been held in a certain contempt by the political leadership of the country. In July 1949, the *Journal of the Film Industry* noted regretfully that "the film industry has suffered considerably due to the negative policy and positive indifference of Government—foreign and indigenous." Besides, freedom of expression as applied to the cinema has never excited the same passions as freedom of the press. What the government did recognize after 1947, was the immense power of the cinema for the spread of information and ideas, as well as the potential of the film industry as a source of revenue. The story of the cinema in independent India was to be one of clashes with a government that set out to establish an increasingly rigid control over it through a series of legislative measures and the imposition of crippling taxes.

Immediate Post-Independence Period

1948 was a year of crisis. Film production had become a losing proposition, when 97 of 134 producing companies of 1947 did not make a single film.[1] In the immediate post-Partition period there was general depression and unemployment, production costs soared; there was an acute shortage of raw film and, in the bitter aftermath of Partition, the market in the newly-created state of Pakistan was closed to the Indian film producer.

Before the war, most States had levied an entertainment tax of $12\frac{1}{2}$ per cent, but by 1949 entertainment taxes in India ranged from 25 to 75 per cent with an average of 33 per cent depending on the gauge, length, colour/black and white, and genre of the film. This was only a part of the picture. Municipalities also began to levy entertainment tax; there were octroi duties on transporting film from one city to another; there were sales taxes under which cinema equipment was taxed at luxury rates, and there were exorbitant import duties on raw film production and equipment.

On 30 June 1949, the film industry went on strike on an All India Cinema Protest Day, during which virtually all cinemas remained closed. The protest was directed mainly against the government's taxation policy: "At every stage of film production taxes are paid. Every industry, every person, pays tax. But the proportion of special taxes borne by the film industry is much more than the general taxes borne by it in common with other industries. All these taxes (excluding income tax) amount to not less than 60 per cent of the gross collections at the box office," wrote the *Journal of the Bengal Motion Picture Association* in 1948. The strike had no tangible result other than that it demonstrated a unity in the film industry and that the government, state and local, was deprived of a day's taxes—a not inconsiderable amount.

At the same time, government recognized the usefulness of the film medium, while rejecting the film maker, and it resolved to exploit film for its own purpose.

In 1946 the Information Films of India had closed down with the end of the need for war effort films. The Indian leadership had demanded its closure as this unit was looked upon as the propaganda agency of a foreign government. But in 1948 the national government revived the organization "for the production and distribution of documentary films and news reels as a medium of education and information."[3] The Government of India Films Division was set up in Bombay in 1948, under the Ministry of Information & Broadcasting, and theatres were once more required to include an approved film of not more than 2000 ft (35 mm) in every programme. But whereas the British had charged the theatres a weekly amount of Rs 2.50 to Rs 30 for this material, the Films Division charge would be steadily increased until it ranged from Rs 5 to Rs 150 per week. And from 1951 onwards, under the revised censorship system, the cost to the producers for having his film approved—or rejected, by the Censor Board, would go up to Rs 45 per 1000 ft (35 mm), from the Rs 5 per 1000 ft of pre-Independence days—an increase of 900 per cent.[4]

Another wartime measure was to be revived, curtailing further the freedom of the film maker. For a short while in the period after Independence, raw film would be freely and openly available. Later, because of foreign exchange shortages, raw film was declared an essential commodity to be distributed under Government control. This position still obtains, and raw film is allocated only on the recommendation of the Regional Raw Film Advisory Committee. Since 1949 there had been attempts to restrict the length of feature films in view of the shortage of raw film. The Film Federation of India was asked by the Government to accept voluntarily a ceiling of 11,000 ft for features and 400 ft for trailers. This was firmly rejected by the film industry which was convinced that the longer the film the more popular it would be. Later, with the raw film shortage reaching crisis proportions, the Central Government was obliged to impose certain limitations. The Indian Motion Picture Producers Association (IMPPA) was informed by the Government of India that all Provincial Governments except Madras, in exercise of the powers conferred under Section 8 of the Cinematograph Act of 1918, had issued orders restricting the length of feature films to 11,000 ft and of trailers to 400 ft as from 1 August 1949. The restriction would not apply to films censored before 1 August, nor to those which were already in an advanced state of production by that date. In Bombay that order was to be effective from 15 September.

IMPPA was most indignant at the manner in which the orders were issued, the *Journal of the Film Industry* writing in September 1949 that:

> What is amazing is the haphazard manner in which restrictions are imposed on the trade. No harm would have been done if they had consulted the trade associations on the procedure to be adopted in this case. This is particularly so when the principle of such a restriction was agreed to by IMPPA and other associations. Instead of doing the correct thing at the correct time, our government just issues orders and leaves all worries to the trade to settle after representations to government, involving considerable waste of time and energy for all concerned.

Eventually it was agreed that the restriction would be slightly modified to 12,000 ft in the case of films in the languages of the Eastern Region, 13,000 in the Western and 15,000 in the South. With the easing of the economic and foreign exchange situation, this restriction was withdrawn—but not until 1964, by which time the public as well as the producers had got used to films of a reasonable length. Another Government measure adopted as a result of economic constraint was to have a lasting impact on film quality. In August 1948, a letter issued to all State Government by the Ministry of Works, Mines and Power, referred to the Prime Minister's statement in Parliament that during the present acute shortage of building materials, steps should be taken to stop the construction of all non-essential structures. The emphasis laid by the Government on the "imperative necessity of taking drastic steps urgently for the conservation and utilization of all building materials" was interpreted by many States Governments as a call for a blanket ban on the opening of new cinema houses.[5] This ban was not to be lifted for almost 20 years,[6] reflecting the continuing disapproval of authorities which deplored the cinema-going habit. For the producer it meant that control over film content—story, theme, choice of star and music director has remained firmly in the hands of the profit-oriented distributor and exhibitor.

From White to Brown

The dilemma of the producer became that while on the one hand the distributor/exhibitor demanded that each film contain all the ingredients of what he considered would have the widest appeal, it was those very elements that excited a reformist zeal in the new regime. In the euphoria of having finally shaken off colonial rule, everything foreign was condemned. There was constant talk of "Our National Culture," "Our Glorious Heritage." The sanctity of principles of morality and behaviour "as laid down by our fore-fathers," was repeatedly invoked. B.D. Garga, film maker and film historian, described the prevailing situation as: "Confusion ensued with the changeover from white to brown democracy. The censor-ship code, if anything, became more rigid, reactionary and rigorous. What did not suit the whimsy of a particular new "nabob" was un-ceremoniously suppressed in theories of national need, in claims of religious inviolability or in pleas for the preservation of our moral and spiritual heritage. Much chicanery was perpetrated under the bogus claims of cultural revival. Fossilized traditions, obsolete ideas and medieval habits were given a shot in the arm. As self-appointed custodians of traditional culture, the censors crankily employed the "culture" stick to frighten the non-conformist, to choke new thought and destroy dissent.

Since much semantic confusion exists in words like "culture" and "tradition," what the censors actually aimed at was a revival of past morés and beliefs. Like the eighteenth century French traditionalists who asserted the claims of the Rights of God as against the Rights of Man, our censors eulogize the Middle Ages and Victorian virtues, ignoring the mainstream of modern thought, its moral and social innovations."[7]

Even before the actual date of independence the movement began, to purge Indian culture of all alien elements. From the beginning of the sound era the Hindi i.e., the all-India film, in its search for acceptability throughout the country, had tended to avoid easily-identifiable characteristics which would place it within the limits of one region. In stressing its all-India nature, the Hindi film kept away from regional traditions in customs, mannerisms, behaviour and even dress, all of which vary widely. In a rural or even an urban lower middle-class setting, this would be unavoidable. The Hindi film, therefore, preferred to set its fantasies against an urban higher-income level background which is stamped by a westernized uniformity. Within this setting, dance and music, both integral elements of Indian cinema, also assumed a hybrid form. Film music composer/arrangers borrowed from folk and classical Indian music as well as from the melody, harmony and orchestration of popular western music. For the purists this was anathema and with independence in sight, pressures began to build up. As early as 1945 the Madras Music Academy passed a resolution recommending to the government of Madras that there should be at least two members of the Music Academy on the Film Censor Board in order to "preserve the purity and standards of Carnatic music." Reporting this in February 1945, the *Journal of the Film Industry* continued: "Nothing is stated as to how the purity and standards are to be preserved. Perhaps the Committee intended that the films which did not guarantee the desired purity and standards should not be certified by the Board of Film Censors?"[8]

The Indian Cinematograph Committee of 1927 had stated that "The object of censorship is strictly limited to preclude that which is definitely undesirable or unsuitable for public exhibition."[9] It had rejected the idea that films should be censored not only on moral and social grounds, but on artistic grounds as well, and said instead: "We do not consider that it is either practicable or justifiable to make one man or one body of men the arbiter of taste for a whole population,"[10] and in pre-independent India this ruling was strictly observed. In the same issue of February 1945, the *Journal of the Film Industry* reported that a few members of a Board of Censors had found that in a film previously certified by the Board, a story was historically untrue. These members therefore, felt that the film should not be exhibited. The matter was referred to the government which pointed out that refusal of a certificate on these grounds was beyond the powers conferred by the Cinematograph Act of 1918.[11]

In post-independence India, however, such niceties were easily dismissed by the self-appointed custodians of traditional culture. They made no secret of their contempt for the cinema, even though in many cases they had not been near a film theatre more than once or twice in their lives. Thus we have statements such as: "I think that the greatest injury is being done to the nation by the cinematograph," by someone who says a few moments later, "I have also been to cinema houses a few years ago, not now. I do not know if they have made any progress."[12] The cinema was held to be a morally corrupting influence, but since it could not be got rid of, it must be rigidly controlled. Another Bombay government body, in a report on music education, condemned current film songs as seriously corrupted by western influence and "alien to the genius of Indian music." It became a grievance of purists that "these cinemas are doing a great injury to our old treasure of music, poetry and art."[13] Discussions were held between IMPPA and the Bombay Board of Film Censors, on the subject of hybrid songs (with a mixture of English and Hindi words) in Indian films. In August 1949 the *Journal of the Film Industry* wrote that "While the Home Ministry and the Board have not raised any objections to the use of foreign words, a ban has been placed on hybrid songs in Indian films in the future. The ban is silly and is unbecoming of our international approach to our problems. It is certainly time for us to shed our inferiority complex and stop making a hue and cry of our art and culture being in danger due to foreign influences."[14] The Journal, however, came out against "vulgarity and low taste" and agreed that "if any song, hybrid or otherwise is of low taste, it should be disallowed."[15]

In 1952 Dr Keskar, Minister for Information and Broadcasting, describing film music as "cheap and vulgar," drastically reduced radio broadcasts of film songs.[16] All India Radio, since the beginning of regular broadcasts in 1935, had been entirely government controlled, as television was to be when it was introduced in 1959. Thus the policy and planning of programmes was well within the powers of the minister. By 1952, in fact, most government agencies dealing with mass media had become the responsibility of the Ministry of Information and Broadcasting. These included the Board of Film Censors, the Films Division, the Mobile Units (travelling cinemas), the Publications Division, the Press Information Bureau, and All India Radio. Dr Keskar, a devotee of Indian classical music, was also moved by the reformer's zeal to revive Indian classical culture, especially its music. He had little regard for film, informing a conference of producers he had been invited to address that "Producers in this line should have a certain background of culture. At present there is hardly any standard maintained by many of the productions we see on the screen."[17] Apart from his personal dislike of film music, Dr Keskar had valid reasons for encouraging classical and folk music. Both had "fallen into decay and somnolence," along with the neglect of all things Indian, and, he added, "it is obvious that music which formerly flourished on account of royal and princely patronage, will not revive and flourish unless the State can extend to them the same or extended patronage."[18] Western style instrumentation, orchestration and harmony run counter to the Indian melodic system. For film songs, Indian musicians were using instruments such as the piano, harmonium, saxophone, and had adopted the western tempered scale. There is no doubt that this did have the effect of desensitizing the listener to the delicacies and subtleties of the 22-note scale of unequal intervals which is the foundation of Indian music. For this reason he felt that the survival of Indian music and musicians called for drastic steps. The steps that AIR took did go a long way towards reviving interest in classical and folk music. But film songs had entered too deeply into the consciousness of the masses. From the beginning of sound, songs had played an important part in films, even those of "social realism." The music director had very early become a major figure and even today, prospective audiences frequently select a film on the basis of the star and the music-director. For five years following Dr Keskar's decision in 1952, All India Radio studiously ignored film music while all over the country listeners tuned into the commercial service of Radio Ceylon to hear Indian film songs.[19] In 1957, accepting defeat, AIR started a new service—"Vividh Bharati," offering "popular music and light entertainment." A regular allocation had had to be made for film songs.

Post-Independence Censorship Policy

Around 1947, various moves were afoot to reform Indian society generally. The provincial governments had several powers and in choosing to exercise them, the government of Bombay decided to introduce prohibition. At the same time it announced that "with effect from 1 April 1947, no scenes showing drinking of any type of liquor will be permitted in any films."[20] Bombarded with letters, protests and delegations, it issued a clarification: "There are films which are avowedly meant to propagate the idea of abstinence. In such films, drinking scenes being meant to condemn drink, will not be cut out.

"If the scenes are meant to ridicule drink, to hold it in abhorrence, to show it as poisonous, to paint the drinking habit as ungentlemanly, unhealthy and anti-social, or to condemn it in various other ways, then such scenes, though they show drinking, will be allowed.

"If the scenes are meant, on the other hand, to make fun of the idea of prohibition, to induce people to become indifferent to such a programme, or to encourage them to break prohibition laws or to glorify drink, to show it as a fashion, or to describe it as a social custom about which there is nothing wrong, to make it popular, to paint it as healthy, honourable or respectable and to make it appear as religious, then such scenes are objectionable and will be removed from films."[21]

The *Times of India* retorted satirically to this clarification, saying:

All this is very puzzling. Apparently the public is to be permitted to see scenes depicting the 'horrible' effects of drinking, but not those in which drinking is shown as a harmless social custom, or in which it tends to cheer up the tired and the depressed. What the Ministry should now do is to devise a type of blinkers for the public by which they can view only those sights which are supposed to be good for them. The Ministers might even offer a prize for blinkers of this description. Meanwhile, soaring prices, shortage of food and cloth, black marketing and other trifling sins will, one supposes, continue to flourish as usual.[22]

But here the *Times of India* was being less than fair to the film censor. For good or bad, prohibition had been adopted as government policy and where criticism of such a policy would be perfectly valid, it was hardly reasonable to expect that films showing the pleasure of indulging in the very habit the government hoped to discourage could be allowed by the censors.

The general policy of censorship, however, on grounds of "too much frivolity" as the Home Minister of Bombay complained, or obscenity, vulgarity and immoral suggestion, did come in for a good deal of critical comment, and the entire basis of censorship was condemned as narrow-minded and ruinous to the future of the industry. Analyzing the features of the system, a leading producer took strong exception to the "orthodox and narrow views on showing the true aspects of life," and the "prudish and puritanical attitude to harmless, quickly forgotten gaieties."[23] The *Journal of the Film Industry* went so far as to say that "by prohibiting absolutely the portrayal of evil in society, the Home Minister is attempting to foster complacency and put the social conscience to sleep."[24] But *Filmindia*, always imbued with a crusading zeal, was by January 1948 applauding Government policy and even taking credit for having instigated it: "The film censors have been pretty active in the last 3 months, and have carried out most of the suggestions given by *Filmindia* to rid our pictures of their anti-social stuff. If they keep up their present watchful enthusiasm, we shall soon have a clean, instructive and entertaining screen, which will help both the young and old to get correct recreation."

The film censors had carried out their task most zealously, and in the year 1947-48, out of the 195 Indian pictures passed by the censors in Bombay, 82 were approved only after cuts were made, and in Madras out of the 37 foreign films censored, 18 suffered from excisions. Moreover, 13 foreign films and three Indian films were totally banned throughout Bombay province.[25] Deletions were made of drinking scenes, speeches and songs of vulgar suggestiveness, discussions between prostitutes, their agents and customers; brothel scenes; songs and dances accompanied by vulgar gestures; suggestions of nudity; bathing scenes; school-girls reciting love songs; whipping scenes; jokes at the expense of priests and public servants; dead bodies hanging, mutilation of hands, feet, tongue; stabbing; women in labour; talk referring to abortion; workers revolt against millowners; gambling scenes.

In an attempt to ease the problems raised for the producer by cutting or even banning completed films, the Home Minister suggested that producers submit film scripts to the Censor Boards before beginning production, on the lines of the American system, under which a self-regulating censorship body formed by the Motion Picture Producers and Distributors of America, acting in a purely advisory capacity, examined scripts for material that might be considered objectionable. But it was not the practice in India to have final scripts ready before production. Moreover, producers were afraid of their ideas being stolen or plagiarized, and they came out strongly and unanimously against such a step.[26]

To try and appease an increasingly hostile and nervous film industry, the Bombay Home Minister convened a meeting on 27 March 1948, between the Bombay Board of Film Censors and the Indian Motion Picture Producers Association. At this informal conference, many of the problems facing the industry and government were discussed. The Home Minister assured the industry that "at the same time as tightening up the censorship of all objectionable features, Government would soon provide them with a comprehensive code to help them avoid wastage of time, energy and money on features that were bound to be banned by the censors."[27]

At the end of the meeting it was agreed that:

(1) Producers would be given the fullest opportunity to discuss any matters connected with their pictures when presented for censorship.

(2) There would be no discrimination between Indian and foreign films in the matter of censorship.

(3) A production code would be drafted separately by the Board and IMPPA, which would be available for the guidance of producers and censors.

(4) A central censorship organization would be of considerable assistance in ensuring uniformity in all provinces.

(5) Pictures once passed by the Board would be re-examined only if the government and the Board are satisfied that any complaints against them are genuine.

(6) Frequent contact should be maintained between the Government, the Board and IMPPA so that any difficulties arising out of the censorship policy could be solved, by mutual discussion and adjustments.[28]

In August 1948, the Bombay Board of Film Censors, in consultation with IMPPA and with the approval of the Government of Bombay, issued to film producers a set of suggestions for guidance in the production of feature films which will "lead the public to better thought and ultimately to a better life."[28] The change this represented was that in place of the Instructions to Film Inspectors of 1920, the Board now advised producers on what might be found objectionable. The suggestions can be roughly classified under seven headings. (1) Religion and Faith; (2) Peoples, Ideal and Morals; (3) History and Mythology; (4) Law; (5) Crime; (6) Sex; (7) Miscellaneous.

Under these classifications the instructions are specific and detailed.

Films are barred from uttering profanity to God or to religions or faiths, or to their founders; salacious incidents, obscene, ambiguous and irreverent titles, obscenity in talk, songs or gestures distasteful or prejudicial to good taste would not be permitted; presentation of history, mythology, legends and classical works must, as far as possible, be based on recognized documentary evidence and characters of Indian or other mythologies, of gods and goddesses, of historical heroes or of sacred personalities may not be presented in a frivolous manner. Law, natural or human, was not to be ridiculed nor sympathy created for its violation. No crime could be presented in such a way as to create sympathy for it or inspire its imitation. The sympathy of the public was never to be thrown on the side of crime, wrong-doing or evil. Illegal forms of sex relationships such as free love, companionate marriage or "virgin" motherhood would not be permitted, and adultery or illicit sex relationships if necessary for the plot, may not be justified nor presented attractively. Kissing or embracing by adults, or exhibiting passion repugnant to good taste were also forbidden, on the grounds that though common in western countries, kissing and embracing by adults in public "is alien to our country." The instructions also stated that "Dancing is acknowledged as an art. It should, therefore, be presented beautifully, in keeping with the finer traditions of our country. Incredible and crude presentation of feats and stunts shall not be shown. The use of miracles permissible in religions and mythology shall, like the exercise of supernatural powers, be severely restricted."[30]

The film industry was bound by these instructions, and it was left to the press to "beg leave to question the validity of the multitude of 'don'ts' tabulated by the Boards. In place of a discerning analysis of the issues at stake on a cultural and artistic plane, we see the darkening and harmful influence of Mrs Grundy at work.[31] It is the negativeness of the Board's policy that is open to criticism. We suspect that it has over-stepped the bounds of its jurisdiction to the extent of appropriating to itself the guardianship of public morals."[32]

In a nicely balanced editorial in its January 1949 issue, the *Journal of the Film Industry* expressed the dilemma of the film producer.

Our country is today in a transitional stage. National and moral values are undergoing a change in the new set-up of the condi -

tions in free India. It is the but natural that in these transient circumstances, censorship of motion pictures also should be in a transitional stage. In this crucial stage the Press has an important duty to criticize intelligently without venom. It is the duty of Government to lay down a general policy and trust the censor to execute it. It is the duty of the censors to interpret opinion and be guided by the policy laid down by the Government. The producer has the greatest difficulty conforming to a standard which is yet to be laid down. All are agreed that we are aiming at a moral and national standard which in the corrrect democratic sense, has to be interpreted from public opinion. Unfortunately, public opinion is not sufficiently crystallized today on the subject.

Not only was public opinion not crystallized, it varied from region to region. What might perhaps have been valid for Bombay, could be unacceptable in Bengal, or in Madras. In addition to the suggestions to Producers, therefore, the Bombay, Madras and Calcutta Censor Boards, each issued their own Censorship Codes, for the guidance of the members of their Boards. But frequently while judging a film, the censors in their enthusiasm, went beyond even the directions laid down in these "suggestions." In April 1949, the *Journal of the Bengal Motion Picture Association* published a list of films rejected by the Censor Board in Calcutta, along with reasons for the ban. Among these were:

Matlabi (The Selfish One, India, Hindi). Rejected. This is a sloppy stunt picture not suitable for public exhibition.
Jassy (England). Prohibited on the ground that the film having no moral behind it, it not suitable for public exhibition.
The Madonna's Secret (England). Prohibited on the ground that this is a crime picture without any relieving feature.[33]

The *Journal of the Film Industry* in Bombay, attempted to reason with the authorities—"The Boards of Censors under the Cinematograph Act 1918, are meant to examine films and pass them as 'Suitable for public exhibition.' In a recent picture, the Bombay Board directed 'the nurse, Leena, should be made to look older when in the house, as she is supposed to have a grown-up son.' It appears to us that the censor's duty is *not* that of a critic. There may be faults in the story, characterization, technique, etc. So long as they are not *objectionable* from the public point of view, the censors have no business to ask for any cuts. If every member of the Board becomes a critic in addition to a censor, there will be no end to cuts."[34]

Increasingly the Board seemed to be making aesthetic judgements. Sequences that could by no stretch of imagination be considered objectionable, were ordered to be "shortened" without any reason being given for the ruling. In the film *Vairabmantra* (Shiva's Mantra) for example, the Calcutta Censor Board directed the producer to:

—shorten the journey of Bhairab to fetch the heroine
—shorten the chasing scene
—reduce to the minimum the scene of Tantrik gloating over his plans for the heroine
—shorten the fire scenes.[35]

In answer to vociferous protest from the film industry, the Minister for Information and Broadcasting advised producers to exercise self-censorship, saying that since "unfortunately we do not yet have an established standard in India for the moral content of motion pictures, the standard has been varying. In the absence of strong public opinion to lay down this standard, it is being laid down by the censors."[30] The film industry was disgusted, and helpless. The All India Cinema Protest Day, organized jointly by the Indian Motion Picture Producers Association, Bombay, the Bengal Motion Picture Association, Calcutta, and the South Indian film Chamber of Commerce, Madras, on 30 June 1949, had served to draw attention to its woes, but had no other concrete result. On 15 August 1949, the second anniversary of Independence, the Bengal Motion Picture Association's Journal wrote :

Two years ago today, the sun rose over free India's horizon after a lapse of two centuries. . . . (India's multitudes) were happy over the thought that they were free people. High hopes of a better future in the hands of the National Government made them feel happier still. We for ourselves, had felt so. And today two years after, we find all our hopes shattered. Our own government takes no notice of our grievances and all our problems remain unsolved. . . .

The New Statutes of 1949

The government in 1949, did begin to take note of the very genuine grievances of the film industry. On 29 August 1949, a film Enquiry Committee was appointed with directives to, inter alia,

—enquire into the growth and the organization of the film industry in India, and to indicate the lines on which further development should be directed, and
—to examine what measures should be adopted to enable films in India to develop into an effective instrument for the promotion of national culture, education and healthy entertainment.

The committee of six included two eminent representatives of the film world: B.N. Sircar, founder of New Theatres, and V. Shantaram, co-founder of the Prabhat Film Company. Of the other four, two were members of the Constituent Assembly, including the Chairman, S.K. Patil; one was a professor of History and one represesented the Ministry of Information & Broadcasting.

As the Committee went to work, important changes were wrought in the censorship system through two new statutes. The Cinematograph (Amendment) Act, 1949, created two categories of censorship certificates: "A," restricted to adults over the age of 18 years; and "U," for unrestricted universal public exhibition. This was the first time such categories had been used in India. But even this very reasonable amendment was not passed unchallenged by the conservative element in the legislature. Fears were expressed that under the new classification, all approved films would be released with a "U" certificate whereas the kind of films until now rejected by the censors as unfit for public exhibition, would be passed with an "A" certificate. Certain issues peculiar to the Indian social scheme were also raised regarding the proposed 18 year old age classification of adult. The question asked was: "What will happen in the case of a wife who is 15 years old and a husband who is 20 or 21?" But R. R. Diwakar, Minister for Information and Broadcasting, who introduced the Bill, appealed for "reason" and "commonsense," and made an eloquent plea for "not shutting our eyes to modern methods and media."[37] The Act came into force on 1 September 1949, with the hope that some of the problems of censorship would be eased and films that tackled adult themes in an adult manner could not be banned as unfit for children. (In keeping with Indian social behaviour patterns, children below the age of three years were to be permitted to accompany their parents to "A" films.)

In the meanwhile, the anomaly of a film passed by one provincial Board being banned by another, or by a state government, remained. "The film *Lahore*, for instance, ran in several States without any trouble. The government of Uttar Pradesh, however, decided to suspend exhibition. A month later it was seen by the Cinema Advisory Committee of that State, and the order was revoked. The police would not let it be shown in Hyderabad city, although it was shown in 10 other cities of Hyderabad province. Thus a producer has to run after each State and Province," wrote the *Journal of the Film Industry* in September 1949. At this time also another extraordinary proposal—to prohibit film actors playing roles of gods and goddesses was—under the active consideration of the Madras Government, which seemed to feel that the indiscriminate featuring of Hindu gods and goddesses in mythologicals, had resulted in the public losing their veneration for them and that to prevent this, it might be advisable to bring in such a ban.[38]

The industry had been agitating a long time for the establishment of a Central Board, to ensure a uniformity of judgment and to restrain abuse of the powers of Censorship. The Indian Cinematograph Committee had also recommended this in 1927. Finally, in December 1946, the Cinematograph (2nd Amendment) Act 1949, made provisions for the appointment of a single Central Board of Film Censors. The power of certifying films for exhibition was, up to this time, being exercised by the State Governments under the provisions of the Act before the amendment. Since film production was more or less concentrated in three State capitals, Bombay, Calcutta and Madras, and since the import of foreign films was also being handled at these three ports, the first examination of films was carried on mainly by Boards established at these cities. But Boards had been constituted also in the States of Uttar Pradesh, Punjab, Mysore and Travancore Cochin. In Uttar Pradesh, films which carried a valid certificate from any Board could be exhibited without fresh examination, and as there was little local production, the function of the Uttar Pradesh Board had been only to examine those films which raised or were likely to raise any peculiar local problems. In the Punjab, a Board was set up in Lahore before Partition. After Partition, the Board continued to be in existence in the Punjab (India), but it examined mainly the few films in Punjabi which were presented there first. In Mysore and Travancore it was the practice to insist that every film be brought to the Board for certification before it could be exhibited. In the case of imported films, the Mysore Board was usually satisfied with merely levying of a fee while Indian films, particularly those to which unfavourable references had been made in newspapers or journals, were always seen by the Censor Board. In Travancore, films which held valid certificates from other Boards were not scrutinized, and a certificate was issued on payment of a nominal fee.[39]

Each of these Boards consisted of a number of non-official members and a few officials who were there ex-officio, e.g., the Commissioner of Police at Bombay, Madras and Calcutta, and the Garrison Officer in certain cantonment cities. All members of the Board were honorary workers, but the Boards maintained a paid staff in places where the work was heavy. An official was usually the convener of the Board and the practice was to call a meeting when a film was presented for examination. Usually the convener had to ask several members before he could get one or two who could spare the time to see the film. The screening would be arranged by the producer or distributor and the film was seen by at least one official and one or two members of the Board. If those present felt that the film contained nothing objectionable, they recommended the grant of the certificate, which was issued by the President of the Board. If it was felt that certain portions should be excised, the producers generally accepted the decision and made the required changes. When the producer was not prepared to accept the recommendations of the Board, the film was usually seen again by the full Board or as many members as could attend, and their opinion was communicated to the producer. Where he agreed to carry out the Board's recommendations, the film was certified as amended. If, however, the producer refused to carry out the recommendations, the certificate was also refused. In order to prevent such a film being brought up before a different Board without disclosing the fact that it had once been refused a certificate, the application form provided a column where the producer was desired to state whether the film had been shown before any other Board, and what the decision had been.[40]

For the guidance of the members of the Board, a code of general principle to be keep in mind as well as a list of subjects deemed objectionable, was issued by Bombay, Calcutta and Madras, reflecting again the difference of opinion and attitude that existed in the regions. But any code, however, comprehensive of necessity left considerable latitude for the interpretition of the clauses or for its application to any individual case. Consequently, differences of opinion between one Board and another as well as between members of the same Board were inevitable. The set of suggestions issued by the Bombay Board in 1948 as guidance to film producers, were also followed by the other Boards while examining films and did make for more consistency in decision making but where lack of uniformity may be reduced, it can never be eliminated. The centralization of censorship through the 2nd Amendment Act of 1949 was undoubtedly a step in the right direction even though variations due to individual judgement and the personal outlook of the members were bound to persist.[41]

This Act was passed after a good deal of discussion regarding the assumption of control over film censorship by the Central Government. In the Government of India Act 1935, the censoring of films was a concurrent subject. In the 1950 Constitution it had to be included in the Union List in view of the Cinematograph 2nd Amendment Act 1949 making it possible to set up a Central Board. Regional Boards would still function in Bombay, Calcutta and Madras, but under a central authority based in Bombay. The State Governments however, retained their powers of uncertifying a film where this was considered advisable in the interests of law and order. Such a ban could continue for a maximum duration of two months, but any further extension would require the concurrence of the Central Government.[42] The Amending Act came into force in 1951 and was followed shortly after by rules framed under the authority of this Act, which set out the composition of the Board and the manner of its functioning.

In exercise of its powers under Rule 32 (4) (b) of these Cinematograph (Censorship) Rules 1951, the Board decided to grant exemption of part of the examination fee in respect of films that were not of an educational nature in the technical sense, but which nevertheless fulfilled an educational purpose. Films certified as being of a predominantly educational (PE) nature were divided into two categories—

1. Films useful as visual aids to instruction in the classroom.
2. Films not included in Category 1, but which are informative and educational in the general sense.

The entire examination fee was waived in the case of films within the first category and half in the case of the second. No revision was to be made in the case of 35mm films exceeding 200 ft in length and of 16 mm films exceeding 800 ft in length.[43]

Although in the beginning PE certificates were awarded only to short documentary films, this was later enlarged to include feature films as well. The criteria on the basis of which the Central Board of Film Censors was authorized by the Ministry of Finance, Department of Revenue and Insurance, to waive excise levy in the case of Indian films and to exempt foreign films from customs duty were laid down by the Ministry of Information & Broadcasting—

(*a*) Films intended for use in education at all grades;

(*b*) Films for children based on children's stories and folktales and those on activities and interests of children;

(*c*) Films intended for vocational training and guidance, including technical films depicting mechanical operations in the fields of engineering and technology and those relating to industry, business management, farming, etc.;

(*d*) Films suitable for mass education designed to spread knowledge regarding health, hygiene, sports and games, social welfare, community living, citizenship, etc.;

(*e*) Films showing foreign people, their habits, ways of living, their customs etc., from the educational point of view;

(*f*) Films dealing with scientific research and popularization of science;

with the provision that

(*i*) Films falling under any of the above categories but not likely to be of any use in the Indian background may not, at the discretion of the Central Board of Film Censors, be allowed exemption from customs duty;

(*ii*) Films with educational content but not of distinctly high standard in quality of production and treatment shall not be allowed exemption from customs duty; and

(*iii*) The fact that a film is of interest to a limited group shall not prevent it from being declared predominantly educational if it otherwise fulfils the terms specified above;

(*iv*) That the films which contain direct or indirect advertisement of a trading concern shall not be declared as predominantly educational films even though they may be so in character otherwise.

Disagreements did arise, with the Department of Revenue occasinally objecting to a decision of the Censor Board on the grounds that the criteria had not been followed.

Years later, in 1972, a feature film *Jai Bangladesh* (Hail Bangladesh) was granted a PE certificate. The day the Indian government recognized the newly independent country of Bangladesh, the film was banned on the grounds that this government might take exception to it. The producer, I.S. Johar, changed the title and the ban was lifted.

The Central Board of Film Censors had barely started functioning when, on 12 July 1952 the Cinematograph Act 1952 was enacted. This Act repealed the Cinematograph Act of 1918, alongwith all other enactments on the subject and is the authority for the present system of film censorship in India.

However, before the enactment of this Act, but too late to influence its provisions in any way, the report of the Film Enquiry Committee was submitted and we shall consider the report as well as various developments and events in 1951, before taking up the provisions and the significance of the 1952 Act.

The Report of the Film Enquiry Committee 1951

Unlike the 1927 Indian Cinematograph Committee, the Film Enquiry Committee of 1949 dealt only briefly with censorship. The 2nd Amendment Act centralizing censorship had been passed, and its main recommendation on that subject was to propose that all certificates granted to films should automatically lapse after five years, and that the films should be seen again by the Board before the certificates were renewed, on the basis that "we feel that thereby any changes in the cinema habits and tastes of the cinema-goers, current judgements and any evidence of the actual effect on the audience as ascertained by research should be effectively reflected in the granting of fresh certificates. In view of our recommendation that fees for certification should be nominal, this should not in-volve any hardship on the producers. On the other hand, we expect that the crystallization of public opinion, the growing experience of the Boards and above all, intensive study of the effects of films on the minds of the cinema-goers would all contribute towards a more rational application of the principles of censorship."[44]

This was the only recommendation to be adopted, and in 1953 was put into practice. This was because it was thought that "the initial certificate permitting exhibition of a film follows an examination in which the standards applied are conditioned by existing values, fashions and trends. It would be unreasonable, therefore, to expect that a certificate granted once with regard to the then conditions and criteria would never fall out of time with prevalent standards."[45] This measure was very unpopular with the industry and gave rise to a great deal of criticism. In 1958, the period of validity of the certificate was extended to 10 years.

The major recommendation of the Committee also had a bearing on censorship, for it proposed a total centralization of the entire film industry through the creation of a Film Council which would constitute a "central authority to superintend and regulate the film Industry . . . advise the Central and State Governments in regard to various matters connected with the production, distribution and exhibition of films"[46] and which would in course of time, "take up the functions of the Board of Censors."[47] The industry would be well represented on the Council which would also include repre-sentatives from the field of education as well as from the Central and State Governments. It would have under its supervision an Institute of Film Art (Film Institute of India set up in 1961) for the training of new talent. It would give annual awards for outstanding work in films (Government of India Film Awards instituted in 1954). It would foster film libraries (National Film Archive established in 1964) and film societies and, in general, instigate research for the benefit and long term development of the industry.

As an adjunct to the Film Council, the Committee proposed a Production Code Administration on the lines of the PCA of America. This, they suggested, should have four regional branches in Delhi, Calcutta, Bombay and Madras, with five members and a chairman at each branch. A central office should coordinate the work of the regional offices. The PCA would scrutinize scripts which producers would have to submit to it before the commencement of shooting; it would advise on changes adopted later by the producers, and exercise some control over the handling of the film. For this, the PCA would have to be assisted by a "first rate body of experts."[48] It would also examine all publicity material and "it should be possible for it to enforce the production before them for approval, of every item of publicity material to be released with the film as well as advance photographs circulated to film journals."[49] The Committee recommended that the code to govern these functions should be based on the advertising code for motion pictures of the Motion Picture Association of America."[50]

The Committee supported the obligatory showing of documentary films and newsreels, and the required payments for this by the theatres. But it agreed with the industry's complaint regarding taxation. It criticized charges such as octroi and internal customs duties which it said should be abolished,[51] and it recommended that entertainment tax be fixed at a uniform 20 per cent on the gross takings,[52] of which 10 per cent should be made available to the proposed Film Council.[53]

It recommended the formation of an Export Corporation (Indian Motion Picture Export Council established in 1958) to stimulate the export market for Indian films. It also recommended that India consider the manufacture of its own raw film, as well as film equipment (Hindustan Photo Films Manufacturing Company started in 1959, in collaboration with the French Company Bauchet). Apart from the Film Council, the Committee recommended that a government sponsored Film Finance Corporation should be established to finance productions, thereby giving the producers a source of capital other than the money lender and the distributor (Film Finance Corporation set up in 1960).

On the whole, the Committee had achieved the aims with which it was set up. It had clearly indicated the "lines on which further development of the film industry should be directed" and through the years, apart from the Film Council which is still under consideration, most of its proposals were implemented.

The film industry greeted the report with enthusiasm, in spite of its reservation about the powers of the proposed Film Council and Production Code Administration. The Committee had paid tribute to the film world's past achievements and present woes in the words:

It is a pity that industry, which has grown to such proportions on its own, without either state support or patrongage and in the face of foreign competition on terms which were certainly not much to its advantage, should find itself in the present state of doldrums. It cannot be denied that the pioneers of this industry established themselves in spite of the adverse circumstances of patronage of foreign goods, of social stigma that attached to the profession, of lack of high-quality equipment, and of dearth of artistic and technical talent. Nor can it be gainsaid that the contribution that these pioneers and their successors—famous names in its annals, like Prabhat, Bombay Talkies and New Theatres—made to the building up and growth of this industry despite these adverse circumstances was substantial and praiseworthy . . . . [54]

The State of the Film Industry in 1951

The industry had, in fact, grown to very substantial proportions. By 1951 the annual production of films had reached 275, with an average of 600 million spectators a year in 3,250 theatres which included 850 travelling cinemas.[55] The net revenue to the industry was estimated at about Rs 200 million of which Rs 55 million was paid out as entertainment tax alone.[56]

This phenomenal growth had been achieved in spite of black money, astronomical payments to stars and music directors, the power exercized by distributors and exhibitors over film content, the suicidal rates of 60 to 100 per cent interest paid to money lenders and above all, a Government Policy that banned construction of cinemas, collected huge taxes, and imposed foreign exchange controls which made raw film and equipment as precious as gold. Added to this had been the vagaries of censorship which made the harassed film maker hesitate to deviate in any way from the formula film.

The price paid in terms of quality, however, was high. In the atmosphere of 1951, the classics of the 1930s could probably not have been made, e.g. *Devdas* (alcoholism, and prostitution), *Duniya na Mane* (suicide), *Mukti* (adultery). Both *Chandidas* and *Acchut Kanya* dealt with love between a Brahmin and an untouchable, and might even be considered as fomenting social unrest if that were not in keeping with government's policy to eradicate untouchability and the caste system! But with so many pressures and no organized studio system to fall back upon, the film maker in the 1950s cannot be blamed for playing safe and turning out glossy, titillating song-and-dance extravaganzas that drew unsophisticated, unlettered audiences by the millions. The educated elite kept well away from all this vulgarity and prided itself on never seeing an Indian film. And the government in its turn, was pressurized for another decade by social workers, educationists, civic groups, legislators and Parliamentarians, to clean up the film industry or failing persuasion, force it, through ever-stricter controls to make films that would be "healthy and morally uplifting." The Government, realizing well that censorship at best has only a negative function, felt itself uanble to find another solution. Public opinion in other countries had acted as a check on films of excessive vulgarity and poor taste. But India's public, in the absence of any other form of entertainment, relished its cinema and flocked to it in increasing numbers. The film industry tried, for its part, but it was too heterogenous, and too much money was at stake for any form of self-regulation to succeed.

In 1951 a Film Federation of India was formed, to represent the industry in its relations with the Government. In 1951 also, the Indian Motion Picture Producers Association in Bombay, passed a unanimous resolution approving a system of self censorship,[57] and appointed a sub-committee to achieve this.[58] For the next few years desultory efforts were made to impose a form of self-censorship through a Production Code Administration that they themselves set up in 1953. But in 1958 the effort had to be abandoned. "We have been toying with many ideas whereby the industry could self-regulate in the fields of censorship, publicity and finance. So far all such moves have proved abortive either due to lack of sufficient determination, or sabotaged by interested parties," wrote the *Journal of the Film Industry* in June 1958.[59] There seemed to be no solution. The clashed continued.

In August 1951 the chairman of the newly appointed Central Board of Film Censors addressed a communication to the South India Film Chamber of Commerce in no uncertain terms: "The Board views with disquiet the tendency to include in film scenes, songs and dances which offend good taste and accepted standards of decency. In order to check this tendency, it may be accepted that films will be carefully scrutinized and songs and dances of the nature referred to will be deleted. Anything which offends good taste or public decency is as objectionable for an adult audience as for a non-adult audience."[60]

In October 1951, the President of the South India Film Chamber of Commerce, in welcoming the chairman of the Central Board of Film Censors said that while not suggesting that censorship should go altogether, it should be carried out in a liberal spirit and that "we accept certain general principles as guidance, but the detailed directives circulated to the producers are so wide in scope that it would be difficult to produce an entertaining picture if the directives are strictly interpreted."[61]

Earlier, in September 1951 Chandulal Shah (who had founded Ranjit Movietone in the '30s and produced a number of satirical comedies on contemporary themes) as President of the Film Federation of India, addressed an appeal to all producers—"not only for the sake of safe censoring, but also as a duty of our own people, we should try to produce and present clean pictures. Let it not be said of us that when we could approach through the screen millions of eyes and ears we, for the sake of money, influenced young minds in such a fashion that they could say that we were responsible for bringing down the moral calibre and behaviour of our own children."[62] Film makers of an earlier era were in fact appalled at the degeneration of their medium and as early as 1948 the then President of IMPPA had declared publicly that "government should not hesitate to cut portions which are objectionable from a moral point of view."[63]

The authorities had reason enough to be worried. But they persisted in the mistaken belief that better films would come as a result of stricter censorship.

To a meeting of the Central Board of Film Censors in Calcutta on 5 November 1951, the Minister for Information & Broadcasting sent the following message of encouragement :

All educated and cultured people expect greater things from our Central Board of Film Censors. They are looking forward to a distinct improvement in the matter of clearing the Indian screen of (a) exotic love scenes which are not at all normal in our society; (b) scenes which are lewd and licentious and have no other object than a vulgar sex appeal; (c) unhealthy entertainment that tempts people to repeat in their own lives scenes which they see on the screen; (*d*) scenes which have the effect of directly or indirectly glorifying or idolizing evil, wickedness, cruelty, criminal or anti-social tendencies; and (*e*) scenes of gangsterism or barbaric conduct. It would be difficult for the Board to be strict later, once conventions are established. . . . It is necessary to ensure that the Code is a strict one and is strictly administered.

Kempraj Urs, film producer and a delegate to this meeting objected to the entire procedure of censorship, declaring that these directives constituted a heavy strain on productions and were an infringement on the rights of the producers. He claimed that producers were responsible people who knew their jobs.[64]

Notes

[1]*Journal of the Film Industry*, January 1949, p. 14.

[2]E. Barnouw and S. Krishnaswamy, *Indian Film*, Columbia University Press, New York, 1963, p. 131.

[3]*Report on Documentary Film & Newsreels*, Ministry of Information & Broadcasting, 1966, p. 4.

[4]*Report of the Film Enquiry Committee*, 1951 p. 24.

[5]*Ibid*, p. 27.

[6]*Close-up*, No. 5-5/1970, p. 192.

[7]B. D. Garga, "Reflections on Censorship," *Close-up*, No. 3, Jan-March 1969, p. 17.

[8]*Journal of the Film Industry*, February 1945, p. 4.

[9]*ICC Report*, 1927, para 3 p. 1.

[10]*Ibid*.

[11]*Journal of the Film Industry*, February 1945, pp. 4-5.

[12]Constituent Assembly (Legislative) Debates, 8 April, 1949.

[13]*Ibid*.

[14]*Journal of the Film Industry*, August 1949, p. 11.

[15]The ban was never enforced rigorously and gradually it was allowed to be forgotten that such an action had ever been contemplated.

[16]G. C. Awasthy, *Broadcasting in India*, Allied Publishers, Bombay 1965, p. 51.

[17]Barnouw & Krishnaswamy, *op. cit.*, p. 200.

[18]*Report of the Ministry of Information & Broadcasting*, 1956-57, p. 1.

[19]Awasthy, *op. cit.*, p. 110.

[20]*Journal of the Film Industry*, 1 April 1947, p. 6.

[21]*Ibid.*, June 1947, and P. Shah, *The Indian Film*, Motion Picture Society of India, Bombay 1950, p. 247.

[22]Panna Shah, *Times of India*, 10 April 1947.

[23]Shah, *op. cit.*, pp. 242-250.

[24]*Journal of the Film Industry*, October 1947, p. 11.

[25]*Ibid.*, February 1948, p. 11.

[26]*Ibid.*, April 1948, p. 6.

[27]Shah, *op. cit.*, p. 244.

[28]*Journal of the Film Industry*, April 1948, p. 6.

[29]*Film Enquiry Committee, op. cit.*, pp. 244-295.

[30]Shah, *op. cit.*, p. 246.

[31]*Sunday Standard*, 29 August 1948.

[32]Mrs Grundy: Character in a play *Speed the Plough*, by a little known eighteenth century English writer Thomas Morton. The name became synony-mous with an excessive prudery because of the phrase which appears like a lietmotiv through the play—"What will Mrs Grundy say?"

[33]Barnouw and Krishnaswamy, *op. cit.*, p. 133.

[34]*Journal of the Film Industry*, November 1949, p. 17.

[35]Barnouw and Krishnaswamy, *op. cit.*, p. 133.

[36]*Journal of the Film Industry*, October 1949, p. 12.

[37]Constituent Assembly of India (Legislative) Debates, 8 April 1949, Vol. IV, No. 3.

[38]*Journal of the Film Industry*, January 1945, p. 20.

[39]*Film Enquiry Committee, op. cit.*, pp. 19-20.

[40]*Ibid.*, p. 20.

[41]*Ibid.*, p. 21.

[42]*Ibid.*, p. 23.

[43]*Journal of the Film Industry*, February 1952, p. 9.

[44]*Film Enquiry Committee, op. cit.*, p. 222.

[45]*Journal of the Film Industry*, October 1952, and N. M. Hunnings, *Film Censors and the Law*, Allen & Unwin, 1962, p. 231.

[46]*Film Enquiry Committee, op. cit.*, para 529.

[47]*Ibid.*, para 543.

[48]*Ibid.*, paras 543-546.

[49]*Ibid.*, para 550.

[50]*Ibid.*, Appendix XVIII.

[51]*Ibid.*, paras 574-575.

[52]*Ibid.*, paras 569-570.

[53]*Ibid.*, para 571.

[54]*Ibid.*, para 500.

[55]*Ibid.*, para 39.

[56]*Ibid.*, para 43.

[57]*Journal of the Film Industry*, September 1951, p. 21.

[58]*Ibid.*, October 1951, p. 22.

[59]*Ibid.*, June 1958, p. 9, and Hunnings *op. cit.*, pp. 230-231.

[60]Bulletin, South India Film Chamber of Commerce, August 1951.

[61]*Ibid.*, October 1951.

[62]*Ibid.*, September 1951.

[63]*Journal of the Film Industry,* December 1948, p. 9.

[64]*Ibid.*

5

A Case for the Censors

The Constitution and the Cinematograph Act 1952

The question of responsibility and freedom, liberty and license is one that has always exercised the minds of men, and there is still no definitive answer. As far, however, as fundamental rights are concerned, Article 19, Clause 1 (a) of the Constitution guarantees to every citizen of India freedom of speech and expression. But Clause 2 modifies this freedom to "reasonable restriction." Clause 2 of Article 19 of the Constitution of India reads as follows:

Nothing in sub-clause (a) of Clause 1 shall affect the operation of any existing law, or prevent the State from making any law, insofar as such law imposes reasonable restrictions on the exercise of the right conferred by the said sub-clause in the interest of the sovereignty and integrity of India, the security of the State, friendly relations with foreign states, public order, decency or morality or in relation to contempt of court, defamation or incitement to an offence.

This is the constitutional provision that was adopted by the

Cinematograph Act of 1952, as amended in 1953 and 1959.

The terms of the Act as passed in 1952 were very simple. The government was empowered to constitute a Board on the lines already laid out by the 1951 Rules. This Board could give a film a "U" or an "A" certificate or, if it did not consider the film suitable for exhibition at all, it could inform the applicant of its decision. An appeal was allowed against a Censor Board ruling to the Central Government whose decision would then be final.

The Central Government however, took to itself the power at any stage to "call for the record of any proceeding of the Board relating to the refusal to grant, or the grant of, any certificate and in which no appeal has been preferred and to make such order in the case as to the Central Government may seem fit." (Section 5[4])

The Central Government also reserved for itself another power —to unilaterally declare that:

(*a*) a certified film shall be deemed to be an uncertified film in the whole or any part of India, or

(*b*) a film in respect of which a "U" certificate has been granted, shall be deemed to be a film in respect of which an "A" certificate has been granted.

These powers were soon found to be inadequate for in an amendment in 1953 Clause (c) was added by which the exhibition of any film could be suspended for such a period as may be specified. The suspension, however, could not remain in force for more than two months, and no direction could be given under Clauses (a) and (b) without giving an opportunity to the person concerned for representing his views in the matter.

In 1959 the Act was further expanded and amended. The principles of censorship were set out in Section 5-B, and stated:

1. A film shall not be certified for public exhibition if, in the opinion of the authority competent to grant the certificate, the film or any part of it is against the interests of the security of the State, public order, decency, or morality, or involves defamation or contempt of court, or is likely to incite the commission of any offence.

As may be seen, this sub-section 1 contains part of the wording of

Article 19 (2) of the Constitution.

Sub-section 2 of Section 5-B stated that:

"Subject to the conditions contained in sub-section 1, the Central Government may issue such directions as it may think fit, setting out the principles which shall guide the authority competent to grant certificates under this Act in sanctioning films for public exhibition."

A Board of Film Censors was constituted consisting of a Chairman who should be a whole-time paid officer, and not more than nine other members who would not be whole-time paid government officials but would be entitled to allowances and fees to be prescribed the Government. The Act also provided for the appointment of whole-time Regional or Assistant Regional Officers at the three centres which continued to be Bombay, Calcutta and Madras, as well as for the appointment of Advisory Panels at these centres.

The Act also gave powers to the Government to exempt films from censorship in special cases e.g., films for film societies, and films imported by foreign embassies as part of their cultural programme.

Provision was made for the framing of rules for the purpose of carrying into effect the provisions of this Act. The Rules still in force today are the Cinematograph (Censorship) Rules of 1958, as modified upto 1969. These are in effect, the Rules of 1920 which were re-issued with some modifications in 1951 under the provisions of the Cinematograph (2nd Amendment) Act of 1949.

The Rules contain a list for the guidance of the Censor officers of matter which should be considered objectionable. They begin with the statement of three general principles:

1. No picture shall be certified for public exhibition which will lower the moral standards of those who see it. Hence the sympathy of the audience shall not be thrown on the side of crime, wrong-doing, evil or sin.

2. Standards of life, having regard to the standards of the country and the people to which the story relates, shall not be portrayed so as to deprave the morality of the audience.

3. The prevailing laws shall not be so ridiculed as to create sympathy for violation of such laws.

These general guiding principles were followed by a detailed list of what should not be permitted, in order to ensure that a uniform standard was maintained by the three regional centres. It retains taboos dating from 1920 such as "excessively passionate love scenes," "unnecessary exhibition of feminine underclothing," "realistic horrors of warfare," "blackmail associated with immorality," "gross travesties of the administration of justice," as well as material likely to promote "disaffection or resistance to Government."

It is clear that a strict interpretation of these rules would result in almost all films being banned. It is these sweeping restrictions which have provoked so much criticism of the censorship system by the industry as well as the press and public opinion. It has driven producers to resort to indirect, unrealistic, suggestive modes of expression which are often vulgar and unaesthetic and convey the precise impression that the authorities hoped to eradicate. Continually, the Censor Boards emphasized the need for films not to lower the moral standards of those who see them. Excisions ordered reflected the determination not to show crime and criminals in a sympathetic light, as well as to uphold the authority of legal institutions—as, for example:

> *Minimi*—Delete all shots of police officers and constables behaving in a totally improper and incorrect manner. (August 1953)
> *Sarala*—Shorten Ramesh manhanding Gadadhar so as to remove the impression that a prisoner in the lock-up is assaulted in the presence of an officer. (November 1953)[1]

In carrying out the directives issued to them the Censor officers occasionally went beyond what was expected of them, and conducted a censorship policy consonant with their own subjective and personal prejudices. In August 1952, K. Srinivasan, Regional Officer at the Madras Board, at a meeting with the South India Film Chamber of Commerce (hereafter SIFCC) asked producers to avoid scenes which brought rich and poor in sharp contrast, as he said that such scenes tended to create social unrest and class hatred. The Madras Board had in fact made some cuts on these grounds, as in—

> *Sing And March On* (China)—Delete the words 'who cared a

damned thing about us poor workers in the past?' (February 1952, Madras Board)

Out Of Fog And Smoke (Czechoslovakia)—Delete from commentary 'When Czechoslovakia took the path of socialism, all people were provided with jobs.' (February 1952, Madras Board)

Babla (Babla, India, Hindi)—In the trailer omit superimposed title: 'The Revelry of the Rich and the Sobbings of the Poor coming together...,

The SIFCC also felt very strongly about the preoccupation with crime and wrote a sharp editorial in its October 1952 Bulletin: "As a result of these dirty pictures, crime in the country has been on the increase. So many methods of committing crimes and escaping have been shown in these films that the amateur criminal soon becomes a professional, feeling himself safe with his newly acquired knowledge from films. *The Big House, I am a Fugitive from a Chain Gang,* and other crime and prison dramas coming from Hollywood have introduced this new vogue in crime. Indian producers have conspired with the foreigners by copying the productions as quickly as possible, to induce people to take to crime as a profession. This is a case for the censors."[2]

The majority of the cuts were, however, on sexual grounds. An obsession of the mid-'50s was described in the following terms by the *Journal of the Bengal Motion Picture Association:* "Censorship in India is fast becoming a censorship of the female anatomy with the emphasis currently on vogue in cutting the 'emphasized bosom' of heroines in some of our pictures. We deplore any attempt on the part of anyone to exploit the lower emotions of man, but we cannot agree that the female anatomy should be tampered with to please the neo-realist that is the Indian censor. We do not know whether there has been any new directive to the censor which is kept before the mind's eye while examining pictures."

The editorial referred to censorship orders such as:

Dhuaan (Smoke, India, Hindi)—Delete close-up of Geeta's bust in profile from song (replaced with another close-up of Geeta above bust.)

Khoj (Search, India, Hindi)—Delete shots of Dilruba in jumper emphasizing bust.

Manitanum Mrigamum (Man and Beast, India, Tamil)—

Reduce close-ups and side shots of Kamala's bust in the second dance.

Wabash Avenue (America)—Curtail to the minimum shot of Betty Grable's dance in scanty and indecorous costume.

South Sea Sinner (America)—Omit the shot where the heroine while splashing water in a playful mood, lifts her skirt a little too high.

The Indian producers did frequently film the female anatomy in a manner that was lewd and vulgar, and costumes were designed to heighten the effect. But when the depiction of a normal relationship between the sexes was denied, all sorts of devices had to be employed. Where honesty and frankness had to be replaced by suggestiveness, the result was bound to be either puerile, or offensive. Even more disturbing was the false sense of values and patterns of behaviour that these films perpetuated. They aroused heated arguments and invited the opprobrium of many self-righteous defenders of the high principles of purity and wholesomeness. One of the cinema's most impassioned antagonists was Mrs Lilavati Munshi who was a member of the Central Board of Film Censors. In the winter of 1951-52, the first International Film Festival was held in India, and in March 1952, in the course of her Presidential address at the annual conference of the Bombay Presidency Womens' Council, Mrs Munshi said:

As a member of the Central Board of Film Censors, I feel that something has to be done to prevent the unhealthy influences which are in evidence in some of the films produced locally or imported from outside. Films are the greatest weapon which can make or mar the future generation. Drink, crime, sex and brutality, if presented in an attractive form, will influence the subconscious mind of the younger generation and make children with their formative minds, lose more values. The influence of the cinema and the stars was greatly in evidence during the recent Film Festival. Crowds that went to see the film stars can be well envied by the greatest politicians. Their behaviour and acting affect society as a whole without making them in any way responsible for it.

So far, the majority of the films are produced with the primary motive of entertainment and a box office hit, and not with a view to educate people or to present art in an ennobling form. And in the craze for entertainment, it is going down a slippery road. Taking advantage of the many persons connected with the films all over the world who are now in India, I would like to make an appeal to them to stop sending to India crime pictures and unhealthy films arousing the baser instincts of man. I would appeal to our producers also not to produce pictures in imitation of others which are neither Indian nor artistic nor moral. . . .[4]

The confused thinking of middle-class Indian society at this time was a legacy of the puritanism developed in pre-British days and compounded by the Victorian attitudes and morality of the British period. In the '50s, confronted with the fast-changing attitudes and morés in the world, this society took refuge in old-established ideas and condemned any deviation from these as "un-Indian." Principles of ancient Hindu aesthetics were forgotten in what appeared as almost a fear of acknowledging the existence of the body, as evidenced in the letter of the Chairman of the Central Board of Film Censors, inviting the cooperation of the producers in formulating illustrations to the directives already issued. As an example of what he meant by this, he sent the following: (1) Exposing the leg of a woman or girl by lifting the sari; (2) Kissing, or intimate physical contact between the sexes; (3) Bedroom scenes where the participants are strangers of opposite sexes, in which one or more of the participants contemplates sexual intercourse with or without the consent of the other; (4) Scenes suggesting that sexual intercourse is about to take place; (5) Garments of such transparency as to invite attention to the legs or bust of the woman or girl; (6) Swaying or jerking of the hip or bust.

"Reasonable Restrictions"

In fairness to the censors, they were not solely and entirely to blame. There was constant and unrelenting pressure on the government to do something about the state of the cinema. Even D. Pancholi, who became President of the Indian Motion Picture Producers Association (hereafter IMPPA) in 1954, admitted that "Prejudice against films is becoming a national disease like untouchability and other social evils."[5] Dr Keskar warned the film industry that: "Government is receiving increasing criticism against the present trend in production, from the public and the press. I would like to give a friendly warning to the industry that it is not possible for the Government to continue this way unless it finds an immediate change with the standards of films. If the film continues as at present, we will be obliged to have a stricter censorship."[6] In 1954, 13,000 house-wives in Delhi, presented an anti-film petition to the Prime Minister, who replied that "Films have an essential part to play in the modern world. At the same time it is true that any powerful medium like motion pictures has both a good effect and a bad effect. We have to take care therefore, that we emphasize the good aspect of it."[7] On 10 December 1954 a debate was held in the Rajya Sabha on the motion that "This House is of the opinion that moral standards in the country are affected to a considerable extent as a result of the exhibition of undesirable films and recommends to the government to take such steps as are necessary either by legislation or otherwise, to prohibit the exhibition of such films, whether foreign or Indian."

In moving the resolution, Mrs Lilavati Munshi, who was also a member of Parliament, gave an example of why she thought moral standards were deteriorating as a result of the exhibition of these "undesirable films." Prithviraj Kapoor, who had started a long and illustrious career in the theatre with this celebrated Prithvi Theatres, had moved into film where his sons and now grandsons still hold sway, was in 1954, a nominated member of the Rajya Sabha. He took issue with Mrs Munshi in the debate that followed her resolution:

Mrs. Munshi: This morning a friend was giving me one or two instances (of the hold that films have on the minds of the young). There was a picture—I do not say it was a bad picture—and in that picture there was an aunt behaving in a cruel manner to-wards two children. Well, two sisters went to see that picture and came home, but ever since they hated their aunt, who had nothing to do with that cruelty shown in the picture. This was narrated to me this morning because he knew I was interested in this subject and this Resolution was coming up.

Prithviraj Kapoor: Did the honourable member hear it from the aunt or from the children?

Mrs. Munshi: From a person connected with the cinema.
Prithviraj Kapoor: There seems to be something wrong with
the aunt which she does not want to disclose.[8]

In spite of Prithviraj Kapoor, the motion was passed! The majority of the members of Parliament did not care for the cinema.
They continually demanded more controls, more surveillance,
condemning films for historical inaccuracies, or for "trying to distort
the Hindu gods and goddesses and to depict them in such a manner
as to bring them into contempt." The major defence of the government against all the pressures on it was the Constitution. "It is not
possible for the government in view of the Constitutional position
to go any further."[9] "Unless wide powers are given, it will not be
posssible to tell the producer that he must produce in this particular way, or what lines should guide him. Such a thing will be unconstitutional and is likely to be invalidated by law courts."[10]
"The government could not assume wider powers regarding censorship because they could not ignore the constitutional limitations."[11]
These are statements made at different times by Dr Keskar.
Minister of Information & Broadcasting, in both Houses of Parliament. Referring to the protest by Delhi housewives he said: "The
government is in sympathy with strong feelings all over the
country, especially among householders, regarding certain trends in
the cinema." However, "in the matter of film control, the scope of
government action is limited by Article 19 (2) of the constitution."[12]
In October 1954, on the occasion of the first National Film
Awards ceremony, the President of India Dr Rajendra Prasad, said:

The cinema is a very powerful medium for projecting ideas.
Broadly speaking, the cinema may be said to have three main
objectives: education, recreation and propaganda. No service
can be real unless it safeguards the genuine interests of those
who are sought to be served. I would, therefore, request film
producers to ponder over this and ask themselves as to what
their real aim is. Sponsoring of films and their actual production
are jobs that can only be undertaken by enlightened and conscientious people. It will not be too much to hope that rising
above purely personal gains, they will always keep in view the
good of the society as a whole. I would request film producers
to keep this high ideal before them. Till such time as this ideal

is achieved, I am afraid it would be necessary for the government as the guardian of society, to exercise some kind of control over the production of films. Freedom is undoubtedly a great blessing, but it has its own discipline and its own limitations. Unless that discipline is voluntarily adhered to by all, freedom itself would be in peril.[13]

Role of the Central Government

Although film censorship by now was probably more restrictive in India than in any other democratic society, the government was still constantly under pressure to intensify rather than ease it. At virtually all sessions of the Rajya Sabha and the Lok Sabha, members requested the Minister concerned to make renewed efforts to purge the film industry of unwholesome influences, leading Dr Keskar to retort that if Parliament wanted stricter censorship in the interest of the welfare of society the Constitution would have to be amended in order to centralize control.[14] A Bill was introduced by Dr Keskar in 1956 "to provide for the constitution of a National Film Board for the purpose of promoting the development of films as a medium of culture, education and healthy entertainment, and for the regulation of exhibitions by means of the Cinematograph."[15]

It was an attempt by the Government to adopt a constructive approach towards the cinema through the establishment of a Production Code Administration, a film Finance Corporation, and a Film Institute—along the lines suggested by the Film Enquiry Committee of 1949. However, due to the enormous recurring expediture involved and the unhappy state of the country's economy at the time, the Bill was dropped in August 1957. But it was subsequently decided to start the Film Institute and the Film Finance Corporation on a small scale, without necessarily bringing in a new Cinematograph Amendment Bill.[16]

The powers that the Government did have, were considerable. The final appeal against a ruling of the Board was to the Central government which could either uphold the ruling, or revise it in the form of giving an "A" certificate to a film refused a certificate by the Board. But more often it passed an even stricter judgement, as can be seen from some records of the Bombay Board.

1954
	Indian	Foreign
Certificates refused	1	43

Appeals to Government, seven. The Board's decisions were upheld, but two approved films were uncertified.

1956
Certificates refused	1	46

Appeals to Government, twenty-three. Twenty decisions upheld, three revised. Twelve approved films uncertified.

1957
Certificates refused	15	61

Appeals to Government, nine, all decisions upheld.
Three approved films uncertified.

1958
Certificates refused	25	65

Appeals to Government, thirteen. All upheld.

1959
Certificates refused	7	30

Appeals to Government, nine. Seven decisions upheld, two revised.

Projecting India to Indians

All this time, the objectives of the Government to use film to educate and inform were being fulfilled by the Films Division. In spite of constant accusations of Government monopoly leading to dullness and the skirting of controversial issues, these documentary films were succeeding in projecting India to Indians—its history, geography, art—past and present, rural development projects, industry, agriculture. And the weekly newsreels brought an awareness of current events and the personalities who shaped them. All this the feature films had never done. The major contribution of the Films Division's documentaries has been this: to try and bring about an appreciation and the beginning of an understanding between different parts of the country, a slow integration of its many and disparate elements.

These films were shown not only in the theatres, but carried to remote areas through the mobile vans of the Field Publicity Units.

Even though a Government department and a subsidiary of the

Ministry of Information and Broadcasting, the Films Division documentaries were not only not exempt from censorship, but even before being presented before the Censorship Board, they had to be passed by a Film Advisory Board set up in 1949 to scrutinize the films carefully for political and social content. All documentary films, whether made by directors employed on a regular basis by the Films Division or independent producers working on a contract with it, had to go through this procedure.

The Films Division had grown from 28 newsreels in 1948-49 to 132 documentaries and newsreels in 1956-57, in 5 languages. Two years later the number was to go up to 165 in 13 languages until in 1973, 227 films were produced. All films of the Films Division today, whether newsreels or documentaries, are dubbed into the 15 major languages spoken in the country.

In 1954, the Ministry of Information and Broadcasting ventured into another area of public sector film making, by launching a Childrens' Film Society as a quasi-independent corporation with Government funds, to produce and distribute films meant exclusively for children.

In an attempt to establish a meaningful contact between the film industry and officialdom, a seminar was organized in New Delhi in 1955, under the auspices of the Sangeet Natak Akadami (Academy of Music, Dance and Drama). The seminar was conducted by Devika Rani, co-founder in the '30s of Bombay Talkies. (After Himansu Rai's death in 1942, Devika Rani had continued Bombay Talkies for some time. Eventually in 1952, Bombay Talkies also closed down. Devika Rani married the painter S. Roerich and retired from films.) The seminar was addressed by Prime Minister Nehru who described the film medium as "one of the biggest things in the modern world," and of the highest importance "in moulding the people of this country, with an influence greater than that of newspapers and books all combined." Although he provoked a good-humoured response to "I am not at the moment talking of the *quality* of that influence," he went on in a more serious vein to say that he believed that "it is a dangerous thing for a Government to become too much of a judge of peoples' morals. I am still affected considerably by my old nineteenth century traditions in regard to such matters. I do not take favourably to too much restriction or censorship. On the other hand, it seems to me quite absurd for anyone to talk about unrestricted liberty in important matters affecting the public," and he concluded that "a Government must inevitably be concerned with something which has such tremendous and wide influence."[17]

Several eminent film personalities participated in the seminar and for the first time, the two warring worlds of the film industry and Governmental bureaucracy came together in an amicable exchange of ideas and problems. Attitudes towards film were slowly becoming slightly less hostile. S.S. Vasan in describing the conservative reaction to the cinema, quoted the Governor of Madras Sri Prakasa, who had said in the inaugural address to the Radio Sangeet Sammelan (Radio Music Festival), that in his childhood it was felt that those who loved music were obsessed by evil passions, and that the followers of the Muses were the depositories of all that was bad in human nature. Since that attitude to music had altered so fundamentally, Mr Vasan hoped that the feeling towards the cinema would undergo a similar change of heart. He described the difficulties faced by the film industry and pleaded for more open and liberal attitudes towards it.[18]

Although the seminar led to no immediate concrete changes, at least a dialogue had been started.

In 1957, the Central Board of Film Censors sponsored a pilot survey of audience reaction to films. The survey was carried out in Greater Bombay with the assistance of the Tata Institute of Social Sciences. Among the conclusions they arrived at was that although 66.7 per cent male adults held the view that films exert an unhealthy influence, only 40 per cent of female adults were of the same opinion.[19] Considering that only three years earlier 13,000 women in Delhi had submitted a petition to the Prime Minister complaining of the evil effect of films, this would indicate that regional and environmental differences play an important part in shaping attitudes. Since it is impossible to generalize about any aspect of Indian life and no judgments can be made which would hold true for the entire country, the task of the censors, too, becomes extremely delicate and complex.

Notes

[1]Bombay Censor Board Records.

[2]*SIFCC Bulletin*, October 1952, p. 26.

[3]*Journal of the Bengal Motion Picture Association*, November 1954, quoted by Barnouw and Krishnaswamy, *Indian Film*, Columbia University Press, New York 1963, p. 209.

[4]*Journal of the Film Industry*, March 1952, p. 24.

[5]*SIFCC Bulletin*, October 1952.

[6]N.M. Hunnings, *Film Censors and the Law*, London, Allen and Unwin, 1967, p. 232.

[7]*SIFCC Bulletin*, August 1954.

[8]Rajya Sabha debates, 26 November 1954.

[9]Dr Keskar, Lok Sabha, 25 August 1954.

[10]*Ibid.*, 18 August 1958.

[11]Dr Keskar, Rajya Sabha, 18 February 1959.

[12]Dr Keskar, Lok Sabha, 26 August 1954.

[13]*SIFCC Bulletin*, November 1954.

[14]Dr Keskar, Rajya Sabha, 29 April 1953.

[15]*Ibid.*, 10 December 1956.

[16]*Journal of the Film Industry*, August 1957, p. 2.

[17]*Film Seminar Report*, Sangeet Natak Akademi, Delhi 1956, pp. 11-18.

[18]*Ibid.*, pp. 23-34.

[19]Khosla Committee, p. 71.

6

Linguistic Logistics

Living with Compromise: The Hindi Film

The impact of film was not being exaggerated. But it applied most of all to the Hindi film. Language became an issue when the first sound film was produced in Bombay, in Hindi, in 1931. It was clear from the start that Hindi, the most widely-spoken language of the country would be the only medium of an "all-India" film and perhaps eventually the base of a national cinema.

Though the Hindi film subsequently played a major role in spreading the language, it is not the language of either Bombay, Calcutta or Madras. Calcutta remains firmly committed to the Bengali language and culture, and Tamil is the language of Madras, although Telugu, Kannada and Malayalam can also be understood if not spoken here. Surprisingly, in no city in the North where Hindi is the regional language, did a film industry ever develop.

Bombay, with its central geographical location, has always been the hub of a prosperous trade and business community. Although it is the capital of the Marathi speaking state of Maharashtra, it has no overt, narrow, regional characteristics. All languages are spoken here by a wide cross-section of Indians who arrive daily from all over the country. There has been nothing, therefore, to stand in the way of its becoming the national centre of the Hindi film industry.

The immediate and astonishing success of this cinema right from the start, led others to imitate it. Calcutta began producing Hindi versions of its most successful Bengali films, but Madras in 1948 entered the lucrative Hindi film market in a big way and it has since then established itself as a viable rival to Bombay. The Hindi film thus has no cultural links with the environment in which it is produced. In this fact lies both its strength and its weakness.

Because it is not-based in a Hindi-speaking State, it reflects no regional or linguistic characteristics or prejudices, and enables all Indians everywhere to identify with it. But not being firmly rooted in any single tradition or environment, it is forced to abandon nuance and subtlety and adopt a necessarily superficial and general character.

In the cities to which people from the villages arrive in large numbers every day in search of better opportunities, this cinema offers the only relief from loneliness, hunger and sordid living conditions. It fulfils their need for drama, music, farce, dancing, escape into illusions of high living, into fantastic dreams of sin and modernity. In the resulting variety entertainment, there is no time for story telling or for a logical sequence of events. Stock situations provide stock answers and whatever action there is, turns out to be only the preparation for a song. By far the large majority of these films deal with an imaginary urban life in which only rich people and villains live. The film world is glamorous, opulent and easy, far removed from the real world in which the viewers move. The hero and heroine are almost invariably young and handsome and overcome difficulties without any of the worries that are experienced in real life. They are for the most educated, but without any definite occupation or profession. The villains belong to the rich or middle class, but very rarely to the poorer classes. The meeting between the hero and the heroine takes place almost always accidentally, and the emphasis is on romantic love, manifested in songs and dances.

Another set situation is the sickly sentimental family drama with its stereotyped two-dimensional characters—the lost or orphaned child, the suffering widow, the poor, simple village girl and the cigarette-somking (sign of depravity in the semiology of the Indian cinema), westernized city girl. Thrown in for good measure is almost invariably a dance sequence of dreadful vulgarity.

For the average village then, the glimpse these films offer into the manners and dress and extravagant living style obtaining among the affluent, does go a long way towards distorting reality. "They begin to think that towns are a sort of paradise where there is no poverty, no hunger, no difficulties of any kind." According to Chidananda Das Gupta, film maker and film critic and co-founder with Satyajit Ray of the film society movement in India, this cinema is "the most effective obstacle against the development of a positive attitude towards a synthesis of tradition with modern life for a future pattern of living."

The extent and influence of this Hindi film exposes it to problems that the more modest regional language film experiences in much smaller measure: censorship. As the Hindi film is seen by such a wide and varied and cross-section of people, it is the unenviable task of the censor to see that nothing is portrayed which could offend religious, communal, or regional sensibilities. The regional language film with its strong social and cultural identity has a clear advantage over the hybrid Hindi film. The financial pressures on the latter, its astronomical budgets, make success at the box office not a luxury but an imperative. Even those few producers who have attempted serious social comment have felt obliged to introduce irrelevant song and dances with an eye to the mass audience; the Hindi cinema has learnt to live with compromise.

The regional cinema, conceived and produced on a much more modest scale and limited to more homogenous audiences, is able to explore themes and subjects in greater depth. The audiences that such films attract are generally of the educated middle class and censorship consequently tends to be more lenient towards them. In recent years Mrinal Sen has made repeated and bitter attacks on social injustice in his Bengali films, but not even their advocacy of a violent overthrow of society has prevented them from being passed by the censors.

Regional Films: South India

The regional language cinema had grown considerably in size and importance. By 1960, compared to 120 films in Hindi, 197 were made in 10 different regional languages. Dominating the scene was Madras, capital of Tamil Nadu. Sixty-three films were made in 1960 in its own regional language—Tamil. But producers from neighbouring States also used its studies and technical facilities for making 72 films in Kannada, Telugu and Malayalam. In addition, ever since S.S. Vasan broke into the Hindi film market with *Chandralekha* (Chandralekha) in 1948, Madras studios had been turning out a sizable number of films in Hindi. The greater majority of these films in Hindi as well as the regional languages, are the stereotyped song and dance melodrama and mythologicals of the Bombay style film. But serious cinema is more easily possible in a regional language where the audience is more homogenous, united at least by language and custom and associations, if not by economic equality.

Thus, by way of an appeal to regional sentiments, an extraordinary relationship has developed through the years, between film and politics in, particularly, the Tamil cinema. It cannot be called political cinema, nor even a cinema of commitment in the sense of projecting a political ideology; it has served rather, as the forum of a particular party or politician. For the last 25 years, a number of Tamil Nadu's key politicians have been actors or scriptwriters. This trend began in 1949 when a highly politicized screenplay writer, C.N. Annadurai, formed a new political party—the DMK (Dravidian Progressive Movement), and ended by becoming Chief Minister of Tamil Nadu in 1967. The appeal of his party lay in its anti-Hindi, anti-Brahmin and anti-North attitude. It called for a Dravidian resurgence after centuries of Aryan domination. But its message was spread by way of the cinema. Dialogue and songs praised Dravidian values and Dravidian culture.[1] C.N. Annadurai continued writing scripts until he became Chief Minister. Following his example, film people entered active politics and politicians wrote for and acted in films. Inevitably, dialogue abounded with lines such as "O Divine Tamil, we bow to thee who reflect the glories of ancient Dravidistan" or the following between two people lost in a forest.

Man 1: Should we turn North?
Man 2: Never. South is much better.

Man 1: The night is dark.
Man 2: Do not worry. The rising sun will soon bring light

and good fortune.[2] (The rising sun was the emblem of the DMK party.)

These techniques were greeted with such roars of audience approval that other non-political directors, producers and actors began to use them too, allying themselves with one political party or another. Film gossip often became intermixed with political news. Newspapers and magazines began devoting a good deal of space to the activities of the film world while film magazines gave news of politicians, since eminent personalities spanned both worlds. Inevitably for the readers also, the two became inseparable and led to a much greater political awareness in the average South Indian.

Films of this kind created serious problems for the censors. Cutting bits of dialogue, a few scenes, could not eliminate the spirit which infused the entire film. Tamil films extolled the glories of Dravidistan, blaming the northerners for depraving its society and culture. They satirized Brahmanical institutions and heaped invective on those who held them in reverence. It was an inevitable reaction. The South Indian Dravidian had for too long been oppressed by the Brahmins. But these films and the reactions they provoked, led to "grave disorders, including arson, looting and assault."[3] They helped create bitterness and hostility between the South and North. Occasionally a film would be banned, more often it would be passed with a great many cuts.

In 1952, *Parasakti* (The Goddess), written by Karunandhi, was passed with nine cuts. Several complaints were received about the film—that it is an anti-God film and that it contains disruptive political ideology and propagates religious heresy. It was then seen by the Revising Committee whose report together with a print of the film was sent to Delhi in April 1953. The Central Government ordered two more cuts. A Telugu version was made in 1955. The Board gave it a "U" certificate with 34 cuts and made it clear that when the Tamil version was presented for re-certification, it would have to make the same 34 cuts. *Sorgavasal* (Gateway to Heaven) 1969 written by Annadurai, had to carry out 27 cuts as, for example: "Delete the words 'It is not the practice of Tamils to seek merit by performing Dharma,' together with sounds of laughter;" and "In the King's speech to the priests delete the words 'low fellows who smear sacred ashes."

Sorgavasal was passed but the censors were concerned about the unmistakable slant given to the story by the dialogues which revile the traditions and mythology associated with the commoner and less developed aspects of Hinduism and which would appear calculated to wound the susceptibilities of believers in tradition, to hurt them by invective and abuse and to foment ill will against classes of the Hindus who believe in such aspects.

But the censorship rules did not prohibit the display of party flags and emblems, portraits of political leaders, dialogue and songs referring to party leaders. This was in fact the very technique employed by nationalist film producers under the British. Annadurai had become a greatly loved and revered leader. He was popularly and affectionately known as "Anna," which also means "big brother," and any even oblique reference to him brought cheers from audiences. Thus:

He: Believe me, sister.
She: I do, Anna, I do. The whole land believes in you, and will follow you.

I heard in Kanchi what Anna said. I will tell you. He said better times are ahead for the people. (Audience Applause)

Annadurai died in 1971, and his mantle fell on Karunanidhi, a close friend, political ally, and also a screenplay writer. He, in his turn became Chief Minister, and was opposed politically by the immensely popular film actor M.G. Ramachandran. Both had been followers of Annadurai, and many of M.G.R's films had been written by Karunanidhi. In 1973 MGR left the DMK after a disagreement with Karunanidhi, and formed another party—the Anna DMK. The contest for the next elections was carried out through the cinema, and when in March 1977, the Anna DMK swept the polls against a discredited DMK, MGR was installed as Chief Minister.

The first and until this period, the only political film was Cho Ramaswamy's *Thuglak*. A writer by profession and editor of two satiric journals, *Pickwick* and *Thuglak*, he decided in 1970 that film had a more effective and wider reach. His Tamil film with the same title as his journal *Thuglak*, was first written and performed as a play in 1967 and had a record nember of performances. It is a satirical and cynical comment on politics, and abounds with dialogue such as—

A political promise is a promise which shall always be kept as a promise and shall always remain a promise . . .

I don't want people around me who lift their heads up. I only want those who raise their hands.

The references to current happenings were obvious and unmistakable . . .

I nationalized the banks for your own good. Unfortunately the Supreme Court struck it down. So now I have decided to nationalize the Supreme Court.

There are two kinds of socialism. One is making paupers princes. The other is making princes paupers. I have chosen the second method for our country.

Decidedly this was not a film that would be popular with the authorities. The Madras Censor Board—according to Cho quite clearly under instructions—demanded a record number of cuts which would have called for extensive re-shooting. He refused, and appealed to the Centre whereupon the State Government had all copies of his fortnightly *Thuglak* confiscated. But there was nothing to stop Cho, as he is popularly known, from speaking out in public. This was February 1971. Elections for the State Assembly were round the corner, and Cho began campaigning for the Congress O—the party from which Mrs Gandhi's Ruling Congress had broken away in 1969 and to which Annadurai, Karunanidhi and MGR were all opposed. At these meetings which were attended by anything between one and five hundred thousand people, Cho also appealed for support for his film, asking the people to send telegrams to the Central Government protesting against the position taken by the Censor Board. As a result, the Central Government in Delhi was flooded with telegrams. The Ministry of Information and Broadcasting saw the film and allowed it to be released. The DMK nothing loath, organized riots at the theatres where the film was being exhibited, even trying to whip up communal passions by claiming that it was anti-Muslim. But audiences were not taken in and thronged those theatres which were not cowed by threats of violence.

Much later, during the Emergency, *Thuglak* was again withdrawn from public exhibition.

The people of Kerala too, are both highly politicized and have a high rate of literacy (60 per cent in a country where only 30 per cent of the people are literate). Most film people from Kerala are also politically active. Ramu Kariat, a winner of the Best Film Award for his beautiful *Chemmeen* (The Prawn) in 1966, has been a member of the State Legislative Assembly. But no other State in India has used film in quite the same way as the Tamilians.

Regional Cinema: Bengal

The intellectual Bengalis approach cinema in quite a different manner. The Film Society Movement began in Bengal in 1947 when Satyajit Ray and Chidananda Das Gupta founded the Calcutta Film Society. Jean Renoir made *The River* in Calcutta in 1948, and left a lasting impression on those he came in contact with. Pudovkin, two years later, addressed the Calcutta Film Society, and opened another small window on world cinema. The first International Film Festival in India in 1952 which was held in Bombay, Calcutta and Madras, introduced the film industry to Italian neo-realism and European cinema generally. For the first time an awareness began to seep in, of cinema as art. By 1956, Satyajit Ray had made *Pather Panchali* (The Song of the Road) and won the "Best Human Document" award at the Cannes Film Festival. Ray had untold trouble over finances for this film. He pawned his insurance policy and his wife's jewellery, but still did not have enough to complete the film until the West Bengal State Government, in an extraordinary gesture, provided him with the Rs 200,000 he needed.[4] For the first time, the Government had made a positive contribution towards "changing the tone of Indian cinema," and did not exercise its powers only in a negative manner through censorship. Satyajit Ray's contribution to Indian cinema has been immense and immeasurable. He not only placed, singlehanded, India on the map of world cinema; he caused attitudes towards film to undergo a fundamental re-thinking within India; because of his own personality and social background, people began to consider working in the cinema a not unrespectable profession. And it showed the way for the government to play a concrete and positive role. Through the years, Ray's success and prestige have soared, as one after another of his films carried away the highest international honours. All this he has done within the framework of a "most restrictive censorship."

Ritwick Ghatak and Mrinal Sen are two other outstanding names in Bengali cinema. Ghatak in his films shows a burning sense of involvement in today's problems and their effect on the lives of ordinary people. An illustration of the flexibility of censorship is his *Subarnarekha* (Golden Line) which shows a refugee woman forced into prostitution to provide for her family. This film was passed by the Censor Board in spite of Directive No. C (iii) (c): "No soliciting, prostitution or procuration. . ."

Since censorship in the late, '50s, as indeed still today, was largely concerned with sex and morality, Mrinal Sen has been left alone to continue making his highly political, in fact propagandist films, advocating an extreme form of socialism and attacking political and social institutions. In the late '60s and early '70s, his highly inflammable—in the Indian context—*Interview, Calcutta 71, Patadik* (The Guerrilla Fighter) and *Chorus* were all passed by the censors. In 1973 and 1977, two of Mrinal Sen's films—*Chorus* in Bengali and *Mrigayaa* (The Royal Hunt) in Hindi respectively won the national award for the year's best film. But although these films exercise an immediate appeal for a segment of Calcutta's urban youth, they are largely ignored by Bengal's rural population which demands entertainment from its films, not revolution!

Regional Cinema: Western India

In Bombay, the centre of both the Gujrati and the Marathi languages, the Hindi film has swamped the regional cinema. Although the pioneers of Indian cinema, Phalke, Torney and Bhatvadekar, were all Maharashtrians and in the '30s, the Prabhat Film Company's greatest successes were in Marathi, after Independence Bombay became the home of the Hindi film, and the Marathi film suffered a decline. In 1960, for instance, only 15 films were made in Marathi (120 in Hindi), and two in Gujarati. The number has grown slightly in the last few years, but nothing of any particular significance has emerged.

The Positive Sixties

On the whole, by the end of the '50s and the early '60s, India was settling down. Morés, behaviour, social customs, the country in fact, was beginning to find its way. And with this stabilization, came a more mature attitude, less sensitive to imagined threats against the "purity" of "national culture." Another generation too, was growing up, that had not suffered under the taunts and slights of colonial domination and therefore, did not feel the need to assert its "Indianness" quite so aggressively.

The effects of crash programmes of industrializatoin and literacy were beginning to be felt; Indian society was at last showing signs of breaking away from the outworn, outmoded customs and beliefs it had held on to for 500 years as a defence against alien rulers.

The spirit of confidence and maturity was carried over even to the harassed film censors, who became more sure of themselves in dealing with charges of laxity in their judgements as, for instance, in their handling of a complaint received at the Bombay office against an Indian film, in Hindi, with the English title *Evening in Paris*. The Cine Films Reform Association of India had objected to the "depiction of young women in scanty dress" and demanded at the same time, representation on the Censor Boards. The answer sent by the Board was that "the mere fact that a woman is wearing a scanty dress in itself cannot constitute a good reason for its removal, unless the camera is focussed on the bare part of the body in a suggestive manner." Regarding the request for representation on the Boards, the Association was told that "the function of censorship is distinct and different and does not afford scope for effecting reforms in films."[5] This was in 1968. Censorship had come a long from the days when "showing the leg of a woman or girl by lifting the sari" would have been censorable material.

However, it was still not unusual for entire films to be banned for reasons of excessive violence, brutality and sadism, immorality and indecency, glorification of criminal characters, smuggling, crime, rape.

Double standards in judging Indian and foreign films had remained, in spite of the film industry's protests. A report by the Central Board of Film Censors justified this by saying that although the principles applied were the same, the difference in the social fabric and standards of life had to be kept in mind. Thus kissing was permitted to be shown in foreign films, but not in Indian films. In fact, the Board pointed out that "we are more strict with foreign films because we do not hesitate to impose an outright ban on a foreign film, whereas we are more careful in subjecting the Indian producer to a similar treatment." 'It isworth noting here, the names of some of the foreign films banned in recent years: *Boccaccio 70, Le Repos du Guerrier, Manchurian Candidate, Lolita, La Bonne Soupe, Carnal Knowledge* and *The Confession.*

Occasionally the Board felt obliged to give a long explanation for its decision, an explanation which at times sounded suspiciously like an apology, as in the case of Joseph Losey's *The Servant* (England). "Although this is a tour de force of films making, it is utterly nihilistic. It shows evil in action and takes no standpoint on anything. On an immature person it can have a salacious and harmful impact, and on a mature person the effect can be very disturbing. The superb craftsmanship only enhances its evil content."[7] An appeal against this judgement was made to the Central Government, which passed it with several cuts and an "A" certificate.

A number of moves were initiated in the 1960s. The Film Finance Corporation began functioning in 1960. The Film Institute began training students in the art of film in 1961 on the grounds of the old Prabhat Film Company in Poona. And in 1964 the National Film Archive began acquiring film classics from India and all over the world. Thus, serious students of cinema were at last able to see great films, such as *Battleship Potemkin* which had been banned in India by the Censor Boards in 1928. The Government had at last entered the film scene in a big and positive way, even though its impact was not to be felt for another decade.

Notes

[1]R.G.K., "Karunanidhi or MGR," *The Illustrated Weekly of India,* 19 November 1972.

[2]E. Barnouw and S. Krishnaswamy, *Indian Film,* Columbia University Press, New York, 1963, pp. 171-172.

[3]Madras Censor Board Records.

[4]Chidananda Das Gupta, "Contemporary Trends in Indian Films: Eastern Region," *Indian Cinema 1965,* Publications Division, New Delhi.

[5]Bombay Censor Board Records, 1968.

[6]Bombay Censor Board Records.

[7]*Ibid.*

7

The Rules of the Game

With the setting up of film organizations as recommended by the 1951 Film Enquiry Committee, a need was now beginning to be felt for a far-reaching investigation in the specific area of film censorship.

On 7 May 1965, S.B. Bobdey moved the following resolution in the Rajya Sabha:

Although we accept that the Code of censorship was formulated with the utmost good faith and the safeguard of social sanctity, I am now convinced that the existing censorship procedure requires a radical change. The working of the code administration and censorship during the last 10 years has revealed many serious drawbacks in its implementation. If this state of affairs continues further, the day is not far off which would witness the defeat of the purpose of the Code.

The Resolution was accepted and adopted in the following form:

This House is of the opinion that Government should appoint a Committee consisting of literary men, educationists, members of Parliament and representatives of the film industry, more parti-

cularly producers, directors and artists of note, to enquire into
the working of the existing procedure for sanctioning of cinematograph films for exhibition, and the effect that these films have
on society, keeping in view the development of the film industry,
and to make recommendations to effect improvements therein.

The Resolution was adopted, but the Enquiry Committee on
Film Censorship was set up only in March 1968.

In the meanwhile, in 1966, three informal panels of producers were
constituted and attached to the Censor Boards at the three regional
centres in Calcutta, Bombay and Madras. These committees, composed in each case of four eminent film producers, acted as con-
sultative bodies to which both the Censor Officer and the producers
could refer. The formation of these panels was greeted with great
enthusiasm, even though in the long run they did not prove to be
useful.

*The Estimates Committee, 1967, and The Enquiry Committee on Film
Censorship, 1969*

In 1967 the Estimates Committe completed an exhaustive enquiry
into the functioning of the Censor Boards and submitted its report
and recommendations to Parliament. Before any Government
action could be considered on the basis of these recommendations,
the report of the Enquiry Committee on Film Censorship was submitted in July 1969. Under these circumstances it would be as well
to consider the recommendations of both committees together.
The composition of these committees is of particular interest in
this context; the Estimates Committee consisted solely of elected
members of the Lower House of Parliament (Lok Sabha), whereas
the Enquiry Committe on Film Censorship was set up under the
Chairmanship of a former Chief Justice of the Punjab High Court
and comprised eight members of both houses of Parliament, and
four representatives of the film industry—K.A. Abbas (Bombay),
A.V. Meiyappan (Madras), Tapan Sinha (Calcutta) and Nargis Dutt
(immensely popular Hindi film star of the '50s). On the committee
also were three eminent intellectuals among whom was the brilliant
novelist R.K. Narayan. This committee came to be known by the
name of its Chairman as the Khosla Committee, and shall be so
referred to hereafter.

The areas in which both Committees made recommendations were : (1) The principles of censorship; (2) Classification of films according to age groups; (3) Constitution of the Board and qualifications for membership of the Board as well as the advisory panels; (4) Censorship fees; (5) Pre-censorship of scripts; (6) Double standards concerning Indian and foreign films; (7) Censorship of Indian films for export; and (8) Improvements in the general quality of films.

(1) The Estimates Committee made no suggestions for a change in the manner of application for censorship, saying merely that any complaints from producers against charges of rough treatment by the Board should be carefully looked into and the Board should satisfy itself that the criticism was not justified. It showed how attitudes had improved by indicating a marked sympathy for the film industry, and suggesting that "better results might be achieved by associating the film industry in developing a set of norms and criteria which are socially acceptable." It urged joint meetings between the representatives of the Ministry of Information and Broadcasting and the film industry, "so that such of the clauses of the directive principles or the censorship code as do not reflect the spirit of the times could be suitably modified." At the same time, it emphasized that film censorship should conform to certain social standards so that a "deletrious effect may not be created on the impressionable minds of young people." The totality of the impact of a film on the audience should be considered, and not simply the deletion of a scene or two.

The recommendation of the Khosla Committee was radical and sweeping. After examining at length the constitutional legality of censorship, it concluded that, in the case of films, "censorship can be deemed to be a reasonable restriction on the right of freedom of expression" provided that "the nature and extent of this control or restriction is related to the matters mentioned in Article 19 (2) of the Constitution. If the restriction is of a kind that would not be declared reasonable by a Court of Law, the restriction will not be justified .... It is clear that many of the rules which are at present in force have no legal sanction behind them, nor can they be said to be reasonable or rational. Censorship must be authorized by law, and must be confined within the limits permitted by law and the provisions of the Constitution. To extend the scope of censorship to considerations of public taste and ban a matter which does not fall within the ambit of the reasonable restriction clause would not be legal." In the light of these conclusions, the Committee declared that the General Principles and the Application of General Principles of censorship currently in force would have to be done away with. In their stead should be Censorship Guidelines framed by the Board of Censors. The Code must be in general terms, following closely the provisions of Article 19 (2) of the Constitution. The application and interpretation of the Code should rest with the Censors themselves who would then exercise their discretion in judging films along generally accepted norms of morality and conduct, taking into account that these norms change from time to time. It was felt by the Committee that "the abrogation of the present General Principles will make for greater freedom in the production of films both in the matter of subject and in the matter of treatment.

(2) Having proved that a person cannot be restrained from producing a film that does not transgress either the penal laws or the Constitution and, at the same time, that an adult individual can lawfully claim to see a film which may be vulgar or in bad taste but which complies with the requirements of the law, the Committee went on to look at the question of the suitability of films for children. Article 39 (f) of the Constitution requires the State to ensure "that children and youth are protected against exploitation and against moral and material abandonment." The State thus has the right to declare that some films are not suitable for children under a certain age. The Estimates Committee suggested that the Government seriously consider raising the age limit for adults to persons above the age of 21 instead of 18 as at present. It also suggested that the Khosla Committee take up the question of three categories of films instead of the current classification into "A" and "U" only. This the Khosla Committee did do, and recommended:

(1) 'U' films, for universal exhibition including children under the age of 16.

(2) 'G' films, which may be seen by adults and also by children under 16 provided they are accompanied by their parents or guardians.

(3) 'A' films, only for adults above the age of 18. Children between 16 and 18 may see the films if accompanied by

adults, but childern under 16 may not view these films under any circumstances.

Such a classification, it was felt, would prevent the baneful effect if any, of the cinema upon children or adolescents. As far as raising the age limit for adults to 21, the Government rejected it saying that 18 is quite mature enough an age and moreover, "in India, a large number of girls marry between the ages of 18 and 21. It would lead to odd situations if wives of this age group were not allowed to go to the movies with their husbands."

(3) To carry out censorship along the lines it suggested, the Khosla Committee proposed a fundamental reorganization of the manner of its application. The Estimates Committee had made a mild suggestion to the effect that three of the nine honorary members of the Censor Board should be from the film industry, one each from Bombay, Madras and Calcutta, since such an association would be conducive to the maintenance of better liason between the Board and the industry. The Khosla Committee condemned altogether the present functioning and organization of the Board in very strong terms, singling out as a major defect the lack of responsibility entailed in the decisions, where the Board merely carried out the instructions laid down in the Code drawn up by the Government. It stated that "it is important, therefore, that State censorship should be exercised not by a department of the State, whose decisions are subject to revision, appeal or interference by the government, but by an independent body which has been given sufficient authority and responsibility to deal with the matter finally and irrevocably." It went on to describe in detail the composition and functions of the Board it envisaged:

We feel that a Central Board of 20 members drawn from various regions, and familiar with regional languages, will be able to discharge this work competently and expenditiously. Not less than 6 of its members should be familiar with English, Hindi and Urdu . . . . 4 members should be drawn from the Eastern States, all of whom should be familiar with Bengali, Oriya and Assamese . . . . 8 members should be drawn from the Southern region and of these, 2 at least must know Gujarati and Marathi, and 4 should know the 4 principal languages of the South, viz. Tamil, Telugu, Kannada and Malayalam. All members of the

Board should be full-time paid members, and each film should be seen by not less than 3 Censors .... The Censor Board itself, and not a Government department, should draw up a panel of non-official advisors whom they may call upon for advice in exceptional cases relating to local customs, conditions or language. In case of a difference of opinion between the Censors viewing a film, the matter will be referred to the entire Board and as many members as possible should see the film and give their views. The quorum for a full meeting should be 7. This will ensure uniformity and consistency in censorship policy.[1]

The Committee also suggested that the headquarters of the Board should be either Bangalore, Hyderabad, or Nagpur all these cities being near enough to the main film industry centres and far enough to be impervious to the constant influence of the industry.[2] The Estimates Committee had also been in favour of locating the headquarters of the Board, even in its present form, in a central city away from the three main centers of film production.[3]

(4) Both the Estimates Committee and the Khosla Committee favoured the appointment of a public figure with a judicial background as Chairman of the Board. The Estimates Committee also recommended that the Chairman have a "wide understanding of the movie medium, and appreciation of the film as a medium of art." The Khosla Committee stated that it was desirable for the censors to be "persons with discrimination, possessing a knowledge of Indian art, culture, traditions and above all, persons with a liberal and modern outlook."[4]

(5) Both the Committees emphasized the desirability of making the Censor Board financially self-supporting. The fees charged for censoring films were not enough to ensure this, but whereas the Estimates Committee suggested that the Board may examine the feasibility of reducing its administrative expenditure, the Khosla Committee recommended raising the fees on the basis that "the film industry can well afford to pay higher fees for certification of feature films," as this would still only be a small percentage of the total budget of the film.[5]

Regarding pre-censorship of scripts, both committees felt that the prevailing system whereby the producer could ask the advice of the Board if he wished to do so, should be continued. Compulsory pre-censorship was not considered practicable as "the final shape of the film can be totally different in mood and manner from the original script."[6]

(6) It was felt that double standards in judging films of Indian and foreign origin, would have to be maintained. The Estimates Committee expressed itself in agreement with the Board of Film Censors that the "customs, traditions and culture of the Indian people being different from those of people in the West, there is need for according different treatment to foreign films."[7] (It must be kept in mind that only 3 per cent of the total number of films shown at this time were of foreign origin.) The Khosla Committee endorsed this opinion, but added that "having regard to the boldness with which many foreign producers treat human problems, it will be advisable to categorize films containing too frank and intense a discussion of human relationships as films deserving an 'A' certificate, instead of banning them completely."[8]

(7) Concerning the censorship of films meant for export, the Estimates Committee urged that the existing Cinematograph Act be amended, so that "it may be verified by the Censor Board that films intended for export do not contain anything derogatory to our national ideas, culture and traditions, or disparaging to the economic and political policy of the Government."[9] The Khosla Committee also recommended that "to discourage and, if possible, eliminate a distorted image of our social, political and cultural life being presented to other countries through exported films, only films approved by the Censors and granted a certificate for exhibition abroad, should be exported."[10] (Here one is tempted to wonder what would have been the fate of the then unknown Satyajit Ray's first film *Pather Panchali* if he had been obliged to get clearance before sending the film to the Cannes Film Festival, which began a legendary career that brought high international honours to him and prestige to India. Under such a ruling, the chances are that the export of the film might well have been stopped for its intensely moving portrayal of poverty. By a literal minded censor, it could have been judged "a distortion of the image of our social, political and cultural life"—an opinion about Ray all to often expressed in India even today.)

(8) It was, however, in the general field of principles of censorship, relating to questions of decency and morality that the Khosla Committee made suggestions which raised such an outcry for and against them both within the film industry and from the gene-

ral public, that all the far-reaching changes it proposed were temporarily lost sight of in the welter of reactions that followed. The Estimates Committee had confined its remarks on the subject of improving film content to making a general appeal to the Government to evolve a new national policy in regard to production and censorship, which would ameliorate the content and artistic quality of films. It had no concrete methods to suggest as to how this could be achieved. But the Khosla Committee, in advocating strongly that greater freedom should be permitted in the theme and content of films, and that producers should be allowed to deal with social and political questions as well as the subject of sex, stated that unless a film is "against the interest of the security of the State, friendly relations with foreign States, public order, decency or morality, or involves defamation or contempt of court, or is likely to incite the commission of an offence" (Section 5-B [1] of the Cinematograph Act 1952), it cannot be refused a certificate. Thus, "while a film in which violence is shown as a source of pleasure, erotic or otherwise, may be deemed objectionable on the ground that it amounts to an incitement to commit an offence, kissing or nudity cannot be banned unless a Court of Law judges the scene to be obscence."[11] It said, therefore, that "If, in telling the story it is logical, relevant or necessary to depict a passionate kiss or a nude human figure, there should be no question of excluding the shot, provided the theme is handled with delicacy and feeling, aiming at aesthetic expression and avoiding all suggestion of prurience or lasciviousness."[12] This is the sentence that was singled out from the entire report, and it led to a furore; articles in the press, interviews, statements, endless debates and discussion; the whole country became involved in India's kissing crisis. The Censor Board has not so far changed its stand and although no longer so heated, the question is still discussed—"To kiss, or not to kiss," and "Is kissing un-Indian?" Most of the film stars refuse to consider it for a variety of reasons—it is embarrassing, unnecessary, unhygienic, bad for the public image, people from "good families" will no longer want to take up film acting as a profession as lately they had started doing. The issue has still not been resolved.

Legal Position of Censorship: Supreme Court Ruling 1969

Another and much more significant outcome of the Khosla

Committee's Report was that the legal standing of censorship was challenged by a film producer through the Supreme Court for the first time. This committee had conceded that reasonable restriction upon the right of freedom of speech and expression may be imposed under the Constitution. In the case of film censorship, however, it is an executive officer who determines that the restriction he is imposing is reasonable. In fact, reasonableness is a justiciable issue and the test of the reasonableness of a restriction must ultimately rest with a Court of Law. It went on to say:

> The fact that no one has so far chosen to question the censorship code or any of the General Principles or their application contained in the notification of the Central Government Cinematograph (Censorship) Rules 1960, cannot be taken to mean that these principles are all lawful and constitutional. We heard, in the course of our inquiry, murmurs indicative of dissatisfaction with the present system of censorship and a vaguely expressed desire to challenge the censorship code by taking the matter to the Supreme Court on the ground that the notification stifles the propagation of ideas.[13]

The intention of challenging the Code had remained only "a vaguely expressed desire" because no producer or director could afford the financial risk of the delay entailed in legislation. The budget of a feature film is inordinately high and long before the film is completed the date of release is decided upon, so that even a day's delay at the censorship stage can be ruinous. The free-lance documentary film maker is generally sponsored by a government body. Even when a private industrial concern commissions a film, its distribution remains in the hands of the Government of India Films Division, which is under no obligation to take up the film. The making of short film on speculation is, therefore, a rare and hazardous undertaking.

It was left to K. A. Abbas to take up the issues that the Khosla Committee—of which he was a member—had brought out into the open. K. A. Abbas, who began his film making career in 1946 with *Dharti Ke Lal* went on to win a President's Gold Medal for the best film of the year with *Shehar aur Sapna* (Cities and Dreams) in 1963, and a host of other honours both national and international. At the same time he continued writing—

articles, screenplays, short stories, novels, biographies (of both Nehru and Mrs Gandhi). He was, in 1968, a member of the Khosla Committee, a member of the Committee of Experts of the National Integration Council, and a member of the Executive Council of the Children's Film Society. An unshakeable idealist, gentle and charming, he has always been a fighter for causes, a champion of the underdog. In 1969, while the Khosla Committee was pursuing its investigations and deliberations, he decided to challenge the Censorship Code through a short film, knowing that in all likelihood this might, and did, represent a considerable financial loss in view of the high cost of making even a short film, and the improbability of the Films Division ever distributing it.

Since this was the first case in which the censorship of films was contested in a court of law, it is worth examining in detail. The film, called *A Tale of Four Cities,* purported to contrast the luxurious life of the rich in the four cities of Calcutta, Bombay, Delhi and Madras, with the squalor and poverty of the poor, particularly those whose hands and labour built these cities. The film is in black and white, with no commentary. It is a series of contrasts between palatial buildings, hotels, beautiful homes, and the shanties and huts of the poor. In one sequence a fat and prosperous customer is shown sitting in a rickshaw which is pulled by a thin, scrawny little man. In the next scene, the same rickshaw puller dreams that he is sitting in rickshaw, being pulled by his former customer. This scene epitomizes the theme of the film.

In another sequence, a very brief, very fast panning shot shows the red light district of Bombay with women waiting at the doors and windows. Some are dressed in very short skirts. The shot is evidently taken from a moving car. A few quick shots pick out details. A woman inside a house closes a window. In a close-up of her hands we see her holding some money which a male hand takes away, leaving her just a few notes. The man and woman are not shown. In the next scene the woman is sitting at a dressing table. She combs her hair, glances at two birds in a cage, and looks round the room as if that were her cage. She goes behind a screen to change her clothes, comes out, and goes to bed. In her sleep she dreams of her life before she entered the hateful world of prostitution. This is the sequence that was responsible for the controversy.

The Examining Committee of the Censor Board gave the film an "A" certificate. Abbas refused to accept this decision and asked that the film be seen by the Revising Committee, which upheld the earlier decision, but took 45 days to do so. In questioning this verdict, Abbas quoted the relevant Clauses IV (I, II, & III) of the Censorship rules, claiming that this film did not Contravene any of them. He was told that if he were not satisfied, he may appeal to the Central Government. This he did, only to be informed four months later on 3 July 1969, that the Ministry of Information & Broadcasting had decided to offer a "U" certificate to the film, subject to the following cuts: "Shorten the scene of woman in the red light district, deleting specially the shots showing the closing of the window by the lady, the suggestive shots of bare kness, and the passing of the currency notes."

The Ministry quoted two clauses of the Censorship Rules as the authority for this ruling, i.e.,

C (iii) (b) deals with the relations between the sexes in such a manner as to depict immoral traffic in women, and (c) soliciting, prostitution or procuration.

IV It is undesirable that a certificate for unrestricted public exhibition shall be granted in respect of a film depicting a story, or containing incidents unsuitable for young persons.

In his long reply to the Ministry, Abbas contested the interpretation given to these brief shots (total length 12 ft), charging that "the cuts ordered are arbitrary, unwarranted and are not at all covered by the above clauses." He ended his letter with: "Since it is arbitrariness, and not principles that govern this decision, I think someone sometime has to challenge the thoughtless, unconsidered and unwarranted decisions of the Board, and I am glad that that opportunity and that privilege has fallen to my lot."

A writ petition was filed in the Supreme Court and admitted on 28 November 1969. In it, Abbas claimed that his fundamental right of free speech and expression was denied by the order of the Central Government. He claimed a "U" certificate, without cuts, as his right.

The film was screened for the Supreme Court in the presence of the lawyers of both sides (including the Attorney General), and the petitioner. At the preliminary hearing, the Attorney General appeared and stated that the Government had decided to grant a "U" certificate to the film *without the cuts* previously ordered. Abbas then asked to be allowed to amend the petition so as to be able to challenge pre-censorship itself as offensive to freedom of speech and expression, and the provisions of the Act (Cinematograph Act 1952) and the rules, orders and directions under the Act, as vague, arbitrary and indefinite. The Supreme Court allowed the application for amendment, stating that "the petitioner was right in contending that a person who invests his capital in promoting or producing a film must have clear guidance in advance in the matter of censorship of films, even if the law of pre-censorship be not violative of the fundamental right."

When the mattter came up for hearing, the petitioner raised four points: (a) that pre-censorship itself cannot be tolerated under the freedom of speech and expression; (b) that even if it were a legitimate restraint on the freedom, it must be exercised on very definite principles which leave no room for arbitrary action; (c) that there must be a reasonable time limit fixed for the decision of the authorities censoring the film; and (d) that the appeal should be to a Court, or to an independent tribunal and not the Central Government.

At the hearing, the Solicitor General conceded points (c) and (d), and stated that the Government would introduce legislation to effectuate them at the earliest possible opportunity. The petitioner was satisfied by this assurance, and the Court did not take them up.

In its final judgement, the Supreme Court, in considering the first point, went into the question of whether censorship of films was necessary at all and if so, what was its legal and constitutional standing. The Court concluded that "censorship in India (and pre-censorship is not different in quality) has full justification in the field of the exhibition of cinema films," and that "the censorship imposed on the making and exhibition of films is in the interest of society. If the regulations venture into something which goes beyond the legitimate opening to restrictions, they can be questioned on the ground that a legitimate power is being abused. We hold, therefore, that censorship of films, including prior restraint, is justified under our Constitution." In passing its judgment, the Supreme Court quoted an article 'Creative Expressions.' Abbas himself wrote in the July 1963 issue of the monthly magazine *Seminar:*

Even if we believe that a novelist or a painter or a musician should be free to write, paint and compose music without the interference of the State machinery, I doubt if anyone will advocate the same freedom to be extended to the commercial expioitation of a powerful medium of expression and entertainment like cinema. One can imagine the results if an unbridled commercial cinema is allowed to cater to the lowest common denominator of popular taste, especially in a country which, after two centuries of political and cultural domination, is still suffering from a confusion and debasement of cultural values.

Freedom of expression cannot, and should not, be interpreted as a license for the cinemagnates to make money by pandering to and thereby propagating, shoddy and vulgar taste.

On the second point, i.e., the vagueness of the principles on which censorship is exercised, the Court said that it did not agree, and that "the words used (in the Censorship Rules 1960), are within the understanding of the average man. But the main argument raised by the Court, and which led to a judgement in Abbas' favour, was:

What appears to us to be the real flaw in the scheme of the directions is a total absence of any direction which would tend to preserve art and promote it. The artistic appeal or presentation of an episode robs it of its vulgarity and harm, and this appears to be completely forgotten. Artistic as well as inartistic presentations are treated alike and also what may be socially good and useful, and what may not. . . .

Although we are not inclined to hold that the directions are defective insofar as they go, we are of the opinion that directions to emphasize the importance of art to a vaiue judgement by the censors need to be included...Even the items mentioned in the directions may figure in films subject to either their artistic merit or their social value over-weighing their offending character. The task of the censor is extremely delicate and his duties cannot be the subject of an exhaustive set of commands established by prior ratiocination. But direction is necessary to him so that he does not sweep within the terms of the directions vast areas of thought, speech and expression of artistic quality and social purpose and interest. Our standards must be so framed that we are not reduced to a level where the protection of the least capable and the most depraved amongst us determines what the morally healthy can not view or read. The standards we set for our censors must make a substantial allowance in favour of freedom, thus leaving a vast area for creative art to interpret life and society with some of its foibles along with what is good. We must not look upon such human relationships as banned in toto and forever, from human thought, and must give scope for talent to put them before society. The requirements of art and literature include within themselves a comprehensive view of social life and not only in its ideal form, and the line is to be drawn where the average moral man begins to feel embarrassed or disgusted at a naked portrayal of life without the redeeming touch or art of genius or social value. If the depraved begin to see in these things more than what an average person would, in much the same way as, it is wrongly said, a Frenchman sees a woman's legs, it cannot be helped. In our scheme of things, ideas having redeeming social or artistic value must also have importance and protection for their growth.

As an example of what would be permissible even for Indian audiences to see, the Supreme Court mentioned the legend of Oedipus, a story containing patricide, incest, suicide, and ending with Oedipus putting out his own eyes. In much the same way, some of the Indian epics contain instances of adultery, sexual immorality, and cruelty.

Thus, although the directives in themselves are not defective, the judgement continued: "Parliament has not legislated enough, nor has the Central Government filled in the gap. Neither has separated the artistic and the socially valuable from that which is deliberately indecent, obscene, horrifying or corrupting. They have not indicated the need of society and the freedom of the individual. They have thought more of the depraved and less of the ordinary moral man. In their desire to keep films from the abnormal, they have excluded the moral. They have attempted to bring down the public motion picture to the level of home movies."

Abbas won his case. The film was given a "U" certificate without cuts but the Government of India Films Division, sole distribution agency for short films, did not buy it, and the film was never publicly shown.

The Cinematograph Act 1974

At the first hearing, the Solicitor General had given two under-takings—that the Government would fix a reasonable time limit for the decision of the authorities censoring the film, and would also make a provision that an appeal against a decision of the Central Board of Film Censors would lie with a Court or an independent tribunal, not with the Central Government. These commitments had to be honoured. The Ministry of Information and Broadcasting had carefully studied the recommendations of the Khosla Committee, soliciting the views also of the State Governments. After consultations with the Ministries of Law and of Finance, the Cinematograph (2nd Amendment) Bill 1973 was placed before the Rajya Sabha and passed on 27 August 1974. It received the assent of the President at the same time and was to be notified in the official gazette on 1 July 1975.

The changes wrought in censorship by the Act and its accompanying Rules, were in six areas: (1) Composition of the Board; (2) Application of censorship, which now included films intended for export; (3) Formation of an Appellate Tribunal to hear appeals; (4) Censorship fees; (5) Time limit on decisions at every stage of censorship; and (6) The censor certificate, and the manner in which it was to be used.

(1) The new Board was to be composed of a Chairman and five members who were to be full-time paid Government employees, appointed for a three-year period. Six honorary members, including three from the film industry (one each from Calcutta, Bombay and Madras) would be appointed by the Government, and paid certain allowances and fees. In addition, not more than seven assessors would be appointed for two years in each of the three Regional Centres, to assist and advise the Board about language and local customs. They would also receive allowances and fees. One or more Regional Officers would be appointed by the Government at each regional centre, and would perform purely administrative functions. The Board was not to be located in one city, but would function from the three centres: the Chairman, two full-time and two honorary members in Bombay, two full-time and two honorary members in Madras, and one full-time and one honorary member in Calcutta.

(2) Each film would first be seen by an Examining Committee

composed of one full-time member and two assessors. For cases where the producer professed dissatisfaction with the decision of this Committee, the film would be shown to a Revising Committee which would comprise the Chairman (or one full-time member designated by him), one full-time member, and one honorary member.

The classification of films would still be for either unrestricted public exhibition ("U" Certificate), or restricted to adults above the age of 18 ("A" Certificate). However, another category was now added: the sanctioning of films for export. The Board could either certify the film as fit for exhibition outside India, direct the applicant to make certain excisions or modifications before sanctioning the film for exhibition outside India, or refuse to approve it for exhibition outside India. From now on, no film would be allowed to leave the country without an export certificate. A mandatory clause was also inserted, making it compulsory to deposit a print of each certified film with the Censor Board for one year, at the expiry of which period the film would be returned to the producer. The excised portions, in both the negative and the positive prints, were to be surrendered to the Board. At the end of six months, these would be sent to and preserved at, the National Film Archives in Poona.

(3) Twelve persons were to be nominated by the Central Government to serve as members of Appellate Tribunals to hear appeals against decisions of the Central Board of Film Censors. These members were to be selected from among persons familiar with social, cultural and political institutions in India, or from those with a special knowledge of various regions of the country, or those with specialized knowledge of films and their impact on society, or persons who have held civil judicial posts or have been practicing advocates for at least 10 years. Each member of the Appellate Tribunal was to be appointed for three years, and paid travelling allowances plus a consultancy fee of Rs 200 per appeal. The Central Government would appoint three members from among the twelve nominated members, to form an Appellate Tribunal to hear each appeal.

Under Section 6 of the new Act, the Government kept its revisionary powers, retaining the right to throw out a decision taken even by an Appellate Tribunal if it was considered necessary to do so in the interests of the sovereignty and integrity of India, the security of the State, friendly relations with foreign States, or public order, decency and morality.

The retention of these powers by the government could be considered a negation of the whole idea behind setting up independent tribunals, the final judge of decency and morality still remaining a government official or the minister concerned.

(4) A complex table was drawn up in respect of fees to be charged for censorship, depending on the gauge of film—16 mm or 35 mm, the length of the film—the longer the film, the higher the price charged per 300m, and different charges for black-and-white or colour. For a normal length feature film i.e., under 3,600 metres in 35 mm, in black and white, the fee was raised up from Rs 45 per 300 mm reel to Rs 80 and for colour to Rs 100. Between 3,600 and 4,500 metres, the charges would be Rs 140 per black and white reel, and Rs 175 colour reel. Above 4,500 metres, the fee would be Rs 280 for black and white, and Rs 350 for colour. These measures were adopted as much to make the Censor Board entirely self-supporting as to discourage overly long films.

(5) A time limit was fixed for each stage of censorship, from the date of application through to an appeal to the Appellate Tribunal. A time limit was also imposed on the producer for the submission of excised portions and a print of the film upon receipt of the censor certificate.

(6) With regard to the Censor certificate itself, the practice until now had been merely to film the certificate, and attach it to the beginning of the film. The excisions and modifications, marked on the back of the certificate, were naturally not indicated in the film. In order to stop the practice of producers re-inserting the censored portions in prints of the films shown outside the main theatres, it was now made obligatory to display a copy of the certificate with the cuts and modifications marked on it, in the hall of the theatre where the film was playing, and where any local official could verify them.

The film industry objected very strongly to this Act. It felt it should have been consulted when the Act was being framed, but the government's position was that the Act was based on the recommendations of the Khosla Committee which had drawn its conclusions on the strength of extensive interviews with representatives of the industry when it had been given ample opportunity to express its views. The judgement of the Supreme Court in the Abbas case had also led to other changes in the Act which should have pleased the industry.

But the antagonism and the hostility persisted and at the first opportunity, a few days after the Emergency was proclaimed and the new Minister took over, the industry made a strong representation that the enforcement of the Act be stopped, and reconsidered after further discussion.

What the Audience Wants the Audience Gets

The conflict had instensified in recent years with the government's determination to curb the "sex and violence" tendencies at odds with the industry's insistence that its films only mirror the needs and desires of the audience. In a sense these films possibly do reflect life today, with people looking for escape from pain and frustration into a violence which they feel but cannot give way to. In this cinema may well have a cathartic effect, preventing an explosion of real-life violence. Sexual repression in a society still ruled by ancient tenets of behaviour also possibly finds an outlet into uninhibited cinematic licentiousness.

At the same time there is a definite dichotomy in the definition of terms too easily and loosely employed. "Vulgarity" and "obscenity" mean different things to different people, depending on the economic and social background of those using them. Government officials as well as members of the advisory panels of the Censor Boards are usually from the affluent, well-educated, urban, upper-middle class. They are appalled at the "obscene" displays of the female anatomy, at the "vulgarity" of the song-and-dance sequences. Protected from a world of crime and violence, they think it does not exist, and are generally ignorant of the fear in which the impoverished majority lives, whether the dispossessed in rural India or the down-trodden in city slums for whom particularly, prostitution, dancing girls, crime and brutality are a part of life. It is this majority that makes up the mass audience for particularly the Hindi cinema, and which presumably is not shocked by it.

In any case, producers of these Hindi films claim that the violence they portray is a form of adventure, even of valour. It is fantasized; its heros indulge in extraordinary feats, doing double somersaults upwards to land on a balcony and slay the villain.

This is not the kind of violence audiences take seriously; they thrill to it, applauding it with enthusiasm. These same producers maintain that the new, small-budget non-commerical films do much greater damage because the violence they show is real and therefore has much greater impact. The suicide in *Garm Hawa* (A Hot Wind), the beating of the poor labourer in *Ankur* (The Seedling), the clash of caste in *Kaadu* (The Jungle), the rape of the school-teacher's wife by the landowners in *Nishant* (Night's End), this, they claim, is the kind of violence which is dangerous. It pervades the consciousness and remains with the audience, altering its perceptions of society. But then, these films express their makers' concern with the social framework. Their object is to draw attention to its injustices, to create awareness and set their audiences thinking. Whereas the commerical cinema, in emphasizing mindless entertainment, conveniently ignores the role played by all cinema as a medium almost of education.

It is painfully evident that there is no clear idea about the cinema—what it can do, what it should do in its role as a medium of art, of education, entertainment and information. "Violence" and "vulgarity" are like red rags to a bull, but no study has been made either by the government or by the industry, to discover why audiences enjoy this violence as much as they seem to.

As the government's drive against vulgarity and violence strengthened, some films were banned, others containing much the same ingredients were given a "U" certificate. Even the censors themselves appeared uncertain by which yardstick to measure their standards. The incidence of violence seemed to be increasingly reflected in films from Hollywood to Hong Kong. Where nudity and sexual violence were taking over international cinema, in India it was still forbidden to show a couple kissing. With the world on one's doorstep, it becomes impractical and impossible to remain wrapped up in a cocoon, protected by outworn, outdated modes of behaviour, particularly when more and more festivals of uncensored films are opening up a whole new world to Indian audiences.

It needed time, research and careful thinking to evolve a rational policy taking all these factors into consideration.

The government thought that by encouraging "art" films, the general quality of films could be improved. There is a great deal to be said in favour of this view, but by the manner in which it has been done, a polarization has been artificially created between protagonists of the "new wave" and the "commercial" cinema. In actual fact there is room for both, but government and elitist patronage of these films caused the established industry to draw further away into its own world.

In this atmosphere of uneasiness and tension, the Cinematograph Bill was passed by the Rajya Sabha and was awaiting consideration by the Lok Sabha when the Estimates Committee 1973-74 presented its Report on Films to the Lok Sabha on 25 April 1974. The broad scope of its investigations covered the practical difficulties faced by the film industry—finances, taxation, exhibition, export, film festivals, regional language production as well as the star system. In an overall survey of film policy, it went into the relationship of the government to the film industry—the formation of a Film Council, raw stock allocations, construction of new cinema houses and censorship.

Although the Report was not published until August 1974, and the Ministry's replies to the Lok Sabha indicating the actions taken on the recommendations spread over the next ten months, it is to be presumed that the Report was studied in the Lok Sabha before it, in its turn, passed the Cinematograph Act.

Starting once again with a statement on the important place occupied by the cinema in the lives of the people, the Report continued: "Determined efforts should be made by government, in consultation and coordination with the industry, to ensure that films produced in the country, while providing healthy and wholesome entertainment to the masses, make a valuable contribution in building up national character reinforcing moral values, achieving socio-economic objectives, and (that they) channelize the energies of the masses, particularly of the youth, in nation-building activities." It felt that as since 1973 all important functions relating to the film industry like import and export of films, import of raw materials and equipment, had been centralized with the Ministry of Information & Broadcasting, there was no reason why this Ministry should not now be able to play a more effective role "in the matter of developing and assisting the growth of the film industry on healthy lines." It went on to say: "What is actually needed now is concerted and coordinated action on the part of the government, followed by a substantial financial intervention, to help the growth of the film industry in the country." It urged that as the government was becoming increasingly aware of the vast potentialities of this medium of entertainment and communication, a definite and comprehensive policy for the proper development of the film industry must now be drawn up and requisite follow-up action taken to implement this immediately.

To this end it recommended initiation of a programme for the construction of cinema houses which would double their number during the Fifth Five Year Plan period, adding, however, that the government should carefully evaluate the experiment of running Film Finance Corporation films in art theatres in Bombay and other metropolitan towns, before embarking on a scheme of constructing specifically art theaters. Mobile cinemas on the other hand, should be increased, and encouraged to show award-winning and purposeful films in rural areas by charging nominal admission tickets. In noting that the government proposed to create a fund for the film industry by imposing a 5 paise cess on every cinema ticket, the Committee stressed that specific guidelines should be provided, laying down the purpose for which the fund should be used. It wanted a percentage of the amount to be used for assisting "eminent and junior artistes and technicians who are in adverse pecuniary circumstances," and for suitable financial assistance from this fund to be provided to "producers of award-winning films which may not prove such a draw at the box office so as to cover the costs and sustain such laudable productions."

It was sympathetic to the film industry's representation against the amortization formula of charging income tax on the earnings of a film, a formula based on the results of the cost and earnings study made by the government. However, since the government had said that if it were presented with different facts, it would be prepared to reconsider the position, the committee hoped that the film industry would avail of the offer and make the necessary material available so that the possibility of changing this could be studied. It wanted the government—at the Centre and in the States—to encourage the regional film industry to sustain quality production, and to finalize and implement a scheme of dubbing at least national award-winning films as a start.

It wanted the government to explore fresh markets for the export of Indian films, to take strong steps to end the smuggling of films outside the country, at the same time taking concrete measures in conjunction with the industry to see that films which are exported are of "high quality and depict the culture and life of our people in an artistic and presentable manner." (To this the government replied that the Cinematograph Bill 1974, contained a provision necessitating certification of films for export.)

It also wished to see a greater participation of Indian films in international festivals as well as the organization of festivals of Indian films in other countries.

On the question of censorship, the Committee considered that "censorship by government is necessary and must be contiuued" as, from its personal viewing of the cuts imposed by the Censor Board, it was left with the impression that "there is an increasing tendency on the part of film producers to include unnecessary scenes depicting sex, violence, nudity and rape, thus debasing the quality of our films which may have a deletrious effect on the viewers, particularly youth and adolescents." It said it was not convinced by the arguments of the film industry that it is necessary to include these ingredients in order to make a film successful at the box office, pointing to the number of widely-acclaimed films that are free of these traits.

As for the complaints of film producers that "censorship policy is often dictated by the whims and fancies of the high-ups in the Government," it hoped that the constitution of the Board and the Appellate Tribunals as envisaged in the Act would remove many of these complaints. It pointed out that "the film producers in Calcutta and a number of film producers in Bombay who are known for the production of quality films, had no reason for complaints against the censorship policy of the Government." It however, urged that while appointing members to the new Board of Film Censors and to the Appellate Tribunals, care should be taken to see that only persons of proven integrity and knowledge of the industry are included.

All of these recommendations were accepted by the Ministry, the idea being that the proposed National Film Development Corporation would ensure that they were implemented. It stated that all formalities for the setting up of this Corporation had been completed and that it was likely to come into existence by 31 March 1975.

Other recommendations were not pursued in view of the Government's replies, but at least one of these provides an interesting sidelight into the manner in which it was thought film quality might be helped to improve. The Committee was of the opinion, which it said it shared with the 1951 Film Enquiry Committee and the Khosla Committee, 1969, that one of the evils of the film industry was the star system. It found fault with the government for not having taken concrete stepts to "eliminate this evil from the film industry." It blamed the star system for "the rise of the domination of black money in the film industry" and believed that it was the stars' practice of taking up a number of assignments simultaneously that caused production costs to soar by delaying completion of films, and leading to a loss in quality. It wanted action to be taken limiting the number of films in which one star could work at a time. The Government's reply was that such a step was not feasible but that the proposed Film Corporation may be able, in consultation with the industry, to evolve a code of conduct to regulate matters of this nature.

The Committee also, in welcoming the suggestion made by representatives of the film industry, wanted the government to take the initiative in setting up a Trust fund for a kind of old-age pension scheme for film people—actors and technicians. The Ministry, in replying to this, said that the film industry had not yet put forward such a proposal before the government but that when the Film Fund created through the cess on cinema tickets came into being, it should be possible, with the help of the industry, to use it for this purpose as well.

So far none of these suggestions have been implemented, even the National Film Development Corporation still exists only on paper. But as we have seen earlier, all developments in the cinema seem to have consistently been overtaken by political upheavals. The Cinematograph Act 1974 was to come into force on 1 July 1975, but four days earlier, on 26 June a state of Emergency was declared in India, and strict censorship imposed even on the normally free press. The Cinematograph Act was set aside, and the entire country waited in trepidation to see what would happen under a form of government so alien to the aspirations and principles which had inspired the founders of modern India.

Notes

[1]Khosla Committee, para 7.14, pp. 100-101.
[2]*Ibid.*
[3]Estimates Committee, para 83, p. 36.
[4]Khosla Committee para 3 (ii), p. 148.
[5]Khosla Committee, para 7: 18, p. 103.
[6]*Ibid.*, para 6: 6.
[7]Estimates Committee 1967, para 74.
[8]Khosla Committee, para 8: 81, p. 132.
[9]Estimates Committee, para 115.
[10]Khosla Committee, paras 8: 70-8 : 74, p. 130.
[11]Khosla Committee, para 8: 45, p. 122.
[12]*Ibid.*
[13]Khosla Committee, 1969, para 4: 14 p. 51.

8

Zero for Conduct

It is impossible to leave an analysis of censorship and cinema at this stage without referring to some of the incidents that took place in the 19 months of the Emergency and which illustrate government interference with the film world, and the desire to subjugate as well as to exploit it. The application of censorship under the Emergency lost all semblance of rationale and logic. It was used as a stick to beat the industry with, and the fear that a censor certificate would be withheld was enough to overcome the strongest reluctance to comply with the Ministry's most outrageous demands. At the same time, whenever a censorship certificate was not the issue, producers, directors, actors and musicians always had hanging over them the threat of retribution, or charges of income tax evasion to ensure that they toed the line.

A confusion of widely divergent reactions greeted the declaration of the Emergency. Relief at the stringent measures adopted to stem the slow, steady decline into chaos and lift the despondency of the preceding two or three years; shock and panic at stories of the massive scale of arrests and repressive actions; a despairing conviction that the end of democracy was in sight. Rumours ran rife as a rigorous press censorship saw to it that no news critical of government actions found its way into print.

As law and order returned to the streets, and strikes, protests and demonstrations were banned, as the shackled press carried reports only of the benefits or the new rule, the average person was lulled into a sense of security. But slowly, as chilling accounts began circulating of ruthless enforcement measures and the erosion of civil rights, a pall of fear settled over the whole country.

Always at the mercy of governmental will, the film industry wasted no time in sending a telegram of congratulations to the Prime Minister, lauding her "decisive action" and pledging her its full support. Another telegram to V.C. Shukla welcomed him to his new appointment as Minister of Information & Broadcasting.

But it did not take long for the welcome to turn sour as the Minister left no doubt that the state of Emergency would carry the impact of the government far beyond the reach of censorship. The Emergency was to demonstrate more clearly than ever before the combination of scorn and suspicion with which the government has always tended to view the film industry. The period started quietly enough with the industry's satisfaction that there was no longer any question of the unpopular new Cinematograph Act being enforced. There was also the feeling that a new minister, quite unfamiliar with the film world, might lend a more sympathetic ear to its difficulties. With this thought, the leading members of the film industry arrived in Delhi on 14 July 1975, to meet V.C. Shukla and present him with a detailed memorandum listing their grievances and proposing possible solutions. Shukla's response was not unfriendly. But he said that since the film industry posed no immediate problems, he would look into it in a month or so. For the moment he had a number of things to deal with, first and foremost being the press which "had to be tightened up."[1]

The memorandum went into the difficulties the film industry faced in all areas—raw stock, export, taxation and censorship. On the last point once again, it did not take issue with the idea of film censorship as such. On the contrary it stated that "while we have nothing to say on the basic need for censorship of motion pictures, which is socially justified, we do say that the procedures and the conditions should be so made as to take care of the pattern of film distribution and exhibition in the country without upsetting the objective of censorshp. . . ." However, when Shukla did turn his attention to the film industry, it was with the firm intention of using it to the government's advantage. He was little concerned with its problems which were to increase substantially in the coming months. What the government was concerned about and had been for some time, was the steady proliferation of a sex-crime-and-violence dominated cinema.

On 13 June 1975, a letter had been sent by the then Chairman of the Board of Film Censors, V.D. Vyas, to the All-India Film Producers Council, IMPPA and the Film Producers Guild in Bombay, to the SIFCC and the Film Producers Guild of South India in Madras, and to the Eastern India Motion Pictures Association in Calcutta, warning them "that the Government and the Censor Board had on several occasions expressed deep concern over the increasing dose of vulgarity and gruesome violence contained in films that came up before the Board for certification. . . . If this tendency continues to exist, the Board, in accordance with its declared policy, will have no alternative but to treat such films in a stricter manner as provided in the Directions issued by the Central Government."

The government's determination to stamp out "violence and vulgarity" had been in evidence since 1973 when the then Minister of Information & Broadcasting I. K. Gujral had stated in Parliament: "We will not tolerate vulgarity, we will not tolerate perversion, we will not tolerate violence. These trends have to be discouraged, whatever the motive, whatever the profit."[2] But in fact, confronted with a cinema that seemed to rely more and more on a sex, crime and violence formula for success at the box office, the government seemed powerless to put an effective end to such a trend. Short of banning entire films which it was reluctant to do as it would have spelled bankruptcy for a number of small producers attempting to emulate these highly profitable films, the Censor Board could do little more than appeal for cooperation. The removal of the more glaringly offensive scenes (frequently included for this specific purpose by wily producers in order to demonstrate their willingness to follow instructions and equally, to distract the censors from only slightly less objectionable ones) could not remove the tone and texture of violence from the greater majority of these films. An habitual practice among producers was also to shoot the more violent and sexy scenes in two different ways. If one was found to be unacceptable by the censors, it was promptly replaced by the other and presented the following day. Any delay in getting the film ready to meet its release deadline was thus reduced to a minimum. At the same time, there was always the attempt to put one over the censors, and it occasionally worked!

After the imposition of the Emergency the fear that the authorities would now be much more strict, was quickly dispelled when *Sholay* (Flames) was passed by the censors with a few minor cuts and a changed ending. The release of *Sholay,* one of the greatest all-time box office successes, technically impeccable but saturated with violence, gave the film industry the welcome impression that the new regime too, while paying lip service to the idea of eliminating violence would, in actual practice, turn a blind eye towards it. Consequently, shooting was rushed through on a number of crime and violence productions. But *Sholay* was the first indication that films would be passed or stopped at the whim and will of the government, with no regard for consistency in decisions, nor for long established procedures.

Censorship of Film Journals

On 14 August 1975, V. C. Shukla who the next day was to attend the gala premiere of *Sholay*, met with members of the Film Journalists Society and informed them that whatever is not allowed in films will not be allowed in film journals either, and "all types of scandal-mongering, character assassination and malicious reports will have to go." He advised the journalists to evolve a code of self-regulation with the assistance of the Chairman of the Censor Board and the Chief Press Censor. "The film journals," he said, "cannot ignore their responsibility towards the development of the film industry and the country." He was to say later in the Lok Sabha (on 26 April 1976) that:

Most of the film magazines, rather than seriously discussing the technique of film production, the various good points and bad points of the film industry are, under cover of film industry, running some kind of a semi-pornography business, and they are being run mostly with the motive of making money. These film magazines are not running for creating better taste among the viewers of the films, they are not being run to create any awareness among the film goers that good pictures and better pictures should be seen and that these formula films should be discouraged. These two matters—the taste of the film goers and the kind of trends that are generated by these film magazines, are interconnected matters and we are treating them as such. We are taking steps to see that these film magazines improve their trend of writing and they do not run purely for profit and pornography. . . .

Since the Minister made it clear that this Code, which would be permanent and not confined to the period of the Emergency, must be put into practice within a month, a meeting was held on 18 August between the editors of film publications, the Chairman of the Central Board of Film Censors and the Chief Press Censor, at which a code was drawn up in the following terms:

(1) The film journals have the inherent right to exercise freedom in publishing reviews, comments and assessment articles about films and film personalities in their professional capacity.

(2) The film journals should avoid defamation, scandal-mongering and character assassination. They should not be used as vehicles for ventilating personal prejudices and maligning innuendos. The film journals should also eschew any news item or comment which panders to base public curiosity without fulfilling any public interest. This relates even to verifiable news. Harmless gossip is however permissible.

The editors pointed out that film journalists by themselves cannot bring dignity to film and film makers. Therefore, films have to become worthy of a dignified and disciplined India, and the behaviour of film people must be commensurate with these high ideals. On their part, they agreed to "strive to bring about the desired change in the film industry."

There is no doubt that a plethora of fan magazines subsisted on an undiluted diet of gossip, excited a prurient interest in a growing reading public, and went a long way towards propagating an image of the cinema and its stars as vainglorious, empty-headed and sensation-seeking. Rarely, except in a tiny minority of trade journals, was an attempt made at critical analysis, or credit given to those who sought to use the medium as an art form expressing serious concerns. "Thinking as a pastime" was still at a discount!

In September, the Press Information Bureau drew up a set of guidelines based on the film industry's own code, on what would and would not be allowed in film journals. For the remainder of the Emergency period journals would not comment on or even mention, films that were refused certificates by the Censor Board, or make any reference to difficulties faced by individual producers or actors as a result of government orders.

Guidelines for Publicity

Shukla informed the increasingly uneasy film industry that control over film journals was to be extended to publicity material as well. After another discussion with the Minister in Delhi on 6 September 1975, the Indian Motion Picture Distributors Association sent a letter to all its members telling them the Government's latest directive that "the indecent, obscene display of publicity while advertising will not be permitted." As the President of the Association had given an assurance to the Minister that its members would "regulate themselves" on this issue, they were advised to see that this instruction was "rigidly followed by each and everyone. In the event we do not regulate ourselves, the authorities have indicated that they will step in and the members then will have to go through the strenuous and difficult process of getting all publicity materials censored before their display."

In the December issue of their journal, the SIFCC published the guidelines drawn up by its executive committee "in response to the appeal of the Minister of Information & Broadcasting and the Chairman of the Censor Board, and in pursuance of the assurance given to them," guidelines which themselves show that the Government's action was not entirely unjustified:

(1) Posters shall be such as would not offend the restrictions on them, over and again reiterated by the Government of India.

(2) No poster shall contain pictures indecorously or indecently dressed or in voluptuous poses as would corrupt the minds of the youngsters, nor shall their very sight be disgusting.

(3) Nudity in any form, and partially covered bodies which would arouse the baser instincts should be scrupulously avoided.

(4) There shall not be any pictures of highly sexy or passionate embraces in posters.

(5) Semi-nudity in lying poses of women, leading to suggest sexual excesses shall not be portrayed in posters.

(6) Violence in any form should not be portrayed in pictures or posters as to cause terror. Gruesome murders, stabbings and stranglings should not find a place in the posters.

(7) Whipping, caning and crushing with stones or rods should be eliminated.

(8) Suggestive murders and other heinous crimes should also not be portrayed.

(9) Bleeding, injuries and acts like severing the limbs or slaying should not be portrayed in posters.

(10) Striking blind or lame shall not form a part of posters.

(11) Animal or human sacrifices with pictures of frightful gods or goddesses accepting them shall not form part of posters.

The Eastern India Motion Picture Association in Calcutta also reminded its members of the existing voluntary agreement with the Government of West Bengal, regarding pre-censorship of publicity material.

(a) Publicity materials such as hoardings, posters, still photos, show cards, inserts, cinema slides, picture publicity and press advertisements are subject to the scheme.

(b) Certain categories of press advertisements are exempted, and these include extracts of reviews of newspapers and journals, details of film shows, appearance of stars, handbills, although their copies are required to be submitted to the Censor Officer.

(c) No film publicity materials as described above shall be displayed. Directions of the Censor Officer about covering up of objectionable portions if any, must be complied with.

(d) Any member who is not satisfied with the decision of the Censor office has a right to appeal to the Advisory Committee.

Although the Association emphasized the voluntary nature of the scheme, the members were told that fines would be levied for any violation of the rules.

On 29 December another circular letter went out to all film associations and film chambers of commerce from the Chairman of the Censor Board, saying: "We had impressed upon producers' organizations the growing concern of Government over deteriorating standards of publicity through film posters, hoardings, etc.

We would like to draw your attention to provisions of the recently promulgated ordinance to provide against the printing and publication of incitement to crime and other objectionable matter. According to this ordinance, words, signs and visible representations which are grossly indecent or are scurrilous, or intended for blackmail, would be considered as objectionable matter. The ordinance further provides that in considering whether any matter is objectionable under this ordinance, the effect of the words, signs or visible representations, and not the intention of the keeper of the press or the publisher or editor of the newspaper or news sheet shall be taken into account. . . ."

The government's long dissatisfaction with film publicity, stretching over forty years,[3] had finally come to a head. But whereas even the British government of India had abandoned the attempt to regulate and supervise film publicity material, now there was no hesitation. Orders were issued by an absolute authority, and had to be obeyed. There is, at the same time, little doubt that the portrayal of sex and violence in films and in publicizing them, had increased in the last few years and frequently, as has already been pointed out, lurid posters and advertisements displayed and played up scenes that had to be removed from the films themselves. But it was the dictatorial tone of the authorities that reduced the film industry to a state of fear and helplessness. The message had come through clearly and unequivocally that old attitudes and methods would no longer prevail.

The Net Tightens

At the meeting on 6 September, the Minister also informed the industry that "new and rigid censor rules would be introduced shortly." While assuring the industry of his cooperation in solving other problems that it faced, he stated in no uncertain terms that "violence, rape and degradation of womanhood will not be permitted in any movie and that in case this is found beyond reasonable proportion, the film may be totally rejected."

In the course of 1975, 33 Indian films were refused certificates by the Censor Board, but of these 16 were later passed in a revised version, 13 continued to be rejected, and appeals on 4 were still pending at the end of the year. According to the Censor Board's Annual Report for 1975-76, the overall quality and quantity (475) was no different from preceding years. Crime, vendetta, violence, the exploits of smugglers and dacoits, continued to dominate the popular cinema.

However, since most of the films completed in 1975 had been started at least one if not two years earlier, it could hardly be expected that they would alter their preoccupations to keep up with what they still thought was a passing phase.

By early 1976, the Government as well as the country had started to come to terms with the new reality. A framework for the efficacious implementation of the provisions of the Emergency had been built up, and there was now no longer any hesitation in passing new laws, regulations and ordinances. A constitutional amendment passed later in the year was to modify even the fundamental rights clause.

The Film Finance Corporation

One of the early casualties of the Emergency was B.K. Karanjia and through him the Film Finance Corporation of which he was then Chairman.

In 1968 when Karanjia took over as acting Chairman, the FFC was felt to have been a failure. Its initial capital was gone, no returns were coming in from the 30 odd films that had been financed since its inception seven years earlier, and there was a move to wind it up. But that year Mrinal Sen's Hindi film *Bhuvan Shome* (Bhuvan Shome) that the FFC had financed as an experiment, proved unexpectedly successful and two others that followed soon after *Kanku* (The Vermilion Mark) and *Sara Akash* (The Whole Sky), put the FFC back on its feet. Under B.K. Karanjia's chairmanship, major policy decisions were taken—to finance low-budget films by promising newcomers who would not get finances from conventional sources, and to encourage them to film the works of contemporary Indian writers.

By 1975 the FFC was in the proud position of having sponsored a number of award winning films which even though not yet commercially successful, had won considerable critical acclaim and helped create a climate in which serious film making became possible. Suddenly there was talk of a New Wave Indian cinema and films began to be talked about, discussed, waited for, even by the intelligentsia which until now had disdainfully dismissed the whole exercise of making films.

In addition to his honorary chairmanship of the FFC, Karanjia continued as editor of *Filmfare*, the only serious, yet popular English language monthly on films. Neither his professional activities nor his personal predilections allowed for the flattering attentions that V.C. Shukla had evidently come to expect, for it was conveyed to Karanjia that the minister was displeased because on the four occasions he had visited Bombay, Karanjia had not been at the airport to receive him. In September 1975 Shukla informed Karanjia that the Board of the FFC would be reconstituted and a new policy framed. Since the message was clear, Karanjia sent in his resignation on 1 October. Shortly thereafter and before the resignation was accepted, while addressing a newspaper editors conference Shukla made a statement to the effect that the experience of his Ministry with the FFC had not been a happy one, and followed this with factual errors relating to its functioning. At the instance of the Directors of the Corporation, Karanjia wrote to the Minister pointing these out, and asking him to clarify his statement. There was no acknowledgement of this letter and on 3 December 1975 after a meeting called to discuss the issue the Chairman and the directors of the Corporation, all sent in their resignations to the Prime Minister.

Evidently concerned at these developments, Mrs Gandhi called Karanjia to Delhi were he explained the background to her. She promised to look into it, asking in the meanwhile that they all continue until after the International Film Festival which was to be held in Bombay in January 1976 under the FFC's auspices.

Instead of the situation improving as a result of this meeting with the Prime Minister, petty humiliating acts of vengeance against the FFC followed. During the Festival, the FFC was entirely ignored; at the eleventh hour Karanjia was replaced by G.P. Sippy —known to be a close friend of the Minister's, as Chairman of the Festival Managing Committee. But more important, and in contravention of the Company Law under which the FFC had been set up, no general meeting was held because Ministry officials, principal shareholders representing the President of India, would neither come to meetings convened by the FFC nor indicate a date that would suit them.

In the months since the imposition of the Emergency, other causes for friction had arisen. The Minister wrote to an official of the Corporation directing him to sanction a loan for a film that the well-known novelist Rajinder Singh Bedi, wished to make. The official repelied that since the Board had turned down Bedi's application on the grounds that this was not the kind of film the FFC would like to sponsor, the decision could not be reversed and that in any case an official of the Corporation had no authority to sanction a loan. "This was the first time during my tenure that the Ministry sought to influence the FFC's discretion in granting loans," B.K. Karanjia remarked later, adding, "Immediately after my colleagues and I resigned almost the first thing the Corporation did, in violation of the resolution of the Board was to sanction a loan for Mr Bedi."

Another serious difference of opinion fundamentally affected the policy the FFC had successfully pursued in the preceding years. The Ministry began to insist that collateral security of the amount asked for, should be demanded from the applicant as a pre-condition for sanctioning the loan. The FFC's reasoning that talented young newcomers it wished to sponsor would find this an impossible condition to meet, carried no weight with the Ministry. And largely on the issue of collateral, the FFC's financing activities came to a virtual standstill. Nor could any decisions be taken on any level since the Board was legally advised to postpone consideration of all business, including the application for loans, until a general meeting was held.

In spite of repeated reminders, there was no response from the Ministry regarding this meeting. Under the circumstances, on 5 April 1976, Karanjia together with five members of the Board, resigned as from the end of April. As a final humiliation they learnt that the resignations had been accepted "with immediate effect" only when the Special Press Adviser instructed all daily papers to make no mention of this. But this censorship effort came to naught when the newspapers carried the declaration of the Association of Film Directors (with K.A. Abbas as chairman) deploring Karanjia's resignation!

After April 1976 the FFC virtually ceased to function although J. A. Parekh, one of the directors of the Board who had resigned with Karanjia replaced him as Chairman and still continues in this position. But where under Karanjia the Corporation had moved a long way towards fulfilling its earlier objective to encourage the emergence of good cinema without emphasizing returns on investment, this seems to have given way to a desire to generate revenue by supporting films that would have wider audiences and thus recover their costs. The question of collateral too, remains but is not always insisted upon. Somewhere along the way the FFC has lost sight of its uniquely inspiring ambition to raise cinematic sensibilities in both filmmakers and audiences.

The "Drinking Crisis"

For the film industry, 1976 was punctuated by a series of arbitrary orders which were issued with little or no warning, keeping producers, distributors, and exhibitors in a permanent state of suspense. On 6 January instructions were sent out by the Censor Board to the members of its Advisory Panels that "the scenes showing degradation of women through visuals or dialogues must be completely eliminated from films." This directive did not unduly worry the producers, but the one that followed shortly after, created a crisis situation in the industry. On 27 February, a Ministry of Information & Broadcasting notification stated that the existing Direction No. II (XV) of the Cinematograph Rules which reads "drunkenness or drinking that is not essential to the theme of the story" has been substituted by "drunkenness or advertisement of alcholic drinks." Hence, "no scenes of drinking or drunkenness or of display of bottles containing alcoholic drinks are to be permitted in films." In 1947 too, at another momentous moment in India's history, a zealous government attempted to ban drinking scenes from films, but at that time the declared policy of the government was to introduce prohibition throughout the country. In 1976 no steps had been taken although discussions were being held, to once again arrive at and implement a policy of prohibition. In fact, prohibition was never imposed and after desperate and repeated representations by the film industry, it was decided that the new directive would also not be applied to films either completed or three-fourths of the way through production. Subsequently, although the ban was not lifted, a characteristic Indian way was found to circumvent the problem: without it ever being explicitly stated, it was understood that showing the effects of alcohol would not be forbidden, and characters in films could be shown taking a drink as long as it was in an opaque and not a transparent glass!

The Television Trauma

The film industry barely had time to breathe a sigh of relief at the outcome of the "drinking crisis" when it was dealt a bigger blow—and trade journals rang with cries of "despair," "panic," "ruin." At the end of March a meeting was held between the television officials and the film industry to negotiate a new agreement on feature films for television in view of increased producttion costs. The same evening, before an accord had been arrived at, V.C. Shukla, who happened to be in Bombay, called Shree Ram Bohra at the Film Producers Council, to tell him that there was no question of negotiation as the Ministry had decided that brand new, just-completed films would have to be shown on television before their theatrical release, before even a censor certificate had been issued. The normal practice for some years had been for five year-old films to be shown on television, for a fee of eight to ten thousand rupees. Now that was all to be changed. Producers would have to give the films as and when they were asked for, and for no fee. The fee was hardly a bone of contention since it just about covered the cost of one print, but televising a new film where a prospective cinema audience of tens of thousands could see it at no cost to itself, and for no gain to the producer/exhibitor, would make all the difference between success and failure at the box office. With so much at stake, the normanly biddable industry for once dug its heels in and said "No." At a meeting of the All-India Film Producers Council on 6 May, the industry, in a rare moment of unity, determined to stand firm come what may. V.C. Shukla, apparently unaware of the ramifications of his demand, expressed bewilderment at this attitude. But when his claim that he was being helpful in giving free publicity to new films was brushed aside, he was furious and ordered the Censor Board not to pass films, to make more and more cuts, and generally to harass the producers.[5]

The hapless film industry lobbied for support among Members of Parliament, and sought the good offices of the Bombay Pradesh Congress Committee President, who flew to Delhi to reason with the Ministry.

In a strong editorial on 15 April, the *Film Industry Journal* wrote of the "fatal blow" that this demand represented. Not only did the Government not offer any financial support to films as it did to other industries, but it "gravely affected" State Government revenues in that it would cut down considerably the amount of entertainment tax collected because audiences would necessarily be reduced. It pointed to the long, uninterrupted cooperation of the film industry in participating in and organizing fund-raising drives for government programmes—most recently for the Prime Minister's 20-point programme. Where it was "hoping against hope to get some small mercy from the authorities," it found it had been "virtually throttled by the new directive aimed at economizing the expenses of TV network and popularizing it among people at the same time."

Every conceivable argument was used to try and make the government see the harm it would cause. Examples were cited of the collapse of Hollywood, and even of the much smaller British film industry as television began to take over the entertainment world. Hindi film producers themselves said that where once they had regularly taken their families to the movies on weekends, now they all stayed home to watch the Sunday-night film on television. As a last resort, the established industry even took up the cause of the low-budget non-commercial films which it generally disdained but which the government had all along been supporting, saying: "The idea of compulsory or even 'optional' showing of the latest feature films on TV can do more damage to the film industry than any single thing has done so far. The biggest sufferers will be the makers of off-beat small-budget films like *Rajnigandha* (Tuberoses), *Chhoti-Si-Baat* (Just One of Those Things), *Ankur* and so on. These low-budget films do not provide huge sets, tremendous action and grandeur and the type of visual appeal that would be lost, or substantially reduced, by showing a film in black-and-white on a 20-inch screen. People might again like to see a film like *Towering Inferno* on a big screen in the theatre after seeing it on TV; but a film like *Chhoti-Si-Baat* would exhaust its audience once it is shown on TV . . . .

"It seems that the Government took the decision in a hurry without studying the implications in showing the latest films on TV. The industry leaders should use all their contacts, good offices and persuasion to save the industry from any decision that might destroy the very pedestal on which the film industry and the film people are standing."

All of these arguments would have been familiar to anyone

versed in the literature, research, debate, relating to the media. But Shukla was out of his depth in a world totally unrelated to the politics in which he was so much at home. He practically admitted as much when he told the Film Producers Guild of South India on 6 May in Madras, that "If by showing new films on TV it hurts the cinema industry we shall adjust the timing in such a way that you are satisfied that your industry is not hurt."

As an experiment for Shukla's satisfaction, a three year-old film, *Shor* (The Din), which had had a successful first run, was telecast in Delhi on 4 April 1976, and on 16 April it was released commercially in the Delhi cinemas. It went on to collect a meagre Rs 10,000 plus, at the box office, as against an estimated earning capacity of Rs. 47,600. When officials asserted that this was due to comparatively little publicity rather than to its showing on television, they were shown bills for publicity and advertising which the distributor said had been much more than the film warranted. B. R. Chopra in his regular column, "Blow-Up," for the *Film Industry Journal*, wrote that he thought Manoj Kumar the producer/actor, "would lose a minimum two lakhs in the experiment because, on the basis of its grosses at the Delhi theatres, the circuit will not book the picture."[6]

In the face of the film industry's despairing obduracy the Minister finally capitulated. Agreeing that perhaps it had not been such a good idea, he asked for a counter proposal. "We were so frightened by now that we said we were ready to give two-year-old films, but that it was up to individual producers to give new films if they wished. We were also prepared to accept the old rate of payment," said Shree Ram Bohra.

The film industry had reason to be worried because on 6 April, at a meeting with the State Ministers of Information, the Prime Minister had said; "I am sorry to say that the majority of films exhibit violence and crudity. . . .To me they are implausible. We hardly ever see a normal person. They give a stereotyped interpretation of life, generally degrading women and our society as a whole, lauding superstitious beliefs and portraying goodness, if not stupidity, at least as dimness of the mind. A better-off person is invariably shown with a glass of whisky in one hand and a cigarette in the other. It is true that in the end virtue triumphs, but that is not sufficient to wipe out the impact of two hours or more of continuous vice, crime and violence. The morality at the end is only a cloak."

Clearly neither film quality nor official attitudes had changed in the 30 years since Independence.

The film industry's forced association with television did not end with the resolution of the new films issue. The Ministry had launched a drive to improve and popularize television, and ordered that the film industry must assist in that effort. TV, like radio and the Films Division, was entirely in government hands. It had been started in 1959 with the aim of "informing and educating" primarily rural audiences. The Film Institute in Poona had been expanded in 1974 to include training in television as well. The one-year Satellite Instructional Television Experiment was launched in August 1975 after two years of intensive preparation. Fully equipped studios and trained staff existed in Delhi, Bombay, Madras, Calcutta, Lucknow, Srinagar and Amritsar. But in spite of the money and effort poured into it, the one programme that attracted the largest number of viewers remained the weekly Hindi feature film. Deciding to draw upon the popularity of the cinema to win audiences for television and help disseminate government policies on All India Radio, at a meeting in Delhi on 29 April, the Secretary, Ministry of Information & Broadcasting informed the representatives of the film industry that, feature films for television apart, there were specific areas where the industry was expected to cooperate. Producers would be required to make films for TV, writers and actors to do radio and television plays, and musicians to compose songs specifically for radio and TV which singers should be prepared to record. An agreement was drawn up and sent to Motion Picture Associations all over the country. It was the responsibility of these Associations to get actors, directors, singers, musicians, producers, to sign this document according to which they engaged to contribute their services as and when "requested" to do so.

The enormity of this action once again sent waves of shock, anger and fear through the film world. But their mildly-worded protests brought accusations of "unpatriotic," "unnationalistic," together with barely concealed threats of retribution, this time not only of harassment at the censoring stage, but the possibility of arrest under the Maintenance of Internal Security Act, plus charges of income tax evasion. They signed. Asha Bhonsle, one of the most sought-after and highly paid playback singers, appeared repeatedly on television. Top stars performed as commentators and programme presentors. Documentary films were made about actors like the perennial favourite Ashok Kumar, for which they had to find time in their crowded schedules. B. R. Chopra, one of the biggest names in that same commercial cinema the government was continually chastizing, made a documentary on the five-point programme and gave it to the Films Division. Kidar Sharma, another producer/ director of note, made a one-hour feature film for television *Bhigi Palkhen* (Tear-filled Eyes); Atma Ram, the well-known producer of, among other successes, *Yeh Goolistan Hamara* (This, My Garden), made 13 TV films of 20-30 minute duration on prohibition, family planning, and other subjects related to the government's economic and social development effort. The crew, equipment and costs were taken care of by the television station, but Atma Ram's own services as director were donated. However, as he himself says, at the time he genuinely believed in what the government was trying to do, and the positive results of some of its programmes were clearly impressive. It was only later, when the dark side of the Emergency became public knowledge that many of its supporters turned against it. In the meanwhile, even those who were in favour of its achievements, resented the coercive methods employed. Once it was established that film producers would, when called upon, do for television what it had not been able to do for itself, the Film Producers Council received repeated calls for more participation. The Council, to show the authorities it was doing its best, sent circulars to all its members inviting them to come forward to contribute their time and talent, and left it at that.

However, it is easy to forget today, in the general indignation at the government's high handedness, that even in those days, actors and actresses were more than eager to appear on television. In Bombay alone with its estimated 500,000 viewers, exposure on television does provided free publicity for stars and would-be stars, winning them fans and fame with little effort. For the producers, television meant a lot of work with no returns and they were understandably furious at being pushed around.

The Regional Cinema

Through all this turmoil, the regional cinema was barely affected. In Calcutta and Madras too, producers were asked to give new films for television, and offer their services to it. But their protests met with a more sympathetic reaction and no element of compul-

sion entered into their dealings. It was the Bombay cinema that bore
the brunt of both the Ministry's displeasure and its demands. For
those coming into contact with it for the first time, the combination of the wealth and glamour and fame of its stars and their life
styles is just what would attract both envy and opprobrium. Although the Tamil cinema particularly, does not lag far behind in
wealth and glamour, its fame and influence still remain restricted
to one area, whereas the names of Hindi film stars are household
words and Hindi film songs are heard everywhere.

In Bengal the state of the cinema improved under the Emergency.
Producers were delighted that the all-too-frequent electricity and
power cuts which had been a common feature earlier and had
played havoc with shooting schedules, were stopped completely. A
scheme was developed by the State Minister of Information to encourage the building of more cinema houses and give a fillip to
the Bengali film. A year's entertainment tax was given to the theatre
owner if in the course of the first year, 60 per cent of the films
shown were West Bengal productions. In its 1972-73 budget the
State Government also provided for an annual outlay of Rs
2,500,000 for loans to be given to producers at 12 per cent interest plus a commission of 1 per cent—appreciably less than the 15
per cent interest asked by the banks. In addition, where previously
some form of security had been required, under the Emergency that
provision was waived. Thus if a film failed to recover its cost, the
loss was absorbed by the State.

The Bengali cinema, never inclined towards the sex-crime-and
violence formula nor towards the earlier one of song-and-dance,
also did not suffer unduly from new censorship strictures, even
though it did have to follow the directive on drinking scenes.

In her 6 April speech to the State Ministers of Information, Mrs
Gandhi had had a word of praise for the regional cinema saying
that these films had been specially successful in dealing with worthwhile social themes and in "reflecting our literary and cultural
wealth."

This is more true of Bengali films and those of the Eastern region
as a whole, than the South Indian films. There too, a distinction
would have to be made today between the four language areas of
Tamil, Kannada, Telugu and Malayalam. In spite of the political
interests of many of its actors, producers and screenplay writers,
the Tamil cinema remained detached from politics. Censorship

decisions show that the largest number of cuts in Tamil as in Malayalam and Telgu films were of shots and scenes of overt sexiness and vulgarity—and of violence. For example producers were directed to remove "action of Prabha touching dancer's breast," "girl in Malayalam costume with bust exposed," "P's action of gently uncovering her bust," "close shot of Usha with her bust overexposed," "close shot of dancer's action in bouncing her breasts," "Ram Varma's action of caressing Kalyani's neck with his mouth," "man and woman in bed" and "blood ebbing from mouth of Madhu," "dagger being withdrawn from abdomen of Indira" and, "gas chamber in which Neelu is being gassed."

One Telugu film *Telugunadu* (Telugu Homeland), attempted social comment on a political situation. Its clash with the regional Censor Board in Madras took it to the Central Government in Delhi via the Censor Board in Bombay, and finally up to the Delhi High Court. It is discussed in detail later.[7]

The Kannada cinema shows a slightly different trend. With the State government of Karnataka offering subsidies up to Rs 150,000 many more films are being shot in the State, leading to a revival of Kannada literature and proving that there is a market for serious drama as well. A film like *Chomanadudi* (Chomana's Drum) for instance, which won the national award in 1976 for the best film, was produced on a shoe-string budget of Rs 200,000, made double that amount and ran for a 100 days, as did *Kaadu*, another award winning, low-budget film. Both films are in black and white, and both in very different ways, deal with the destructive aspects of caste on individuals and communities. But *Sholay* realized Rs 3,000,000 in Karnataka alone! And in Karnataka alone, a film and theatre actress, Snehalata Reddy was imprisoned under the Maintenance of Internal Security Act, for suspected knowledge of the whereabouts of George Fernandes—then a wanted trade union leader and now a Cabinet Minister. An asthmatic patient who went through appalling suffering through her nine months in jail, she died a week after her release. Snehalata and her film producer husband Pattab-hirama Reddy, had formed a centre for intellecutal and artistic activity in Bangalore. In 1975, their own interest in urban social problems, led them to take up as the subject of a film, the growing fascination of the young with violent revolutionary activity. Since the problem was primarily urban, they decided to shoot an English as well as a Kannada version of the film. Based on a story by the well-known Kannada writer Lankesh, *Wild Wind* (*Chanda Marutha* in Kannada) probes the dilemma of a college professor who preaches revolution and anarchy in the classroom. One of his students, Dinakar, deeply moved by these stirring speeches, joins the Naxalites. His pledge of commitment to the cause involves the murder of a blackmarketeer. In the encounter a policeman is also killed. Dinakar flees to the professor's house and for the first time the professor is confronted with the reality of violence. He and his wife (Snehalata), reluctantly accept the moral burden of hiding Dinakar. Events that follow convince the professor that revolution can only be effected by non-violent methods.

Pattabhirama presented the idea to the Film Finance Corporation which liked the script very much and agreed to help finance the film. Without waiting for the money to actually arrive, they went ahead with the shooting, finishing the film just before the Emergency was declared. Correctly surmizing that the FFC money would no longer be available, and doubtful whether under the changed circumstances the film would be passed by the censors, all further work on it was suspended. Subsequently they learnt that instructions had been received by the Madras Censor Board from Delhi that the film should be banned.

Nandana, Pattabhirama's and Snehalata's daughter, said later how prophetic the film turned out to be. Most of those connected with it were plunged into almost exactly similar situations in real life, working with underground dissidents. It was almost as if the film had anticipated events.

In March 1976, Snehalata was arrested. Shortly afterwards, an official from the department of films in Bangalore came to the Reddis with instructions to see the film even though a censor certificate had not been applied for and without which no film can be released. Positive that the intention was to seize the film, Pattabhirama managed to convince the official that the film was lying unedited in bits and pieces and that there was no question of completing it.

After the March elections the promised funds from the FFC did materialize and on 4 October 1977 the finished film was presented to the Censor Board in Madras—and refused a certificate! On 12 October, it was turned down by the Examining Committee in Bombay and on 22 October by the Revising Committee as well. It was thought to be a film that under the clauses of the censorship guidelines, "is likely to promote disorder, violence, a breach of the law or disaffection or resistance to government," and "is liable to incite people to acts of violence, tends to encourage subversive activity with a view to overthrowing established authority or institutions." Under the guidelines the picturization of subversive methods or guerilla techniques is in any case prohibited.

At each refusal, Pattabhirama Rama Productions wrote to the Chairman of the Censor Board, saying that the film had been totally misconstrued, that its purpose had been "to probe deeply into the psyche of violent revolutionaries and while sympathizing with their motivation for urgent social and economic changes, makes it a point to show that violence is self-defeating. Those who preach the cult of the sword, die by it" (4 October). "The message that the film endeavours to convey is that violence does not pay and that violence should not be used as a method of social change" (13 October). "The film has been expressly made to condemn violence" (27 October).

On 28 October the Censor Board wrote to say that the Board had carefully considered the representations but was unable to alter its decision. The same day Nandana, Pattabhirama and Snehalata's volatile daughter wrote a scathing letter to the Minister, questioning the calibre of the members of the Examining and Revising Committees, and repeating that "the film is an indictment on the futility of violence. . . I feel it is a film that ought to be seen by all students. . . ."

In Delhi, in consideration of the manner of Snehalata's death as a background to its making, the new government must have had to make a political decision regardless of the content of the film in which the violence condemned by official policy is undoubtedly shown. On 11 November 1977, the Ministry of Information & Broadcasting passed the film.

Politicizing the Cinema

Since the producers preferred to keep *Wild Wind* in the can, there was little the authorities could do about it. But *Kissa Kursi Ka* (Saga of a Power Seeker) a telling satire on political conditions completed early in 1975, was to become the cause célèbre of cinema under the Emergency. In 1974 when the film was started, Amrit Nahata was a Congress Member of Parliament, who had produced three films in the last 15 years. His major interest was politics and it was from political discussions with colleagues that the story of *Kissa Kursi Ka* developed. Amrit Nahata said that he felt somebody must speak out from within the party against all that they thought was wrong. But others in the group said no, not yet. He agreed, saying, "I'll keep quiet inside the party but not within my own medium. So I made the film." He wrote a script based on an earlier idea he had had some time before and put aside. With money borrowed from friends and relatives, with actors and technicians from the National School of Drama and the Film Institute, he took on as director Shivendra Sinha who had just one moderately successful Film Finance Corporation backed film behind him. The finished film was a biting indictment of politics and politicians, that "starts out as a farce and takes a very serious turn." Two young people go out to look for an ideal "Janta" candidate to support in the coming Presidential elections. They find that the ridiculous assistant of a roadside quack suits their purpose very well. They pick up Gangu, take him home, shave, wash and dress him up, and present him to their party with a speech of corrosive cynicism.

In "Seth Gangaram's" rise to power, with a small car as his election symbol, ending with his installation as life-long President of Jan Gan Desh, everything that touches politics is satirized—the press, the holy men, socialism, idealism, nationalization, political murders, sex, corruption, with a poor dumb girl standing as the symbol of the unfortunate country.

In colour, with a fantasy dance sequence and the celebrated vioce of Asha Bhonsle, the film was presented before the Central Board of Film Censors in April 1975. The Board's Acting Chairman, unhappy with the majority opinion of the Revising Committee in favour of passing the film, referred it to Delhi.

Time passed and, convinced that the Government was delaying a decision so that the topical interest of the film would be lost. Amrit Nahata filed a petition in the Supreme Court on 12 May 1975, asking the Government to expedite the matter and release the film since no reason had been given why it should not be approved for universal exhibition. He mentioned the provisions of the Cinematograph Act which had received the assent of the President in August 1974 even though it had not yet come into force, as well as the Supreme Court judgement on the Abbas case pointing out that until the new Act came in to change the situation under the existing rules no time limit was set for decisions, and the film could be kept indefinitely in cold storage.

But political events caught up with *Kissa Kursi Ka* and on 5 July, the new Minister V.C. Shukla, ordered that "all prints of the film should immediately be taken possession of and kept in careful custody irrespective of the course of the Court's proceedings." The film was refused a certificate on 11 July 1975. On 14 July, invoking the Defence and Security of India Rules, *Kissa Kursi Ka* was declared undesirable and liable to forfeit by the government.

Amrit Nahata immediately filed another petition in the Supreme Court, seeking a stay on the forfeiture order. On 18 July the Supreme Court rejected the stay petition and directed the producer to hand over the print, negative, sound, even still photos and publicity material relating to the film, at the same time holding the government responsible for preserving the negative and prints in proper condition until the disposal of the writ petition.

At the end of October 1975, after two adjournments, Amrit Nahata, saying that as the government had no arrangements for preserving negatives in addition to prints, he feared that the intention was to destroy it, pleaded with the Court to see the film for itself. The Court agreed and informed the Ministry on 1 November that it would see the film on 17 November. After confirming in a letter on 5 November that it would make the film available for screening on the appointed date, the Ministry followed this up with another communication six days later that the film was not traceable. However, it is reliably learnt that the film and all other connected material were intact on 6 November.

On 19 November the Court instructed the Ministry to arrange for a screening on 12 December, by which time it should be possible to discover the whereabouts of the film. On 11 December, the Ministry claimed that its efforts to find the film had been unsuccessful, at which point the Court directed the government to make another print from the negative for whose safekeeping it had been made responsible under the law.

On 22 March, the Ministry swore an affidavit before the Supreme Court stating that in spite of all efforts, they had been unable to locate this film, print or negative, but that there was nothing unusual in this as such "mix-ups" did occasionally occur. Therefore, the Ministry requested the Supreme Court not to insist on seeing the film, but to prosecute the matter on merit.

The film was never produced before the Supreme Court. The case was adjourned to 1 November 1976 and on 13 July 1976, Amrit Nahata withdrew his petition without even asking for costs.

The whole bizarre incident, redolent of intrigue, factual distortions, mysterious figures, hundreds of cans of vanished film, displays all the trappings of a ninteenth century melodrama. Why did the Minister, for it seems than all orders regarding the film emanated from his office, overreact in this strange manner? Why did Amrit Nahata withdraw his petition? Why did the Supreme Court postpone a hearing for eight months? And above all, why was it necessary to destroy the film? According to Amrit Nahata himself, the film in happier days, probably would have harmed the ruling party. But the Emergency was in force. It cannot have been impossible to find a way of banning, not confiscating it. Such an exteme step had never been resorted to, not even under the British. Even when, in the beginning, the Revising Committee thought the film could be passed, it was with the provision that forty cuts be made. With the required cuts, much of the film's impact could have been wiped out. This, together with delays at all stages, as in the case of so many other films, would undoubtedly have destroyed the topical interest of the film.

In their arrogance, those in power at the time evidently believed they could flout all laws by which any society must abide if it is to survive. And it is under those very laws for which they showed such fine contempt, that they stand accused today. On the basis of a Central Bureau of Investigation enquiry ordered by the new government, a charge sheet was filed in the Delhi High Court on 14 July 1977, according to which V.C. Shukla and Sanjay Gandhi— on the premises of whose car manufacturing plant evidence of the destruction of the film is claimed to have been found, are accused of conspiracy, criminal breach of trust, causing disappearance of evidence and other substantive offences.

Amrit Nahata, now a Member of Parliament representing the Janata party, remade the film this time directing it himself. Minor changes updated the situations and Nahata added an introduction, appearing himself in the film to say that the original version had been confiscated and burnt by the government under the Emergency.

On 1 October the Examining Committee of the Bombay Censor Board asked for 15 cuts to be carried out, mainly of all proper names and incidents in which the reference to actual persons and the identity of the country were obvious. Nahata who had thought that this time the censorship procedure would not be much more than a formality, was quite surprised at the reaction. He took the film to the Revising Committee which also demanded certain deletions. In what must have been ironically reminiscent of earlier events, Amrit Nahata appealed—once again, to Delhi. Here again it must have been difficult for the ministry to uphold the Censor Board's ruling when at the ceremony inaugurating the start of the film (the 'Muhurat') the Janata Party Chairman Chandra Shekhar, had made the impassioned declaration that had the film been shown when it was first made, the Emergency might never have taken place. However, before taking a final decision, the Information & Broadcasting Ministry showed the film to members of the External Affairs and Law Ministries and on 22 November 1977, *Kissa Kursi Ka* was at last cleared for exhibition by the Centre with just one deletion—the sentence in the introduction regarding the destruction of the earlier version had to be removed for legal considerations since the matter was still *sub judice*. On 2 December the film was released all over the country.

Another film, this time in Telugu, was the brainchild of another Congress Member of Parliament. B. Rajagopala Rao had lost an eye in the violent agitation that rocked Andhra Pradesh in 1969, as frenzied demonstrators demanded a partition of the State. When rioting broke out again in 1972 he felt that it should be recorded on film. He got together a group of producers to raise the money and *Telugunadu* was shot over a period of two years as and when finances became available. The finished film which in story form was a plea for unity in the state and in the country, was presented to the Madras Censor Board on 18 March 1975.

The Board rejected it without giving any specific reason for doing so. On 23 May 1975, the CBFC at Bombay confirmed the rejection, stating that the film infringed direction IF II & III of the Censorship guidelines—i.e., that it (IF II) foments social unrest or discontent to such an extent as to incite people to crime, and (III) promotes disorder, violence, a breach of law, disaffection or resistance to government.

Evidently the film, which condemned the futility of demonstrations and agitation that benefit only politicians while the common man suffers, was considered to be a film that "preaches, or is liable

to incite people to acts of violence, or which tends to encourage subversive activity with a view to overthrowing established authority
or institutions." (Explanation first (II) of the censorship guidelines.)

The producers immediately appealed to the Central Government
where a representation was made to I.K.Gujral, then Minister of
Information & Broadcasting. The Minister gave the assurance
that he would pass the film if the Members of Parliament from
Andhra Pradesh were in favour of it. The MPs duly saw the film,
approved it, and wrote a letter to the Minister to this effect. But
the Emergency announced within a few days, saw the removal of
of I.K. Gujral and the installation of V.C. Shukla as Minister.

A considerable delay ensued. Finally Rajgopala Rao appealed for
help to a Cabinet Minister who in turn spoke to Shukla. Ultimately
nine months later, on 5 March 1976, a letter was sent to the producers
from the Information & Broadcasting Ministry that "after having
made the necessary inquiry," the Ministry was of the opinion that
the film was not suitable for public exhibition as "it contravenes
public order, decency or morality and is likely to incite the commission for an offence."

In their answer to the Ministry's letter, the producers reiterated
that their film, on the contrary, dealt with national unity, state
integration, exposed the evils of agitation and their adverse effects
on poor people, brought out the need for united effort and, for
good measure, declared that the film in fact foreshadowed the 20-
point programme. They expressed their willingness to change the
name of the film if that should be found objectionable and to
make any cuts and changes required.

On 20 May this too was rejected by the Ministry which saw no
reason to interfere with the decision of the Board. The film was
banned.

Rajagopala Rao turned for advice to Amrit Nahata whose own
long legal battle with the Ministry was under way. Amrit Nahata
suggested an appeal to the High Court, which would leave open
the possibility to a further appeal to the Supreme Court in case
of an unfavourable decision, and on 9 November 1976, B. Naraya-
namurty the producer, filed a writ petition in the Delhi High Court
to the effect that the film did not infringe any of the rules it had
been accused of and that in any case the producers were prepared
to make changes wherever it was considered desirable.

The petition was accepted but the government had become

adept at employing delaying tactics. The elections were held and not until 11 July 1977 did the Judge rule that there was no case for a total ban of the film. The petitioners asked the Judge to see the film for himself and on 1 October he did so along with the panel of advisers he himself selected from a list of names submitted to him the by government and by the producers. On 10 October he allowed that the film should be passed with no reservations.

After the extraordinary experiences of Amrit Nahata and *Kissa Kursi Ka*, what happened to other films comes as an anti-climax, although for the producers concerned the harassment was harrowing. *Andolan* (The Agitation), for instance, a reenaction of the 1942 Independence movement, was cleared by the Censor Board on 27 May 1975, for universal exhibition. It was given a Predominantly Educational certificate and exempted from entertainment tax for a year in the State of Maharashtra. The release of the film was fixed for 8 August 1975, but immediately upon the declaration of the Emergency, the producers were told—on the telephone—by the Censor Board that the film should be sent to the Ministry in Delhi and could not be released without its clearance. The film was sent, as ordered, to Delhi, and the producers began the long wait for a response. At this time, wrote J. K. Mittal the producer, in an article after the elections, they heard that the opinion in Delhi was that people might be inspired to revolt against the Congress after seeing the film.

For the producers, one of the greatest difficulties occasioned by the delay was the bond obligation they had, according to normal practice, been required to sign. They were informed by the office of the Joint Chief Controller of Imports and Exports with whom the bond is signed, that whether the government permitted the release of the film or not, if the stipulated amount in foreign exchange was not earned, the bond would be forfeit.

It was only after the elections were announced and political leaders of the Opposition released, that a letter came from the Ministry, ordering a number of cuts. The instructions were carried out and on 16 March 1977, the censor certificate was finally issued. With the installation of the new government, the appeal of the producers for a restoration of the excised portions was granted. The new Minister, L. K. Advani, saw *Andolan*, declared it a "national film" and recommended that it be exempt from entertainment tax in all states.

Another film to suffer under the Emergency for what could be considered political reasons, was a feature-documentary *Chhatrabhang* (The Divine Plan). Passed by the Censors with a few minor changes, in December 1975, it was sent as the official Indian entry to the Berlin Film Festival in July 1976.

There the Youth Forum, known to be a very radical group, gave it the award for the best film in the category of films of an exceptional nature dealing with problems in developing countries of the third world. This award plus a review in a German paper praising *Chhatrabhang* as "a sensitive, bold film by a young woman director showing that in spite of political independence social barriers remain," evidently disturbed the Indian authorities who were becoming very sensitive to increasingly harsh criticism in the western press of political conditions in India. It was decided to reconsider the censor certificate given to the film. Since, under the Emergency there was again much talk of progress, change, development, it was felt that such a film only gave India a bad image abroad. After long discussions and appeals by the director (Nina Shivdasani) and producer (Asha Sheth, also a woman) and some more cuts, it was ultimately cleared by the Censor Board in February 1977.

But this incident had put the authorities on the defensive as far as India's image abroad was concerned. In May 1976, India's official entry in the Cannes Film Festival had been a Hindi film *Nishant*, whose theme is the nefarious feudal system. At the time the film was censored the director Shyam Benegal, had been required to open the film with the following texts:

(1) All characters and names in this film are fictitious and bear no resemblance with any person living or dead.
(2) In a feudal state... the year 1945.

At Cannes this widely acclaimed film was seen by the organizers of the Chicago Film Festival and invited by them for the Chicago Festival in November the same year. In October, when the producers asked the Ministry to release the necessary foreign exchange for the English sub-titles which had to be done in Brussels, Shyam Benegal was told that another text would have to be included in the film before it was sent outside India: "This film is a fictionalized recreation of a story of the past when the feudal system was prevalent in British India. It has no bearing with the present day India where feudalism has been abolished and no section of the people suffer from any oppression from another section," at the beginning, and again at the end: "The scenes depicted in this film relate to a period when India was not independent. Citizens of India today enjoy equal rights and status, and working together, are moving ever forward."

On 23 October, by which time screenings of *Nishant* had been scheduled in Chicago for 14 and 18 November and tickets already put out on sale, the producers of the film received a telegram from the Ministry of Information & Broadcasting saying that the Government had decided not to screen *Nishant* at the Chicago Film Festival and therefore the print of the film should not be sent to Brussels. A telegram was also sent to Chicago, offering a replacement for *Nishant*. No reasons were given to anyone at any stage. The Chicago Film Festival organizers objected strongly to this last-minute change, and protested to the Indian Embassy in Washington and the Consulate General [in New York. On 2 November the officials changed their stand, and allowed the film to go to Chicago after all. But it was too late. The sub-titling, without which the film could not have been shown in the Festival, could not be done in time. A print of *Ankur*, Shyam Benegal's first film, was rushed to Chicago and screened in place of *Nishant*, and notwithstanding its extraordinary actions, the Government sent an official delegation to the Festival, consisting of the Information Minister of West Bengal and the Additional Secretary from the Ministry of Information & Broadcasting, Government of India.

Nishant, although in colour, does not by any means enter into the category of the big budget commercial film. It is a bold and moving indictment of social conditions which do still exist today. *Chomanadudi*, a low budget, black-and-white film in Kannada, won the national award for the best feature film in 1975. A very sensitive film dealing with the Brahmin oppression of society, it was the official Indian entry in the Karlovy Vary Festival in August 1976. Now it was decided that two texts must be added to this film as well before any further screenings abroad.

For the beginning: "This film is a fictionalized recreation of a story of the *past* when harijans in rural India suffered from untouchability, serfdom and denial of land ownership. It has no bearing with present day India." And for the end: "The evils of un-touchability, serfdom and denial of land ownership to *harijans* have been wiped out from India as a result of consistent and serious efforts of the people and the government. Today the *harijans* enjoy equal rights and status with other citizens of India."

It seems extraordinary that over-zealous authorities could not see that allowing sensitive and intelligent criticism through films like this could only bring prestige and credibility to India's image. Pretending that there are no problems was not going to make the problems vanish.

With this sort of attitude, it is not surprising that film makers by and large preferred to remain detached from political and even social comment. But Gulzar's *Aandhi* (The Storm) made with Indira Gandhi in mind. It was, however, completed in 1974 and given a "U" certificate by the Censor Board in January 1975. Rumour has it that Mrs Gandhi herself saw it and found nothing objectionable in it. But under the abnormally strained circumstances of the Emergency, sensitivity to any kind of criticism or even comment, intensified. In Madras, one of the two States which still had a non-Congress government until early in 1976, a poster appeared with the announcement "See Indira Gandhi in *Aandhi*." This evidently, was too much to swallow. "Until then the audience, but not Authority, had noticed that Suchitra (Suchitra Sen, the heroine of the film) had modelled herself on Indira in almost every detail," Gulzar himself recalled. The exhibition of the film was suspended for two months in July 1975. The period expired on 9 September 1975. On 1 October 1975, a notice was issued to the producer to show cause why the film should not be banned. This show cause notice, later found to have been issued under a wrong section, was issued on the Minister's orders on the ground that the film sought to bring the system of election by adult franchise into disrepute. The producer appealed to the Minister, stating that he would suffer a loss of Rs 4,000,000 if the film was banned, and offered to re-structure the story. The Minister accepted this idea on 30 January 1976 and on 18 March the film was passed once again with 28 cuts and changes. A sequence in which Suchitra arranges for a stone to be thrown at her in order to win votes and sympathy, had to be changed to show that it was her agent who planned and organized the incident. Most of the cuts were of dialogue such as "Because your father is President of the Congress

Committee . . . ."

Other films suffered on non-political grounds but for no other ostensible reason. In 1973 a sex-education film *Gupt Gyan* (Secret Knowledge) the first of its kind, was made and passed by the Censor Board with 11 cuts. It was given a Predominantly Educational certificate by the Censors and exempted from entertainment tax by 9 State Government. It was shown to a number of members of Parliament, to doctors, to professors, to lawyers. Chandra Shekhar (now President of the Janata Party) wrote: "*Gupt Gyan*...is a very bold attempt in the desired direction for educating our young generation in the knowledge of sex." Atal Behari Vajpayee now Minister of External Affairs, said, "The film *Gupt Gyan* which fulfils an educational purpose and aids family planning to some extent has nothing indecent. It should be made still more interesting and entertaining, so that more and more audiences may be drawn to make its aim of family planning fulfilled." The advocate Ram Jethmalani wrote: "In my opinion the film has a tremendous educational value. It provides information of vital concern to the younger generation on matters of sex and procreation and the hazards of misuse and perversion. The representation of this delicate subject is objective and scientific. It scrupulously avoids the vulgar and obscene." The then Deputy Minister of Law, Justice and Company Affairs Bedabrata Barua, wrote of it as a film that "seeks to educate the public on sex and family planning and is based on modern scientific knowledge. It is a good educative film and should be useful in removing a lot of wrong notions and superstitions that abound in our society on this very vital subject . . . ."

The success of *Gupt Gyan* did not exactly start a vogue of sex education films but in the next two years, three others on issues related to sex education—homosexuality, perversion, venereal disease, frigidity, sexual disorders and impotence, were made. Tamil, Telugu and Malayalam versions were produced of *Gupt Gyan*, *Gupt Shastra* (The Book of Secrets) was shot in Hindi and Tamil, and *Kaam Shastra* (The Book of Love) and *Stree Purush* (Woman and Man) in Hindi. *Stree Purush*, the last of these, was passed in October 1975. Although they claim to be serious films on sex education, the publicity was definitely sensational: "Unusual Sex Games for Loving Partners," "Multi-Orgasms for Men," "Building Sex Confidence in Sex." However, although they enjoyed great success initially, interest in these films was already fading and in March 1977, *Stree Purush* had still not found a distributor when an order came from Delhi banning these films. Since three of these film in these various language versions had already played all over the country, a ban at this stage does seen an unnecessarily extreme step. Some see in it a political motivation, a desire to punish the industry, to show it who was master, as, a few days before the ban, on 10 March the film world and its supporters had come out on the streets of Bombay in a massive show of support for the Opposition, in the coming elections. The ban has still not been revoked in spite of the protest and subsequent promise made to H. H. Jagwani, producer of *Stree Purush*, who went on a hunger strike in front of Parliament House in June 1977.

The harassment was on all levels, sometimes far-reaching, occasionally petty. Ramanand Sagar had a long career as journalist, author, playwright and screenplay writer before entering film production. *Charas* (Hashish), he claims was his first film in the new formula mold of sex and violence. Before it was released, as is the normal practice, publicity and posters had gone on display, incurring the wrath of Shukla who saw the posters on his way into the city from the airport on one of his frequent trips to Bombay. Months later after the elections, in April 1977 *Cine Blitz* wrote with great indignation of what transpired at a meeting held on that visit with the film producers. "Who is this Ramanand Sagar," Shukla is said to have demanded. Sagar rasised his hand like a school kid. The Minister shot at him: "How dare you advertise your picture before it is censored?" The picture was banned and Sagar had to seek the intervention of Sheikh Abduallah to get it passed."

Sagar, in his quiet way, downplays to whole incident without refuting it, although he does deny that he approached Sheikh Abdullah (the Chief Minister of Kashmir) for help.

"Since it is known that I am close to Sheikh Sahib, everyone assumed I must have asked him to intervene," he says.[8] But in fact he carried out all the cuts ordered by the Censor Board, changed the posters by having the guns carried by the actors painted out, held an extravagant première in Delhi, which Shukla attended, donated Rs 51,000 to "a youth Organization," and went on to enjoy the successful run of his film.

Individuals too, even when their film carried no political overtones, were singled out for not personally toeing the government line. The Anand brothers have been in the forefront of Hindi cinema for decades—Chetan and Vijay as producer-director and Dev as a top star. Chetan Anand's *Sahib Bahadur* (Noble Sir) and *Jaaneman* (Dearly Beloved) with Dev Anand as its star were held up for months. *Sahib Bahaduar* dealt with corruption in high places. As such, the reluctance of the Censor Board to pass it, could be considered valid in the prevailing political climate. But there was no possible excuse for withholding the certification of *Jaaneman* for four and a half months. It was finally passed with cuts of $2\frac{1}{2}$ feet. In the meanwhile the producer had to pay Rs 90,000 to the distributor for repeated delays in the release date of the film, plus thousands more for pre-release publicity. On the commercial service of All India Radio for instance, time has to be booked and paid for well in advance. In the case of *Jaaneman*, when the commercials were sent to AIR they were returned to the producer with no explanation of why they were not to be broadcast. When Chetan Anand insisted on knowing why they were rejected, he was told that AIR "could not give a reason."

Vijay Anand's *Bullet*, in which he was very careful to avoid anything that might be construed objectionable, lay around the Censor Office for 28 days. Finally, when there was no more excuses, it was passed by an embarrassed Censor Board which was clearly following instructions from Delhi. The message was finally conveyed to the Anand brothers that the Ministry was displeased because although the Minister had made several trips to Bombay, the Anand brothers had not been to pay their respects to him.

However, the harassment in their case had limits. Dev Anand did go and see Shukla to reason with him regarding the bond that all film artistes were required to sign for radio and television appearances. The Minister seemed amenable to the explanation that appearing in any and every programme on television could ruin an image limit up over many years.

Hema Malini, for instance, had participated in two television shows on order. Although she is today perhaps the most celebrated star of the Hindi cinema her mother-tongue is Tamil, and she is consequently very particular about rehearsing each scene carefully before shooting. In the case of impromptu television appearances there were no reheasals, and she is said to have been very unhappy with her performance. The Minister, although understanding of

Dev Anand's predicament, was still anxious for him to sign the bond with whatever changes he saw fit to make. Shukla also wanted him to ask his brother Vijay to make a film for television. Ultimately Dev did not sign the bond and Vijay made nothing for television, but in neither case was the matter pursued any further.[10]

Kishore Kumar, the renowned actor-singer, was not let off so lightly. But in his case, retribution followed a clash with senior Information & Broadcasting Ministry officials who were in Bombay to obtain the cooperation of the film industry. Kishore Kumar did not conceal his irritation at being ordered to appear on television and radio and to sign the infamous bond. His less than enthusiastic response and insistence that these were matters that could be discussed with him in his own home, were evidently displeasing to authorities by now becoming accustomed to instant obedience. A few days later, the Youth Congress planned a variety entertainment show in Delhi with the participation of some of the Hindi cinema's top entertainers. The purpose of this *Geeton-Bhari-Sham* (An Evening of Melody) on 11 April 1976, was to raise money for the government's family planning drive. Instructions were conveyed to the Film Producers Council along with a list of preformers who were required to present themselves in Delhi. Among them was Kishore Kumar. All the others accepted perforce, but he declined, saying he was leaving for a concert tour of East Africa.

This continued lack of cooperation and his unhelpful altitude were reported to the Ministry. At the end of April a decision was taken and the Director-Generals of All India Radio and Door Darshan weretold to issue orders banning all Kishore Kumar songs from radio and television. Officials were instructed to contact gramaphone companies such as Columbia and HMV and request them not to sell any Kishore Kumar records; to find out under what contract the BBC was broadcasting Kishore Kumar songs and what could be done to stop this; and even to take steps not to issue raw stock for the completion of any films featuring Kishore Kumar's voice of failing that, to see if there were some way by which a censor certificate could be refused to these films. The last threat was never pursued as it was explained to the official in charge that there was no way in which such an action could be legally justified.

On 4 May 1976, all Kishore Kumar's songs were banned from radio and television for a period of three months. The ban had serious consequences not only for Kishore Kumar personally but also for the films in which he was featured. Music being the cardinal element of films, success at the box office often hinges on the songs becoming popular. In addition, songs are the medium for movie advertising on radio, and television puts out a very popular regular weekly programme of song sequences from films. The whole film world was aghast at the unprecedented action of the government and one which had no legal standing at all.

Since Kishore Kumar's plight affected several producers and music directors, they were all concerned with it. The President and Vice-President of the Film Producers Council went to Delhi to plead in vain with the Ministry of Information & Broadcasting for a reversal of its ruling.

Although no mention of this entire story, not even the ban on the songs, was made in any film magazine, the underground press in a circular on 12 June 1976, wrote: "The one person who had the courage to stand up against Madame Dictator has been shown what is meant by a fascist rule. No more Kishore Kumar songs on radio or TV, and any new film with Kishore Kumar songs are to be censored."

The ban was lifted on 18 June 1976, but only after Kishore Kumar, quite unnerved by his experience, promised to cooperate fully, and to hold a "Kishore Kumar Nite" in Delhi. The proceeds of this evening on 23 January 1977, amounted to Rs 1,600,000 and went to the Delhi Flying Club!

New Ways to Curb Old Tendencies

All this time, while looking for ways in which to make use of the film industry, the government was becoming seriously perturbed by its inability to curb the continuing violence and vulgarity of the cinema. Repeated warnings, drastic cutting, even the banning of entire films, seemed to have no deterrent effect. Displeasure with the film industry led to other forms of control over it. In April 1976 the bond every producer was obliged to sign according to which he undertook to earn in foreign exchange, 150 per cent of the amount spent on the cost of imported colour raw stock allocated to him, was raised to 200 per cent. The Minister of Information & Broadcasting disclaimed responsibility for this action stating in the course of a speech to the Film Producers Guild in Madras on 6 May 1976, that it was done under consistent pressure from the Ministry of Industry and Civil Supplies. He attempted to console the producers by saying: "When we can make pictures in black and white raw stock which is produced in India why have the luxury of coloured pictures?

"They will entertain us probably a little less, but nevertheless good quality pictures can still be made in black and white. There is no sense in spending 5 crores of rupees annually in hard foreign currency only to make our actors and actresses look a little better than they do." However, he continued, since the argument of the producers that far more hard currency was earned by the export of Indian films than was spent on importing colour stock, was irrefutable, it was decided that the bond obligation would be raised. This was another blow that the industry had to learn to live with.

In May came another shock. For no manifest reason, and with no warning, a blanket ban was placed on shooting abroad. At a press conference on 13 May, the Joint Secretary of the Information & Broadcasting Ministry disclosed the latest ruling from Delhi that no permission would be given for any shooting abroad, not even to complete such sequences as had been partly shot abroad and had not been completed for however valid a reason. The decision was absolute and final, with no room for argument or appeal.

For some time, there had been warning signs from Delhi that new and strict censorship rules were being drawn up. Addressing a meeting of the All India Film Producers Council on 13 May, V.C. Shukla made it clear that "vulgar, sensual scenes appealing to base elements, and senseless violence, would not be permitted," reported the *Film Industry Journal*. He was not disposed to be lenient even with completed films awaiting censorship, advising producers to reshoot those portions which would not in any case be passed by the Censors. However, he still continued to assert that he was not the enemy of the film industry, that he only wanted the producers to change in their own best interest. As a result of the Ministry's uncompromising stand, the *Film Industry Journal* on 27 May 1976, published a "Four Point Programme of Film-making," advising producers to avoid scenes of (1) Violence (including fighting); (2) Drunkenness or advertisement of alcoholic drinks; (3) Degradation of women; (4) Sex and vulgarity (including rape scenes).

The film industry asked for a meeting with V.C. Shukla to yet again discuss these questions. Articles in the trade journals bemoaned the effect of tightened censorship on, this time, 280 films either in production or awaiting censorship. "Never in the past has the industry passed through such a gloomy crisis affecting the very survival of the producers on whom all the other sectors including lakhs and lakhs of employees associated in various capacities, depend for their very survival" groaned the *Film Industry Journal* in the same issue. In another article, an appeal was made for an extension of the deadline on the basis that, "relaxing the Censor rules for another three months by allowing what has been allowed withing the last six months would save about 30 film producers from total extinction without either creating any disparity between the films censored one month earlier and one month later, or providing an indirect protection to the films released earlier. At the same time another small bunch of the type of films passed with in last six months is not likely to do any significant damage to society."

The argument was always the same. Nothing had changed. The industry, like the proverbial ostrich, could not believe that the government would actually carry out a policy it had been enunciating for some years now. It did not seem to realize, or was not willing to face, the fact that conditions had changed. It kept hoping for a last minute reprieve, endlessly repeating that the fantasized violence of the Indian cinema was not harmful, that the "vulgarity" and "obscenity" were only a matter of definition. The Ministry itself, frustrated by its inability to make the industry see where it was going wrong, finally came to the conclusion that the only way to reduce scenes of violence was to quantify them. For reasons which only the Ministry could perhaps understand, secret orders were issued to the Censor Board that no more than six minutes of violence which would include fights, were to be permitted, with no single sequence exceeding 60 seconds.

Although it did not see the necessity of informing producers of this, it naturally became clear to them when films began to be cut and censored on this basis. In a letter to G.P. Sippy, President, All India Film Producers Council, the Joint Secretary, Ministry of

Information and Broadcasting wrote of the new censorship rules only in general terms:

.... The Ministry has been laying a great deal of emphasis on eliminating undesirable degrees or forms of violence, obscene sex, and undesirable exhibition of drinking. As regards violence, what is to be eliminated is not physical conflicts which are true to life portrayals, but all traces of cruelty, brutality and of unbearable inflictions on the human body in a sadistic or masochistic spirit. Limited and realistic portrayal of physical conflicts as happen in daily life is not objectionable. What is objectionable is the wanton violence and its debasing depiction. If the basic theme of the film involves a lot of physical conflicts such as depiction of war, prior clearance of Censors should be obtained at the stage of finalization of scripts.

As regards sex, what is to be prevented is not the relationships arising from sexual fascination or even beautiful artistic expression of normal and healthy sex itself, such as in *Garm Hawa* and *Siddhartha* (Siddhartha) but the exhibition of sex or the human body in a manner which is lascivious, lecherous, depraving and the serves prurient interests.

As regards drinking, it is reiterated that where it is shown with the intention of condemning it in short sequences, there should be no objection. However, scenes of drinking which tend to glamorize and glorify drinking in any way should be completely eliminated.

Five films already censored and released, were recalled for review by the government. The official reason given was that there had been repeated complaints by the public of an excessive dose of violence in all five—*Dus Numbri* (The Miscreant), *Nehle Peh Dehla* (Oneupmanship), *Barood* (Gunpowder), *Salaakhen* (Iron Bars), *Kalicharan* (Kalicharan)—but in actual fact it was other producers who had complained of the favouritism and leniency accorded to these films. However, *Sholay* the greatest offender in this regard was not touched. Its producer G.P Sippy, it is said, had a special arrangement with the Minister. There must be an explanation somewhere for the special treatment accorded to *Sholay*. On 18 August 1975, the then Chairman of the Censor Board had written to the Ministry saying that although the most objectionable scenes had

been removed from the film, it would be advisable for the
Ministry to examine it, adding that the official policy to ban films
containing violence was not consistent because two films—*Dharma*
(The Sacred Path) and *Pran Jae Par Vachan Na Jae* (A Life for a
Promise) banned by the Board had subsequently been cleared by
the government. He wanted the Board to come down with a heavy
hand on violence even if it meant outright banning of some films,
and felt that with the firm support of the Ministry, it would be
possible to do this. This letter was brought to Shukla's attention
but *Sholay* was allowed to continue. Later, when G.P. Sippy wanted to export the film, it came up for discussion again. The
Ministry found reason to doubt that the export deal contemplated
by the producer was entirely above board, but Shukla, in a note
on 29 September 1975, said he was inclined to believe Sippy, and
added that the film was expected to earn foreign exchange of
Rs 2,500,000. It almost certainly did earn this amount, proving
vastly popular with audiences all over the world. But in order to
allow it to bring in such a large amount of foreign exchange,
larger considerations of justice and consistency in censorship
rulings were swept aside.

It was inconsistencies such as these that provoked the industry,
arousing its anger and hostility. Under the circumstances it is not
difficult to appreciate the film industry's cynicism and firm conviction that the government was not serious about implementing
its no-violence, no-obscenity directive, that it had no real policy
regarding the film industry, that decisions were taken on an ad-hoc
basis and that if you were only lucky enough or clever enough, if
you had the right contacts or enough thousands of rupees to
spare, you could get away with virtually anything.

Parliament Takes a Hand

By early 1976 with the Emergency having moved smoothly into
gear, with the most important areas having been taken care of,
attention was turning towards what were thought of as more
peripheral matters such as the cinema. In January 1976 the
Information & Broadcasting Minister was asked in the Lok Sabha
"if it had come to the notice of the government that Indian
films give a totally unreal picture of the country and their emphasis
is on violence and sex," and whether any guidelines had been

given to the film industry "to give a proper and real picture as it exists today." V.C. Shukla's very general answer that "steps had been taken," to see that "our films not only become more realistic but they portray social and such other development with which the nation and the people are concerned," led Mrs Roza Deshpande to demand whether he had been able to "impress upon the producers as well as the actors that there should be less *mara-mari* (violence) and fights—and scenes of half-naked actresses should be eliminated," and that there should be "more sensible production of films in order to educate our youth especially." Questions were asked in a later session on 24 March on the kind of films being imported, on the amount of sex and violence in them and whether guidelines had been laid down for a basis of selection. On 26 April 1976, when the budget of the Information & Broadcasting Ministry was under discussion in the Lok Sabha, V.C. Shukla made a general policy statement on films, in part taking up the Prime Minister's comments to the State Ministers Conference on 6 April, saying "our policy is one of promoting a healthy growth of the film industry. We want it to grow but not grow towards formula films, towards films which for 90 per cent of the time glorify sex, violence, obscenity, vulgarity. . . and which, in the last 10 minutes undo everything and try to conform to the censorship ideas that good triumphs over evil." He gave notice to the film industry that "that kind of thing will not do . . . if the films do not conform to the censorship guidelines then the Central Board of Film Censors will not be content with only cutting a shot here and there and allowing the rest of the film to go, but the entire film will be rejected. Otherwise a tendency was growing among the film producers that they may have about 2000 ft of sex and violence and even if it was cut to half, the other half will remain and that will be good enough for instigating the baser instints among the people who go to see these films. This kind of thing, I want to warn, will not be permitted. If we find that the theme of the film is such that it cannot be corrected by cuts, if the whole film goes against the very spirit of the censorship policy of the Government the entire film will be rejected and no part of it will be allowed to be shown. Moreover the producers should take this warning into account while planning their productions now and in the future."

As it happens, the new guidelines were not made known officially to the film industry until June 1976. But in the Lok Sabha, other questions were put to the Information & Broadcasting Ministry, ironically enough by N.K. Sanghi, a Congress Member of Parliament and then President of the Film Federation of India, asking "whether government have considered the desirability of enlisting the cooperation of the film industry for the propagation and implementation of the 20-point programme and if so, what steps had been taken." This was in January 1976, at which stage, happily for the film industry, not very much had been done, and V.C. Shukla turned the question aside, saying "this matter has been discussed with some leading producers and their reply is being awaited. . . ." He went on to add that "government are fully utilizing the agency of the Films Division in advancing and screening such documentaries as have a social purpose and have a bearing on the 20-point economic programme. This includes acquisition of such short films made by private producers also."

Sanghi retorted somewhat sarcastically that "From the answer it is very clear that no public announcement has yet been made by the Minister to channelize the producers to do a very vital job." He wanted the film industry to be involved in propagating government policies and, as an incentive, for a national award to be offered to the best film produced on the 20-point programme. To this, Dharam Bir Sinha, Deputy Minister for Information & Broadcasting replied very reasonably that "Basically the main thrust of information in regard to the 20-point programme is through documentaries. As far as national awards are concerned, these are for films as a medium of art. If documentary films are creatively done, they come within its ambit and will be considered." But Sanghi was insistent that feature films should also be used for disseminating the 20-point programme, that a national award should be instituted for the best of such films and that they should be exempted from entertainment tax. Sinha admitted that these were "excellent suggestions for action." As we have seen, the attention thus drawn to the feature film industry resulted in its continuous harassment in a variety of ways, but no incentive was offered by way of national awards, although one film, *Mazdoor Zindabad* (Long Live the Labourer) was exempted from entertainment tax.[11]

Twenty Points

But short of nationalizing the industry, government could not force producers to make films on the 20-point or the 5-point programme. Films Division had made some documentaries that, as Shukla said, had a bearing on these points. But early in 1976, perhaps as a follow-up of the "excellent suggestion," a Committee was formed under the aegis of the Deputy Minister to importune at least the independent documentary producers into spreading the message of the 20-point programme through films. Since all short film producers are dependent on the goodwill of the Films Division for contracts or at least for distribution of their films, antagonizing this all-powerful organization could spell ruin for the independent documentary film maker. In early 1976, a project entilted "Film 20," based on a proposal by S. Sukhdev, was set up, and a dozen eminent documentary producers were invited to Bombay to select a topic from the 20-point programme for a film.

B.D. Garga's film on housing *Roof Above*, was too provocative for the Film Advisory Board to swallow. It was referred to Delhi. The Minister was out of town when B. D. Garga arrived there in December 1976. He met the Deputy Minister who approved the film even though it highlights the glaring discrepancies between reality and Government promises. "It was a miraculous escape," Garga recalls, still marvelling at his luck.

Chidananda Das Gupta was less fortunate. His experience is a perfect example of the impingement of the Emergency on filmmaking as well as the manipulation of the Film Advsory Board to serve political ends. At the first meeting, in spite of his preference for either bonded labour or the status of a women as a subject, he was given "Prices." When the rough cut of *Zaroorat Ki Poorti* (Fulfilling Needs) was shown to the Ministries of Finance, Commerce, Industry and Civil Supplies, Food and Agriculture, there was general approval, some suggestions, and an order to state unequivocally that lower prices were a direct outcome of the Emergency. By the time the changes had been carried out the prices of raw cotton, sugar and edible oils had risen steeply. Chidananda Das Gupta out of a concern for the credibility of his film wrote to Dharam Bir Sinha suggesting that this was perhaps not a good moment to release a film whose statements were in sharp contradiction of the actual situation. There was no answer from the

Ministry, but Films Division, to whom he had sent a copy of the letter, wrote back saying there was no need to rush through the completion of the film. Early in January 1977, the finished film was sent to the Film Advisory Board for approval before censoring. Shortly before the elections in March, the Film Advisory Board told him that the length of some sequences should be reduced. Das Gupta went from Calcutta where he was based, to Bombay, to find out what exactly had to be done. Films Division informed him that some portions where there was no speech, were thought to be too long and should be shortened. In early April the hapless producer arrived with the once-more finished film, at which point he was told that since the Emergency was over and there was no longer any point in releasing the film, he should now find out from the Film Advisory Board if it was prepared to pass it. The Board did not consider that under the prevailing circumstances, the film was any longer suitable for public exhibition. Since in the contract it had been stipulated that the Films Division would accept the film only when it had been passed by the Film Advisory Board it rejected the film and refused to honour its financial obligations.

It was only when the new Minister took over after the elections and Chidananda Das Gupta appealed to him, that the Films Division was told to accept the film with the original changes asked for by the Film Advisory Board regarding shortening the length of some sequences, and honour its contract without reference to the political situation.

The documentary film that caused the greatest furore was Sukhdev's *After the Silence*, on bonded labour. Sukhdev from the start of his film life in 1965, had had a number of encounters with the censors. In 1965 he made *And Miles to Go* on his own, without any sponsorship, and with the hope of selling it when it was completed. When he showed it to the Censor Board it was entitled *The Great Promise*. The title, together with a sentence in the commentary to the effect that the gap between the rich and the poor was widening, led the chairman of the Censor Board to ask him—"Young man, are you trying to change the government?" He was made to carry out a number of alterations, including the title. At the International Film Festival in Delhi in December 1965 he won the special Jury prize for this film, but the members of the Jury were evidently a little puzzled because Lindsay Anderson, the internationally renowned British director, asked Sukhdev how he liked his film. Sukhdev hesitated, "I like the first half," he replied. "Who made the second half?" "The Censor." Both halves were bought and released by the Film Division. But then elections were announced and the film was withdrawn. "I am sorry about that," the then Minister of Information & Broadcasting told Sukhdev. "It is a very good film. But don't worry, after the elections we shall release it again." And they did.

Sukhdev went on to collect several more awards for some outstanding films in a colourful career dotted with clashes with the authorities. When the Emergency was declared, he came out with a 20-minute film *Thunder of Freedom* in February 1976 which, on the whole, supported the measures adopted. He was the moving spirit behind the "Film 20" project but that did not stop him from exposing with a shocking frankness the vicious system of bonded labour, in which many Congressmen in the state of Bihar were deeply implicated. Here again the Censor Board did not feel it could pass any sort of judgement and told him to go to Delhi. Once again, the Deputy Minister, himself a Bihar politician, approved it, and the film was accorded a censor certificate. In the film mention was made by name of an infamous land-owner who had for years terrorized, exploited, and in at least one case, been involved in the murder of a labourer. Arrested under MISA he was released within 12 hours, and his high level political connections led to Shukla's injunction that his name be deleted from the film. One of his notorious associates Narayan Sau, was still in jail where he was filmed by Sukhdev. Sau's statement in the film that but for the Emergency he would not have surrendered even the 55 acres which constituted a small part of his holdings, lent great credibility to the 20-point programme. He remained in the film but ultimately his mentor's name had to go, as the Films Division was not prepared to accept the film otherwise. *After the Silence*, despite initial resistance from the authorities, was in the end allowed to be entered in the International Film Festival at Delhi in January 1977 where it was awarded the Golden Peacock for the best documentary. After the elections and the change of government, Sukhdev wanted to enter it in competition for the National Awards in August 1977, but Films Divison withdrew it. The award for the best documentary in the category of Best Promotional Film—non-commercial— was nevertheless carried away by Sukhdev for yet another film, *New World of Power*, but this time the subject was electrical, not political, power!

Sukhdev however, came in for a great deal of criticism after the March 1977 elections for, in spite of a Films Division proviso that each independent producer be given only one film a year, Sukhdev was assigned four. But the Films Division was only following orders from the Centre which throughout this period showed a nonchalant disregard for established procedure. Films were assigned, bought, contracted, and stopped, at the instance of the Ministry, without going through the normal channels of the Film Advisory Board or the Documentary Film Purchase Committee.

National Film Policy Seminar

By the middle of 1976, having secured an iron grip over the industry, the authorities it seems, now desired a seal of approval. Accordingly, in mid-1976, seminars were organized by the Ministry of Information & Broadcasting to discuss national policy with regard to television and film. The film policy seminar in Delhi on 1, 2 and 3 July was chaired by Satyajit Ray and included as participants journalists, film makers and writers. Throughout the meetings senior officials of the Ministry of Information & Broadcasting were present even though they did not participate in the discussions.

In the all-important area of censorship, this committee endorsed Government strictures on violence—brutality, sadism, torture, cruelty and on the exploitation of women as sex objects or on their subjugation under pretence of upholding tradition. In the main, it upheld the conclusions of the Khosla Committee regarding the constitution of the board, contenting itself with the suggestion that a third category of certificate be considered, whereby a child over the age of 14 accompanied by an adult may be allowed to see "socially committed films."

It is interesting to note that the fact of, or the need for, censorship was not questioned.

While agreeing with the Government's stand in these areas, it nonetheless pointed out that it was the Government's own ambiguous attitude that had contributed in large measure towards strengthening the evils of the film industry. It expressed concern at the "overuse" of commercial cinema on national TV, was firm that films less than two years old should not be shown on TV, that the total ban on drinking scenes was inadvisable, that the special award for the most popular film introduced in the categories of National Awards in 1975 should be discontinued as it established a false dichotomy between "films of artistic excellence and popular films," made out a strong case for the import of Kodak Eastman colour raw stock, and concluded with two statements that could not have been popular with the authorities: One, that "insofar as the aim of education itself is to make every individual citizen the conscience of his society, it follows that films which try to focus on the ills of the society and on the necessity for change and progress should be encouraged." And two, that "in view of the Emergency, a special point requires to be made. It is understandable that the government wishes to prevent any politically subversive films from being produced. But the danger is that a total depoliticization of the cinema may reduce films and its audiences to a state of apathy and indifference towards identifying themselves with the political future of the country. This will also encourage escapist entertainment."

Although in its final sentence the Committee approved of the government sponsoring films as part of a sustained campaign for promoting India's image abroad, the participants in the seminar were not prepared to offer an unqualified endorsement of the government's aims and policy. The report of the seminar was suppressed.

The Emergency Ends

Thus the Ministry continued to issue ad hoc directives as and when they thought these were called for. In keeping with the policy on violence, in September 1976 instructions were issued to the Censor Board that new restrictions in force should also be applied to the old films when they come up for recertification as they had to after every ten years, "so that old films containing violence and sex may not become the rage and thus popular."

Another proposal briefly entertained in this period was in keeping with the spirit of the times. In the last years, smuggling films out of the country had begun to be systematically organized. Different methods of controlling it had been discussed at various moments. Now it was suggested that the producer—for whom this racket represented a considerable loss—be held responsible for any print spirited illegally out of the country, that he be liable to a fine of Rs 500,000 and three years in jail, and that this undertaking be exacted by the Censor Board. Although some producers may well have profited from this bypassing of the Indian Motion Picture Export Corporation, in the end the gross unfairness of making all producers suffer, caused reason to prevail and the idea was dropped.

In the period of the Emergency, the total dependence of the film industry on the Ministry of Information & Broadcasting was exposed more glaringly than ever before. In earlier years, whatever the attitude of the powers that be may have been, there was at least some attempt to formulate and follow a systematic policy which would not be affected by shifts in political appointments at the Centre. However inadequate, unthinking and unjust the application of censorship may have been, even with accusations of corruption and favouritism and lack of uniformity in decisions regarding Hindi, regional and imported films, the industry was not entirely dissatisfied with the system. An appeal to the government against a censorship ruling did frequently meet with sympathetic understanding and in some significant cases, unfavourable decisions of the Censor Board were overruled at the Centre.

But in these 19 months, decisions were based on personal predilection, and confusion, uncertainity and apprehension characterized the plight of the film world.

Incredibly enough, despite the seemingly insurmountable difficulties, chastized and browbeaten as it was, the indestructible film industry continued to grow and in 1976, 507 feature films were produced, as compared to 475 in 1975 and 435 in 1974. Even with the shortage of colour raw stock and the raising of the bond obligation, 260 of these 505 films were produced in colour, 37 more than in 1975 and 52 more than in 1974. However, with Hindi films becoming bigger and more expensive, and with State governments offering incentives and subsidies for the production of regional language films, the Hindi cinema seems to have started a downward trend— as figures for the last five years indicate:

	1972	1973	1974	1975	1976
Hindi	134	140	135	120	108
Regional	280	307	300	355	399

In 1976, 23 Indian and 24 imported films were refused censor certificates whereas only 12 Indian and 6 foreign films were rejected in 1975 and 5 Indian and 2 foreign in 1974.

Among the foreign films whose release was held up for six months was *All the President's Men*. According to the Censor Board, the delay was occasioned by divided opinion within the Examining and Revising Committees and, therefore, a final decision was left to the Centre. Referred to Delhi in January 1977, the file on this film was not dealt with ostensibly for the usual reasons of bureaucratic dilatoriness. But when the question came up of including it in the International Film Festival in January 1977, the Directorate of Film Festivals was told that it was not to be shown. This order followed special screenings of the film for the Ministry at which a number of police officers were present. Quite clearly the inference was that it would give rise to unpleasant comparisons with the current situation in India and that it would "subvert journalists working under press censorship during the Emergency."[12] In March, a few days before the elections, *All the President's Men* was finally cleared by the Censor Board, with no strings attached.

With the announcement on 18 January that elections would be held in March, the psychosis of fear built up over the last year and a half, was not immediately dispelled. On the contrary, as soon as elections were announced, G. P. Sippy, President of the All India Film Producers' Council, took it upon himself to send a telegram to Mrs Gandhi on behalf of the film industry, pledging her its whole-hearted support. But from the start, individual directors, producers, actors, took a stand against this and began campaigning for the Opposition. Prominent in this move was Vijay Anand who was the prime force behind building up support for the Janata Party within the film world. As the momentum built up, as abuses under the Emergency became public knowledge, even fervent supporters of the Congress such as Atma Ram were appalled. Atma Ram rallied to Vijay Anand's side, and "he backed me up splendidly" said Vijay Anand later. Shortly before election day—on 3-4 March 1977—at a meeting of the Film Producers Council, Vijay Anand and Atma Ram objected strenuously to G. P. Sippy's telegram of support to the Prime Minister. G. P. Sippy pleaded helplessness, saying "Do you know what torture I am going through. Every day and every night I am getting trunk calls from Delhi asking me to issue this statement and that statement, bring stars and collected funds . . ."[13]

But on that day in early March the Emergency was still in force, and the proceedings of the Council meeting were reported to the authorities. In the hectic days that followed, threatening calls from the income tax office warned that those who supported the Janata would be "taken care of." The film industry issued a press statement bringing this attempted intimidation out into the open; the government on it part issued a statement saying at no stage had there been any attempt to persecute the film industry. On 10 March five songs from Atma Ram's latest film *Aafat* (Calamity) were banned. "I discovered this only after 15 days when my publicity agent was informed that they may not be broadcast on All India Radio," he said. It was claimed by the authorities concerned that the ban was not motivated by political considerations, that the songs had been rejected by a committee that screens all radio advertising. But in the charged days of election fever this is not an explanation anybody was prepared to accept.

On 13 March, a huge rally by the film industry brought 1,500,000 people out in the streets of Bombay in a massive show of support for the Opposition Party.

In an atmosphere thick with charges, denials, countercharges, the elections were held. The party that had ruled India since Independence 30 years ago, bowed out of power, a victim of the peoples' anger against the last 19 months of its style of government.

The film industry, exhilarated by this second independence, returned with a will to its principal occupation of chasing box office success. *Star and Style* in its 22 April-5 May 1977 issue, described the renewed enthusiastic activity: "Under the Emergency and the new censorship policy, a number of completed films were held up. Now the release of other films also completed, is being held up again. Stars and fight composers are being frantically roped in by film makers to incorporate a few fight scenes in otherwise tame films. Even action-oriented films which had been completed without any *masala* (spice) are now hastily shooting some more scenes."

But although the government was new, the individuals who constituted it were not. One of the first acts of the Janata government vis-a-vis the cinema was to increase the excise levy on films by 300 per cent!

The film industry was stunned. From Calcutta, Madras and

Bombay, the long trek to Delhi to reason with the authorities began again. The scenario was familiar. The fight had resumed.

Notes

[1]"He certainly tightened us up." Shree Ram Bohra, then Vice-President of the All India Film Producers Guild, commented wryly in Delhi in June 1977.

[2]I. K. Gujral, Rajya Sabha, 27 August 1973.

[3]See pp. 51-52.

[4]B. K. Karanjia to the author, Bombay, November 1977.

[5]Interview with Shree Ram Bohra and Atma Ram, New Delhi, June 1977.

[6]*Film Industry Journal*, 13 May 1976.

[7]See p. 173.

[8]White paper on misuse of the Mass Media, p. 85.

[9]Ramanand Sagar to the author, Delhi, July 1977.

[10]Vijay Anand to the author, August 1977.

[11]After the elections, this exemption was withdrawn.

[12]*Film Blaze*, 9 April 1977.

[13]*Cine Blitz*, April 1977.

9

Films and Freedom

To liberal thinkers in India as in other democracies, any form of censorship is anathema. But in recent years, there has been growing recognition even in the most aggressively freedom-seeking countries, that given the rapidly changing structure of society itself and the constantly increasing power of the media a rational, workable balance has to be evolved between liberty and licence, freedom and responsibility.

Neither the recent legislation in various countries, nor the number of public enquiries or attempts at policy formulation in the communications and media field show a coherent, comprehensive approach or understanding. An awareness has nevertheless come about that simple and pat answers are inadequate and that new concepts in the media field require a fresh look at basic attitudes and at traditional rules in this area.

It therefore becomes necessary to place the discussion of government control over the cinema in a wider perspective, both with regard to the socio-economic situation of the country and in terms of an international context.

The International Milieu

It would be beyond the scope of this survey to trace the progression of ideas relating to freedom of expression and the conditions for its exercise. Since, however, all modern media were first developed in a few technologically advanced western countries, it was there that measures of social control and legal safeguards were first formulated.

The precepts contained in international statutes such as the Universal Declaration of Human Rights are based solely on western legal philosophy, stressing the rights of the individual in society. But more recently, the concept of duty—emphasized in both Hindu and Islamic law, has also now been introduced.

In the International Convention of Civil and Political Rights 1966, it is stated in Article 19 that the exercise of the rights defined under freedom of expression "carries with it special duties and responsibilities. It may therefore be subject to certain restrictions, but these shall only be such as are provided by law and are necessary for: (a) the respect of the rights and reputations of others, and (b) the protection of national security or of public order, or of public health and morals.

Article 4 (a) of the International Convention on the Elimination of all forms of Racial Discrimination which was adopted by the United Nations General Assembly in December 1965, says that State parties

(a) Shall declare an offence punishable by law all dissemination of ideas based on racial superiority or hatred, incitement to racial discrimination as well as acts of violence or incitement to such acts against any race or group of persons of another colour or ethnic origin.

Most of the international instruments in this area are conceived in terms of older technologies and mainly with reference to the press. Media based on new technologies are hardly considered. However, the European Convention for the Protection of Human Rights and Fundamental Freedoms, 1960, is more explicit with regard to modern media. In Article 10, the recognition of everyone's right to freedom of expression is subject to a proviso which gives States the right to require authorization for broadcasting, television or cinema enterprises. It is further stated that "the exercise of these freedoms, since it carries with it duties and responsibilities, may be subject to such formalities, conditions, restrictions or penalties as are prescribed by law and are necessary in a democratic society, in the interest of national security, territorial integrity or public safety; for the prevention of disorder or crime, for the protection of health and morals, for the protection of the reputation and rights of others, for preventing the disclosure of information received in confidence, or for maintaining the authority and impartiality of the judiciary."

This formulation lies very near to the one used in the Indian Constitution.

The application of these international codes to national law is left to each country, which will legislate in terms of its own specific situation. Since however, most of these texts have been framed with particular reference to the press, a number of countries have found it necessary to adopt special rules for films and other new means of expression such as video cassettes.

In India a censorship ruling was challenged in a court of law for the first time in 1970. The outcome of K. A. Abbas' petition against the decisions of the Censor Board and its ratification by the Central Government regarding his documentary film *A Tale of Four Cities* was an historic Supreme Court judgement. On a number of points Abbas' position was vindicated, but on a fundamental question the Supreme Court ruled that the censorship of films does not infringe the constitutional guarantee of freedom of expression. The Clause 19 (2) on which the judgement was based, bears remarkable similarities to international statutes dealing with this issue.

There are very few countries where there is no control of any kind over film or television. Even where there is no direct censorship, there is the indirect pressure exercised by political or financial vested interests, sometimes even by concerned citizens groups. In the United States, for instance, where television plays a role similar to that of the cinema in India, the National Citizens Committee for Broadcasting set up by Nicholas Johnson in Washington, through publication of statistics and articles in its monthly newsletter *Media Watch*, has been able to exert moral pressure on American companies to stop advertising on TV shows with excessive violence. This has led to a number of such programmes being withdrawn from television screens. The strong feelings against violence are also the reason for the introduction of a limited form of film censorship in Sweden which has the oldest constitutional guarantees for freedom of the press in the world. In a country like Italy where the influence of the Catholic Church is still very powerful, in November 1975 the government censors banned the showing of Pasolini's *120 Days of Sodom* ruling that the film was unsuitable for Italian audiences who were "not sufficiently mature yet for such movies."[1] The ban naturally raised storms of protest all over Europe, giving further proof that the entire field of communication/information/entertainment media is characterized by confusion, unresolved issues, contradictory attitudes. One reason for this state of affairs is the lack of a generally accepted—or even a generally acceptable—theoretical framework. There are theories of communication, but no particular theory of communication. The public debate in India as well as in other countries shows that there is no clear concept about the effect and impact of media, and research in this area has not advanced enough to provide a basis for firm conclusions.

Development and the Media

Here in India disturbingly little serious thinking, leave alone research, has been devoted to these questions. Film policy, especially with regard to censorship, is based on the findings, since independence, of two high-level enquiry committees and some solemn seminars. Yet cinema is the major modern audio-visual medium to which the population has access and the need to harness information and communication channels in support of the development effort is internationally recognized. As practical experience has proved, popular understanding and participation are absolutely essential if any changes in long-accepted, familiar patterns are to succeed. The initial failure of many development projects whether in education, agriculture, industry, even family planning, have brought an awareness of the power of the media to break down public resistance and lack of understanding.

Until now the government in India thought to do this through running the radio, television and Films Division as government departments. That this has not been in any way adequate and in fact succeeded in creating a credibility gap was forcefully driven home as a result of the blatant abuse of these media under the

Emergency, and today new guidelines are being sought by government established committees to set up all three as independent corporations.

However, another important aspect of the emphasis today on the use of the media is that the classic division between education, information and entertainment is breaking down. It is now widely recognized that even entertainment films for example, carry information on values, behaviour and social morés from which people will "learn." Thus even an avowed entertainment industry cannot escape social responsibility.

The evidence of a number of social workers and educationists heard by the Film Enquiry Committee in 1951 gave convincing proof of the detrimental effect of certain films on women's education. The theme underlying these films was—at one stage—that the educated girl makes a poor housewife. She was usually depicted as a flippant, social butterfly, too busy flirting and playing to have any time to spare for looking after the house, or to care for her children or her old parents. Occasionally the story ended with her reformation, but more often it was the village girl, unschooled and simple, who rescued the family or saved the hero. Taken in conjunction with the almost total lack of themes where higher education for women served any useful purpose, it was hardly surprising that people with little contact with educated women came to the false conclusion that education for women was undesirable, and even dangerous. These films pandered to the convictions of conservative elements who ridiculed the idea of educating women, as well as to those who not having themselves had the privilege of education saw no need for it, particularly not for their daughters.

In today's changed circumstances, women's education is no longer an issue, but other ideas continue to be propagated unthinkingly by the cinema in the guise of entertainment. Among them, as has been indicated earlier, is the glamourization and unrealistic portrayal of city life. This is doing great harm to the vital and stated national goal of discouraging migration to the city.

However, the entire issue of the relationship of the media to the development effort remains largely unexplored. Certain implications have only recently appeared in debate and serious study. What is becoming increasingly clear is that the importance of the media's role in society must be carefully taken into account. In India, this has particular relevance for the cinema whose influence as a major medium of communication far exceeds the impact of the press, radio and television combined.

What Price Censorship?

The sad want of understanding and cooperation between the government and the film industry is especially regrettable in view of the size of the industry (507 film produced in 1976), the accumulation of talent within it, and the undeniable fact that the cinema has a major role to play. The general lack of sympathy for the medium, perhaps aggravated by the physical distances separating film centres from the political centre, the irritation caused by a variety of government controls over an industry primarily in private hands—all have made for an unfortunate and unnecessary conflict.

The government has thus never been able to draw upon the cinema's vast resources, its far-reaching influence, to assist in explaining and popularizing new economic and educational programmes. Not, that is, until the Emergency and then too, in such a heavy-handed, ill-advised manner that instead of obtaining the goodwill and cooperation of the film industry, it alienated it totally.

Censorship therefore, is the only way in which the government is able to check the propagation of ideas in direct conflict with its policies. And even in this, as has been pointed out earlier, is not always successful.

The astonishing lack of protest by film makers themselves against censorship may well be due to a recognition of the vast regional, religious, economic and socio-cultural differences within the country. However, although there has been no concerted move for the abolition of censorship per se, there has been great resentment against the frequently arbitrary and too often ill-informed and narrow-minded manner in which it has been administered. The cinema is in fact, still subject to censorship guidelines which, though several times amended and updated are largely based on the Code drawn up by the British authorities in 1919. Yet, despite allegations of excessive severity, this Code has not stood in the way of the production and distribution of some outstanding films such as those of Satyajit Ray, which are internationally acknowledged as among the greatest in world cinema.

It has been flexible enough to admit of more than one interpretation, allowing for the shift in social and moral morés bound to take place in any evolving society. The final powers until now retained by the Central Government (i.e., the Ministry of Information & Broadcasting) have also left open the possibility of a more liberal as of a more restrictive judgement. This absence of final authority by the censor board has sometimes led it into taking some quite extraordinary decisions out of an exaggerated sense of caution. A few years ago, in 1968, for instance, a one-minute shoe advertisement film was brought before it. In the film a man enters a bank and cashes a cheque for a large amount of money. As he leaves he is followed by a second man who has been observing him closely. Outside the bank the first man, evidently fearful for his money, breaks into a run. He is chased by the second man who finally catches up with him, places a hand on his shoulder and asks, panting: "Lovely shoes. From where?" The Censor Board's first reaction was that this film should not be passed as it "encourages bank robbery." When the absurdity of this judgement was brought home to the Board, it quickly overruled its own decision![2]

In other, more significant instances, appeals against the Board's decisions have led to more liberal rulings by the Centre. In recent years two Film Finance Corporation-supported films, both in colour, both in Hindi, encountered censorship problems—*Maya Darpan* (Mirror of Illusion) in 1972 and *Garm Hawa* in 1974. In *Maya Darpan*, the first feature by a Film Institute graduate, a brief shot of a nude girl was cut out by the Censor Board, reinstated on appeal to the Central Government and in 1973 it was given the National Award for the best Hindi film in the regional films category. *Garm Hawa*, the first feature by a young Hindu director and his Muslim wife, showed the tragic impact of the partition on peoples' lives. It is the story of a well-established, middle-class Muslim family which refuses to leave its home in Agra to emigrate to Pakistan—an emigration that had been forced upon thousands of families on both sides of the border at Independence in 1947. The Censor Board, apprehensive that this very sensitive and humane film might be construed as being anti-Indian by extremist Hindu elements thereby creating a law-and-order situation, referred it to the Central Government. It was shown to the Ministry of Information & Broadcasting, to a cross-section of members of

Parliament, even to the Prime Minister, and approved by them for universal exhibition. *Garm Hawa* subsequently played to full houses all over the country and, at the Annual Film Awards in 1975, was judged the best film of National Integration.

Earlier still, in 1969-70, a low budget, black and white Kannada film, *Samskara* (The Sacrament) produced by Pattabhirama Reddy, was refused a certificate by the Regional Censor Board at Madras on the grounds that it would offend a particular sect of Brahmins. The film shows the profligate life of a Brahmin, his death from plague, and the refusal of his fellow Brahmins to cremate him for reasons not to do with the manner of his death but the manner of his life. It shows a people so blinded by the trappings of religion that they ignore the terrifying reality of a plague epidemic. The film was allowed on appeal by the Central Government and went on to win the gold medal for the year's best film in 1972.

An overly-rigid censorship is thus not the only method by which the cinema is controlled in India. In fact, fear of the censor has caused producers to exercise a strict and much more insidious form of self-imposed censorship.

There is also a tendency to forget that the pressures brought to bear on the Indian cinema come from many sources. There is the economic situation of the country which for many years made it necessary to curtail the construction of more theatres, thereby delivering control over film content and style into the hands of the profit-oriented distributors and exhibitors. There is the difficulty of obtaining financial backing, the chronic shortage of raw film and equipment and, most of all, a parallel economy of "black" money which has been at least partly responsible for raising star fees and film budgets to astronomical proportions.

In view of the above considerations, it would not be incorrect to assume that in general it is financial and other related pressures as much as censorship that have made experimentation difficult and that, with regard to censorship itself, a great deal depends on the interpretation of the Code. The recent trends in film making are also leading to an awareness of the necessity of taking into account the points raised by the Supreme Court in its judgement on the Abbas case.

At the moment the prestige if not yet the commercial success that these new films are enjoying, has caused a polarization between the popular cinema and the loosely-termed "parallel" cinema.

But the fact that in the last few years these low-budget, "non-commercial" films have won most of the National Film Awards as well as recognition at international film festivals, is leading to a relization that there is room, and audiences, in India, for films that provoke thought alongside those that provide entertainment.

Notes

[1]*International Herald Tribune*, 13 November 1975.
[2]S. Sukhdev to the author, September 1976.

R

Select Bibliography

Abbas, Khwaja Ahmad, *I am not an Island,* Delhi: Vikas Publishing House, 1977.

————"Film & Society," *Yojana,* 15 October 1974.

————"Creative Expression," *Seminar,* July 1963.

Ali, Naushad, "Music of the Movies" in *Indian Talkie 1931-56,* Bombay: Film Federation of India, 1956.

Arnheim, R., *Film as Art,* London: Faber & Faber, 1958.

Atreya, B.L., "La Culture Indienne, ses aspects spirituels, moraux et sociaux," *L'originalite des Cultures; son role dans la comprehension internationale,* Paris: Unesco, 1953.

Awasthy, G.C., *Broadcasting in India,* Bombay: Allied Publishers, 1959.

Azad, Maulana Abul Kalam, *India Wins Freedom,* Calcutta: Orient Longmans, 1959.

Bahadur, Satish, "Screen Education at University Levels in India. A Survey of Facts & Possibilities," Paris: Unesco, 1966.

————"Indian Cinema and the Film Theories of Pudovkin and Eisenstein," Poona: Film Institute of India, 1970.

Barns, Margarita, *The Indian Press. A History of the Growth of Public Opinion in India,* London: Allen & Unwin, 1940.

Barnouw, E, and S. Krishnaswamy, *Indian Film,* New York: Columbia University Press, 1963.

Bardeche, Maurice, and Robert Brassilach, *The History of Motion Pictures,* translated and edited by Iris Barry, New York: W.W. Norton, 1938.

de Bary, W.T. (ed.), *Sources of Indian Tradition,* New York: Columbia

University Press, 1958.

BMPA Journal, Calcutta: Bengal Motion Picture Association (monthly).

Bose, Debaki Kumar, "Films Must Mirror Life," *Indian Talkie, 1931-56*, Bombay: Film Federation of India, 1956.

Bowers, Faubion, *Theatre in the East*, New York: Grove Press, 1956.

Cambridge History of India, Vol. VI, reprinted in New Delhi: S. Chand & Co, 1958.

Chopra, B.R., "Film and the Censor," *Filmfare*, 1 December 1972.

Choudhri, R.S., "Teething Troubles of the Talkie," *Indian Talkie 1931-56*, Bombay: Film Federation of India, 1956.

Close-Up (Special Number on The Indian Film Scene), Vol. 3, Nos. 5-6.

Communications, Number 9, Special issue "La Censure et le Censurable." Revue of the Ecole Pratique des Hautes Etudes-Centre d'Etudes des Communications de Masse, Paris: Edition du Seuil, 1967.

Congress Presidential Addresses, from 1911 to 1934, Madras: G.A Natesan & Co.

Das Gupta, C., "Indian Cinema Today," *Film Quarterly*, Vol. XXII, No. 4. Summer 1969, University of California.

Darshini, P., "Dilemma of Film Censorship," *Vidura*, Vol. 6, No. 3, August 1969.

Desai, A.R., *Social Background of Indian Nationalism*, Bombay: Popular Book Depot, 1946.

Desai, Chimanlal B., "Sagar was Ten Years Ahead," *Indian Talkie 1931-56*, Bombay: Film Federation of India, 1956.

Devi, Kanan, "Rise of the Star System," *Indian Talkie 1931-56*, Bombay: Film Federation of India, 1956.

Dhingra, Baldoon, *Le Cinema Indien et la Civilisation Indienne*, Paris: Unesco, 1963.

Dipali, Calcutta weekly, discontinued in 1950.

Dogra, Bharat E., "Regional Cinema, The Struggle for Survival," *Patriot*, 15 June 1975.

Esoofally, Abdulally, "Half a Century in Exhibition Line," *Indian Talkie 1931-56*, Bombay: Film Federation of India, 1956.

Estimates Committee, *2nd Report*, (*1967-68*), New Delhi: Lok Sabha Secretariat, 1967.

————*9th Report* (*1969-70*), New Delhi: Lok Sabha Secretariat, 1969.

————*58th Report* (*1973-74*), New Delhi: Lok Sabha Secretariat, 1975.

————*59th Report* (*1973-74*), New Delhi: Lok Sabha Secretariat, 1975.

Evidences, Indian Cinematograph Committee, 1927-28, Vols. I-IV, Calcutta: Government of India Central Publications Branch, 1928.

Fathelal, S., "Prabhat was a Training School," *Indian Talkie 1931-56*, Bombay: Film Federation of India, 1956.

Film Seminar Report, New Delhi: Sangeet Natak Akademi, 1955.

Filmfare, Bombay (weekly).

Filmindia, Bombay (monthly); succeeded by *Mother India,* 1961.

Fulchignoni, Enrico, *La Civilisation de l'Image,* Traduction de l'italien par Guiseppe Crescenz, Paris: Payot, 1969.

Film Enquiry Committee Report 1962-63, Government of West Bengal, 1968.

Four Times Five, Special Publication to celebrate 20 years of documentary film, New Delhi: the Directorate of Advertising and Visual Publicity, Government of India, 1968.

Gandhi, M.K., *The Collected Works of Mahatma Gandhi*, New Delhi: The Publications Division, Ministry of Information & Broadcasting, 1966.

Garga B.D., "Beyond our Frontiers," *Filmfare*, 3 November 1961.

—— "A Critical Survey," *Marg* (documentary film issue), June 1960.

—— "Historical Survey," *Seminar*, 1 May 1960.

—— "50 famous Indian films," *Filmfare*, 19 December 1969.

—— "Thoughts on Censorship," *Close-up*, No. 3, January-May 1969.

—— "Fifty Years of Indian Cinema," *Filmfare*, 8 March 1963.

——*The Present Day Situation and Future Prospects of the Feature Film in India*, Paris: Unesco, September 1961.

——*Sound Track in the Indian Film*, Paris: Unesco, August 1966.

Gargi, Balwant, *Theatre in India*, New York: Theatre Arts Books, 1962.

Gokhale, B.G., *Indian Thought throughout the Ages*, Bombay: Asia Publishing House, 1961.

Gopal, Ram, *British Rule in India*, Bombay: Asia Publishing House, 1946.

Haskell, M., *From Reverence to Rape*, New York: Holt, Rinehart & Winston Inc., 1974.

Hunnings, N.M., *Film Censors and the Law*, London: Allen and Unwin, 1967.

Inglis, R.A., *Freedom of the Movies. A Report on Self-Regulation*, Chicago University Press, 1947.

Indian Cinema. A Profile, New Delhi: Research and Reference Division, Ministry of Information & Broadcasting, 1974.

Indian Census Publications, New Delhi: Office of the Registrar General of India, Ministry of Home Affairs.

Indian Cinema 1965, New Delhi: Ministry of Information & Broadcasting, Government of India.

Indian Cinematograph Year Book 1938, Bombay Motion Picture Society of India, Division Branch.

Indian Motion Picture Producers Association, Silver Jubilee Souvenir, *25 Years, 1938-1963*, Bombay: IMPPA, 1963.

Indian Talkie 1931-56, Silver Jubilee Souvenir. Special number on the 25th anniversary of the sound film.

Indian Motion Picture Almanac, Calcutta: Shot Publications, 1971.

Isaakson, F., and L. Furhammar, *Politics and Film*, London: Studio Vista, 1971.

Jag Mohan (ed.), *Two Decades of the Film Division*, Bombay, Films Division, Ministry of Information & Broadcasting, 1969.

Jarvie, R. C., *Towards a Sociology of the Cinema—A Comparative Essay on the Structure and Functioning of a Major Entertainment Industry*, London: Routledge and Kegan Paul, 1970.

Jeanne, R., and C. Ford, *Histoire Encyclopedique du Cinema*, Paris: Robert Laffont, 1947.

John, K. C., "Helping Malayalam Cinema," *Times of India*, 14 October 1975.

Journal of the BMPA, Calcutta (monthly).

Journal of the Film Industry, Bombay: IMPPA (monthly till 1962, then weekly). In 1975 its name was changed to *Film Industry Journal*.

Kabir, Humayun, *The Indian Heritage*, Bombay: Asia Publishing House, 1955.

Lok Sabha Debates, New Delhi: Lok Sabha Secretariat.

Lindgren, E., *The Art of the Film*, London: Allen & Unwin, 1963.

Majumdar, R. C., (ed.), *History and Culture of the Indian People*, Vols. 9 and 10, Bombay: Bharatiya Vidya Bhavan, 1963.

Majumdar, R. C., H. C. Raychaudri and Kalinkardutta, *An Advanced History of India*, London: Macmillan, 1948.

McLame, John R., (ed.), *Political Awakening in India*, New Jersey: Prentice Hall, 1967.

Masani, M., *Broadcasting and the People*, New Delhi: National Book Trust, 1975.

Mahmood, Hameeduddin, "Regional Cinema deserves a Better Deal," *Sunday World*, 13 February 1972.

Montage, Special number on Satyajit Ray, July 1966.

———Special Number on The Cinema Situation, December 1974, Bombay: Anandam Film Society.

Mukherjee, H., *India Struggles for Freedom*, Bombay: Kutub Publishers, 1946.

Mujeeb, M., *Islamic Influence on Indian Society*, Meerut: Meenakashi Prakashan, 1972.

Natarajan, S., *History of Indian Journalism*, Part II of the *Report of the Press Commission*, New Delhi: Publications Division, Ministry of Information & Broadcasting, 1955.

Nehru, J., *The Discovery of India*, London: Meridian Books, 1956.

Powdermaker, H., *Hollywood, the Dream Factory. An Anthropologist Looks at the Movie Makers*, Boston: Little, Brown & Co, 1950.

Parrain, Philippe, *Regards sur le Cinema Indien*, Paris: Editions du Cerf, 1969.

Radio & Television, Report of the Committee on Broadcasting and Information Media, New Delhi: Ministry of Information & Broadcasting, 1966.

Rakesh, Mohan, "Film Censorship," *Filmfare*, December 1972.

Randall, R. S., *Censorship of the Movies. The Social & Political Control of a Mass Media*, University of Wisconsin Press, 1968.

Rajya Sabha Debates, New Delhi: Rajya Sabha Secretariat.

Rangoonwallah, F., *Seventy Five Years of Indian Cinema*, New Delhi: The

Indian Book Company, 1976.

Ray, Satyajit, *Our Films, Their Films*, New Delhi: Orient Longman, 1976.

Report 1972-73, Government of India, Ministry of Information & Broadcasting.

Report on Documentary Films and Newsreels, Committee on Broadcasting & Information Media, New Delhi: Ministry of Information & Broadcasting, 1966.

Report of the Enquiry Commitee on Film Censorship, New Delhi: Government of India Press, 1969.

Report of the Film Enquiry Committee, New Delhi: Government of India Press, 1951.

Report of the Indian Cinematograph Committee, 1927-1928 Madras: Government Press, 1928.

Rotha, Paul, and Richard Griffith, *The Film Till Now*, London: Vision Press, 1960.

Sarkar, K., *Indian Cinema Today*, New Delhi: Sterling Publishers, 1975.

Schacht, J., *Introduction to Islamic Law*, Oxford University Press, 1964.

Screen, Bombay (weekly).

Seminar, New Delhi (monthly). Special Numbers, "Film," May 1960, "Censorship," July 1963.

Sen, Mrinal, *Views on Cinema*, Calcutta: Ishan Publication, 1977.

Shah, Panna, *The Indian Film*, Bombay: Motion Picture Society of India, 1950.

SIFCC Bulletin, (monthly), Madras: South India Film Chamber of Commerce.

Sitaramayya, Pattabh, *History of the Indian National Congress*, New Delhi: S. Chand & Co., 1969.

South India Film Chamber of Commerce, *20 Years of Service, 1939-1959*, Madras: South India Film Chamber of Commerce, 1959.

Studies in Film History, A Compilation of Research Papers devoted to D. G. Phalke (1870-1944), Poona: Film Institute of India 1974.

Vasan, S. S., "Pageants for our Peasants," *Indian Talkie 1931-56*, Bombay: Film Federation of India, 1956.

Vijaylakshmi. S., *The Impact of Film*, Madras: Centre for Social Research, 1974.

Vizzard, Jack, *See no Evil*, New York: Simon and Schuster, 1970.

White Paper on Misuse of the Mass Media, New Delhi: Government of India, August 1977.

Index